THE AMERICAN DREAM OF SUCCESS:

**The Search for the Self
in the Twentieth Century**

THE AMERICAN DREAM OF SUCCESS:

**The Search for the Self
in the Twentieth Century**

Lawrence Chenoweth
University of Wisconsin - Green Bay

DUXBURY PRESS
North Scituate, Massachusetts

Duxbury Press, North Scituate, Massachusetts
A Division of Wadsworth Publishing Company, Inc.

ISBN-0-87872-059-6

L. C. Cat. Card No. 73-890882

Printed in the United States of America

The American Dream of Success was edited by Jay P. Bartlett and
designed by Duxbury Press.
The cover was designed by Pat Sustendal.

1 2 3 4 5 6 7 8 9 10–77 76 75 74

To
My Mother,
Mrs. Pauline Chenoweth

PREFACE

Modern middle class Americans have become increasingly frustrated in their attempts to find a satisfying life in an understandable society. This dissatisfaction stems from and is made more acute by the discrepancies between the promises of our culture and the realities of our nation. We believe that the individual in America is important, yet we feel insignificant. We assume that the individual can control his life in a democratic society, yet we feel unable to influence our political and economic institutions. Out of loneliness, hope and despair we listen to sermons and songs which asssure us that love can solve our problems, even though we deeply sense an absence of care which accentuates our fear that love has disappeared or, even worse, is a hoax. We have been promised that America is the best nation in which happiness can be pursued, and yet our increasingly frantic search for pleasure reveals the stress which Americans experience. As our tension increases, we look for peace of mind only to become more restive and violent as a nation.

Americans have been unable to change their values adequately in response to massive social transformations. Simple advocacies of particular values have been illusory responses to our paralysis. As a nation always wanting answers rather than willing to question beliefs, we have only become more lost. Thus, this book is directed not towards offering the way out of our problems but towards exploring what our problems are. If such an approach seems unsatisfactory, we should remember that before we can alleviate our stress, we must understand the causes of our confusion today. It is through the process of asking questions rather than in the desire to be guided that we can move towards a sense of freedom in our lives.

To understand the problems involved in the search for the self, I have used an interdisciplinary approach based on history, psychology, popular cultural analysis, sociology and economics. Specifically, I am concerned with how the retention of our traditional guides to living in the face of massive social change has led to an increase of fantasy, helplessness, loneliness and insignificance. I also am interested in how the concept of free will has been distorted into a device which encourages obedience to political and corporate leaders. And why have individual citizens become increasingly passive even as the nation has become domestically more violent and internationally more arrogant?[1]

I have introduced the book with a chapter on the varieties of middle class values which influence our search for the self. Subsequent chapters are structured on a double matrix use of history. To understand the causes of our contemporary stress, I chronologically discuss the effects which the rise of industrialism, the depression, World War II, the cold war and the turbulent Sixties have had on our beliefs. Concurrently, each chapter focuses on particular problems which persistently afflict many Americans' search for the self.

Those problems are: Why do our values related to success, pleasure, morality and care fail to alleviate and often enhance our confusion? How do our personal beliefs make us vulnerable to national leaders unconcerned with our self interests? Why has our faith in rationality, individualism and free will led to fantasy, conformity and paralysis? How do our unwarranted feelings of shame and guilt blunt the imagination and limit cooperation? What are the responsibilities implicit in our conflicting desires for individualism and community? How can the need for optimism impair

the quest for identity? Why were the Sixties such a disillusioning experience? Why is it difficult for us to sustain a
spirit of care? Finally, why is our need for answers and a release from tension so often a cause of our problems?[2]

Although this approach encourages generalizations, as
a historian I believe that social criticism necessitates evidence.
Since I am concerned with the feelings of conventional
middle class citizens as opposed to intellectuals, radicals, the
rich and the impoverished, I have used popular cultural
materials on the assumption that public opinion both shapes
and is shaped by vehicles of mass communication.[3]

The basic sources I have used are 1140 articles published
in *Reader's Digest* sample issues from 1926 through 1969
and 707 articles and stories published in *The Saturday Evening Post* sample issues from 1917 through 1967. In addition to these 1847 articles and stories, I have studied the 47
best-selling self help books published between 1917 and
1969. Discussions of comic strips such as "Superman,"
"Little Orphan Annie" and "Peanuts" also are included as
well as occasional references to other facets of popular culture. Finally, I have correlated this information with social
mobility and organizational studies, political and social
histories, sociological surveys and psychoanalytic evaluations
of individual and group behavior.[4]

Even with all of this material, I recognize that my sources
do not cover the entire range of middle class life. However,
if we wait until all the data is in, as the Social Darwinist
William Graham Sumner argued in the 1890s or Richard
Nixon advocated to a troubled nation eighty years later, we
would never gather enough evidence to assess our problems.

If a social scientist can make too much of his sources,
he also can feel so restricted by his research materials that
he fails to discuss the broader implications of his findings. To
cope with the issue of evidence and generalization, I have
assessed the statements of self help writers, politicians, businessmen and average citizens in and of themselves. When

such statements have suggested larger national issues, I have used these sources as springboards from which to speculate on how American culture affects us.

In studying popular culture, an author is subject to two types of criticism. He always is asked why he did not include some source which nostalgically appeals to an individual reader. In writing this book my research had to stop at some point. While believing that the material I have gathered sufficiently documents my conclusions, I hope other writers will study different popular sources to explore our contemporary dilemmas.

Unfortunately, popular cultural studies also come under attack from those who debate the relative merits of highbrow and lowbrow literature. I have no desire to become part of that dispute. I am equally disturbed by both mass communications enthusiasts who display a distaste for philosophic thought and academics who consider popular culture unworthy of consideration. Strictly intellectual sources offer a rich appreciation of the mysteries of human experience. Popular cultural studies reveal how strongly our folklore influences everyday life.

While I have relegated certain methodological issues to this section's notes, it is necessary to explain why I have chosen *The Saturday Evening Post* and *Reader's Digest* as my basic sources. Over the span of the twentieth century, the two magazines have been the most popular weekly and monthly publications in the United States. Their pervasive influence is indicated by the following facts. In 1928, one out of ten families read *The Saturday Evening Post.* In 1946, the same magazine was read by 12 percent of the population. Since at least 1956, one out of four families reads *Reader's Digest.* The number of *Reader's Digests* distributed in public schools alone in 1946 was more than the combined national circulations of *Fortune, Nation, New Republic, Harper's* and *Atlantic Monthly.* Moreover, while *Reader's Digest* reprints articles selectively and thus is not a representative anthology of American publications, its reprinting approach does make

it a useful source for studying articles which reached the
public through many mass media channels. In my footnotes,
I have cited the sources from which *Reader's Digest* reprinted its articles to indicate further the scope of materials
which appear in this study.[5]

I have considered *The Saturday Evening Post* and
Reader's Digest as indicators of public opinion because both
publications consciously attempted to reflect popular
sentiments to increase sales. *Reader's Digest* queried four
thousand subscribers monthly on their likes and dislikes
of specific issues. *The Saturday Evening Post* conducted
monthly readership interviews to ascertain which values the
magazine should espouse.[6]

Both publications mainly reflect conservative attitudes.
Still, it is possible that readers having different political
views agreed with or were influenced by many of those
magazines' discussions of guides to living. Both magazines
did publish articles in which John F. Kennedy, Adlai Stevenson, Harry Hopkins and Hubert Humphrey endorsed various
tenets of the success ethic. Furthermore, *The Saturday
Evening Post* published many liberal articles on poverty in
the 1960s and *Reader's Digest* supported the New Deal until 1935.

As for the readers themselves, *The Saturday Evening
Post's* followers came from middle and upper middle classes.
In 1946, for example, *The Saturday Evening Post* reached
23 percent of the upper class, 15 percent of the upper middle
class, 11 percent of the middle class, 8 percent of the lower
middle class and only 4 percent of the poor. While *Reader's
Digest* reaches all classes, it is a predominantly middle class
publication. The "1972 Starch Demographic Report" indicated that *Reader's Digest* was found in almost one-third
of all American homes with incomes of $8000–14,999.
Forty percent of the homes receiving *Reader's Digest* have
incomes of $8000–14,999, 25.6 percent have incomes
of $15,000 or more, and 34.4 percent have incomes under
$8000. The magazine is read by slightly less than one-third

of all high school graduates and slightly more than one-third of all college graduates.[7]

Because best-selling self help books have a smaller number of readers than the two magazines, they are less convincing sources of popular opinion. Nevertheless, social trends can account partially for a book's popularity. Moreover, the notoriety of success writers such as Dale Carnegie and Norman Vincent Peale suggests a large following which accepts their opinions. Carnegie's *How to Win Friends and Influence People* was so popular that it was in one out of ten American homes by 1948. And Peale's numerous books do much to explicate the beliefs he preached to an estimated thirty million Americans each week in 1957. Since self help books were more expensive than magazines, less affluent Americans probably did not purchase them.[8]

During the preparation of this book, I received assistance from several individuals and institutions whom I wish to thank. An earlier version of this work was submitted as my dissertation at the University of California, Berkeley. Walton Bean, Michael Rogin and Lawrence Levine, by serving on my dissertation committee, offered valuable criticisms and suggestions. I am especially grateful to Laurence Veysey of the University of California, Santa Cruz, for voluntarily reading the dissertation and offering extensive advice. Moreover, the opportunity afforded me by Laurence Veysey and Henry Nash Smith to teach courses on "The American Dream of Success" at Santa Cruz and "The Theme of the Self in American Culture" at Berkeley helped immeasurably. A postdoctoral fellowship offered by the Center for Twentieth Century Studies at the University of Wisconsin-Milwaukee allowed me to devote an entire year to the preparation of this book. During the final stages of the manuscript's completion, Rollo May, Moses Rischin, John Cawelti, William McLoughlin, D. S. Carne-Ross, William Kaufman and Thomas Bender offered many beneficial suggestions. The collaboration between my editor, Jay Bartlett, and me was both enjoyable and highly rewarding. I also would like to thank Paula Orth, Florence Moore, Mary Ecker and Stephanie DeNatale for their assistance. Finally, a special note to my wife, Kathi, who shows that marriage can bring happiness in a society which demands so many meaningless forms of success.

Lawrence Chenoweth

Green Bay, Wisconsin
September, 1973

TABLE OF CONTENTS

PREFACE   vii

1. *THE AMERICAN DREAM OF SUCCESS AND THE
   SEARCH FOR THE SELF*   1

   The Self and Society. The American Dream of Success.
   Economic Opportunities: Dreams and Realities. Psychological Costs: A Life of Pretense. The Pleasure Ethic. Moralistic and Humanistic Guides to Living.

2. *PASSIVITY AND FANTASY: THE IMPACT OF
   CORPORATISM ON THE AMERICAN DREAM*   31

   Harmony and Instability. The Sublimation of the
   American Dream. The Emergence of Fantasy. Ambivalence and Escapism in Postwar America. Power, Reassurance and Submissiveness. Materialism, Moralism and
   the Corporate Messiah. The Triumph of the Corporation.
   The Rise of the Consumptive Pleasure Ethic.

3. *THE DEPRESSION: SHAME, GUILT AND THE
   SEARCH FOR THE SELF*   63

   The Consequences of Shame and Guilt. Guilt as a Means
   of Escape. The Politics of Guilt. Values in Doubt.
   Imagination and Ambivalence: Franklin Roosevelt and
   and the American Dream. Cooperation and Individualism.
   Myths, Masks and Submission: The Defense of a Faltering Dream .

4. *INDIVIDUALISM AND COMMUNITY*   90

The War Attacks the American Dream. Superman, Will'e and Joe. New Directions in the Search for the Self. The Limitations of Idealism. Autonomy and Care. The Return of Submission and Success.

5. *FANTASY AS REALITY: THE DESPERATE RETENTION OF DOUBTED BELIEFS*   109

The Growth of Ambivalence. Anomie and Paranoia. The Uncertainties of Optimism. Hope Versus Optimism. Religion, Retreat and Resignation. The Crisis of American Culture.

6. *THE RHETORIC OF CARE*   131

Charlie Brown and the Changing American Dream. Image as Reality. New Goals—Old Behavior. Care, Individualism and the Liberal Dilemma. Pleasure, Passivity and Death. Love, Will and the Generation Gap. The Retreat to Illusion.

EPILOGUE   165

APPENDIX   179

NOTES   192

BIBLIOGRAPHY   216

INDEX   227

Chapter 1

THE AMERICAN DREAM OF SUCCESS AND THE SEARCH FOR THE SELF

Plagued by a need for purpose and control, millions of citizens read self help books, inspirational stories, biographies of successful figures and articles purporting to give guides to living. However, self help philosophies often offer more of a confusing array of requirements for the good life than a clear set of solutions to problems. Americans are told to compete with and still love their neighbor, strive for future goals and yet live in the present, work hard and yet relax, achieve financial goals and yet be moral rather than materialistic.

Undergoing such tension, many quests for identity paradoxically have become escapes from the self. To retain American values and ignore the conflicts among our basic beliefs, self help writers increasingly have resorted to rationalizations which have made our philosophies of life outdated and contradictory to the point of absurdity. The concept of success, which formerly was connected with individualism, effort and victory, has become equated with conformity, resignation and, for some self help writers, defeat. From a nation which admired Horatio Alger's Mark, the Match Boy, we have become a people who often identify with Schultz's confused, lonely and passive Charlie Brown.

To understand the causes of our confusion today, we must first realize a fundamental paradox in our concept of self. While we tend to think of the self as an individualistic concept developed by a conscious choice of beliefs, in large

part the self is formed in the individual without his knowledge by his culture and social institutions. In effect, Americans generally act in response to implanted assumptions
rather than out of a clear understanding of the consequences
of their beliefs.

All societies operate within a cultural framework.
Social reality and the cultural forms that give meaning and
significance to our lives are not always in phase. It is the
argument of this book that the dream of success, particularly
since the onset of industrialism, while partially successful in
directing the energies of the American people, has significantly failed to give meaning to the full range of our personal
and social experience.

Since much of the stress which Americans experience
results from culturally ascribed beliefs, this chapter seeks to
understand the formation of the self by our society and
explores how cultural values influence our actions, precipitate
our anxiety, direct and limit our ability to think, and prevent
us from adequately responding to personal and national
problems.

The Self and Society

Essentially, the self is concerned with the questions
"Who am I?" "What is the nature of the society in which I
live?" and "Where am I going?" To cope with these questions, an individual uses values, goals and a conception of his
potential power which he assumes to be true. The values
provide him with a set of standards to evaluate whether his
actions and those of his society are good or bad, desirable
or repugnant, functional or dysfunctional. The goals help
him to measure personal significance and societal progress.
And his self-conception of power affects the degree to which
the individual believes he can participate in his society and
achieve his goals. Together, these inner beliefs, aspirations
and self-conceptions form a philosophy of life which, held

with an almost religious conviction, provides the individual's sense of identity.[1]

While an individual consciously selects some of his values, the immediate concerns of family and occupation prevent him from thinking too deeply about his beliefs. Instead a person usually assumes that the uncomplicated statements and clichés transmitted by popular culture clearly explain man and his relationship to society.

As a child, the individual is imbued with values and aspirations promulgated by parents, churches and schools which are accepted without question and become articles of faith difficult to dislodge in later life. As the individual matures, he is forced to conform to roles demanded by his employer and neighbors to retain his income and community acceptance. And throughout his life, an American is continually deluged with magazines, popular books, songs, movies and television programs which strongly suggest that Americans act in certain prescribed manners.[2]

The unperceived relationship between the acculturation process and the development of personal philosophies has a very definite social function. Since physical coercion towards conventional middle class values is not tolerated, citizens have to be motivated internally to control themselves. Thus, political, religious and economic leaders phrase ideologies as if they were philosophies of life to persuade individuals to act for the benefit of institutions.[3]

Internalizing these ideologies compels the conventional middle class American to accept four different guides to living. The most popularized is the American dream of success, which envisions a world of individual competition in which a man should work for his self interest and defer present gratification in the hope of attaining future wealth, fame and power. The second guide to living, the pleasure-oriented consumption ethic, encourages citizens to be happy in the present by cultivating friendships and concentrating on leisure, entertainment and the purchase of material products. Together these two guides help drive Americans

to produce and consume, thereby increasing the material
prosperity by which our culture measures social progress.
Moreover, while the success ethic calls upon persons to work
for the interests of their economic and political leaders, the
pleasure-oriented approach to living provides Americans with
outlets for frustrations which might otherwise prod citizens
to reform their society substantially.

Two other sets of beliefs, the moralistic and humanistic
guides to living, are also offered to Americans in their quest
for the self. Both guides prefer cooperation to competition
and posit that brotherly love and societal peace are preferable
to material progress. The two philosophies, however, are
founded on distinctly different assumptions. Moralistic
philosophies, promulgated by conservative clergymen,
demand that behavior be judged and guided by religious rules.
Such philosophies deem materialism potentially sinful, consider social problems the result of personal sin, require the
repression of evil emotional urges, and demand that Americans engage in community social work while leaving national
problems to God's will.

In contrast, humanistic guides, preached by liberal
religious and secular leaders, are based on ideals presupposing
man's capacity for kindness. Humanistic guides consider
materialistic outlooks on life unsatisfying but not immoral,
ask people to act out of love rather than guilt, call for
tolerance and individuality of expression, and urge support
of liberal national political reforms to alleviate suffering
caused by environmental inequities.

Both sets of values not only assist Americans in satisfying personal spiritual and humanitarian desires but also
help our society define acceptable channels for political
reform. Moralistic guides inculcate a guilt-ridden fear of
punishment which restrains citizens from committing acts
which our culture deems inappropriate. Humanistic guides
foster a faith in idealism and consensus politics which often
blunts a more radical acceptance of conflict.

Each of these guides to living is aimed at fulfilling conflicting desires for money, pleasure, spirituality and humani-

tarianism felt by most Americans. Since the individual
is driven to act simultaneously in different manners towards
different goals, he understandably becomes tense. It is
difficult for him to discard any of these ambivalent beliefs,
however, because ideological advocates often use moralistic
rhetoric to make him feel obligated to accept divergent
philosophies of life. The American dream of success is often
referred to as the gospel of success to suggest that a life
without diligence is potentially sinful. Church leaders
threaten God's wrath if the individual does not conform to
religious dictates. And humanitarians often attempt to make
him feel guilty if he does not support social reforms.[4]

To lessen tension and gain direction, an American often
is forced to establish priorities by repressing certain feelings.
This process, however, can be highly dissatisfying. Success-
oriented people may become lonely and religious zealots
often lose their humanitarianism. Just as serious, an individual
might resort to rationalizations and escapist actions which
heighten rather than alleviate his anxiety. Positive thinkers
often celebrate fantasy to the extent of lending support to
paranoid movements and "get away from it all" pleasure
seekers may flee only to a sense of greater isolation.

The process whereby the self is culturally developed
makes the individual vulnerable at many points. If the
citizen attempts to retain all four guides to living, he can be
torn apart. If he represses certain desires, he inevitably loses
part of himself. Since philosophies of life are often promulgated by ideologues seeking to motivate people, the average
citizen may be manipulated. And because guilt often prevents
Americans from discarding their beliefs, they may enhance
their stress by resorting to psychological defense mechanisms
to retain dysfunctional values.

The American Dream of Success

The manner in which the American dream of success is
internalized best illustrates the process by which individuals

are unwittingly obliged to accept a philosophy of life, repress
personal desires, become distraught and yet continue to
support society's leaders. From childhood, many Americans
are unconsciously led to accept the success ethic as a guide
to living by parents and teachers who, often unknowingly,
serve as transmitters of this basic American ideology. By
telling children the story "The Little Engine that Could,"
in which a small locomotive learns to climb a mountain by
quickly repeating "I think I can, I think I can," parents
implant into a trusting child a formula for positive thinking
quite similar to the dictums of Emile Coué and Norman
Vincent Peale. As little boys learn to gain parental affection
by emulating their fathers' actions, they begin to consider
work and achievement as means to gain attention and love.
When the child goes to school, he is further acculturated with
the success ethic by being encouraged to compete for grades
and study diligently so that he can advance to college or get
a job.

As adults, many Americans have been entertained by
books and magazines such as *The Saturday Evening Post*
and *Reader's Digest* which consistently proselytize the success
ethic in highly religious terms. Anne Morgan told readers of
The Saturday Evening Post that "we in America have always
had a more or less materialistic religion" and Judge Henry
Neil celebrated "the great American religion of success" in
Reader's Digest. Christa Winsloe preached the "holy, insepa-
rable trinity" of "work, earning and saving." Will power and
self-control were "important moral qualities" for Albert
Wiggam. Dale Carnegie equated salesmanship with the Golden
Rule. Similarly, the return to religion which Henry Link
called for in the title of his best-selling self help book was
largely the development of extroversion and salesmanship.[5]

The ascription of goodness to work made relaxation
potentially evil. Since leisure might be construed as laziness,
the moralistic tenor of the gospel of success could lead an
individual to feel compelled to work to calm his conscience.
Arthur J. Wiltse told *Reader's Digest* subscribers that work

and success were "soul-satisfying," while Vash Young explained in his self help book that "keeping busy is an important part of my religion." Similarly, articles in *The Saturday Evening Post* often spoke of retired men who felt so uneasy that they had to return to their jobs.[6]

By demanding that Americans continually work and only relax so that they could produce more efficiently, success advocates asked Americans to be future-oriented and thus further repress desires for enjoyment. Henry Link believed that self-determination required "habits of subordinating impulsive tendencies to a more distant goal." "The sacrifice of immediate desires and inclinations for the performance of some less pleasant task, leads to a steady increase in the individual's range of interests, likes, and successes."[7]

Emotional repression is a consistent theme in success literature because the achievement ethic encourages a material frame of reference in which people are commercial objects rather than sensitive beings.

Carnegie's formula for success encouraged Americans to repress their feelings and package themselves as marketable commodities. Realizing the value of a dynamic personality, Carnegie implored his readers to assess themselves. In *How To Win Friends and Influence People*, he included a diary in which his readers could list personality assets and liabilities. Finally, Carnegie instructed his readers to eliminate irritable traits, simulate modesty and enthusiasm, and develop "the kind of a smile that will bring a good price in the market place."[8]

Such personality manipulations and compulsive diligence dehumanized achievers' lives. In praising Connie Francis's success, Dean Jennings wrote in *The Saturday Evening Post* that the popular singer was "a very big business, and in the relentless process of creating a commercial image the manipulators have infused her with a shrewdness and glacial poise rarely found in one so young." But, Jennings went on to say, "the processing seems to have squeezed the youth out of her, leaving a pervading sense of loneliness.

'There are only twenty-four hours in a day,' she says wist-
fully, 'and there is no time for me to have joy and to live.
I feel guilty when I'm not working hard.' "[9]

Besides sacrificing spontaneity and friendships, ambitious
individuals often made marriage secondary to success.
Jennings believed that Connie Francis's business affairs left
her with "little time for serious suitors." Similarly, Elvis
Presley, characterized by friends as a lonely devotee to
success, was quoted in *The Saturday Evening Post* as saying,
"There just doesn't seem to be enough time in my life for
getting serious with women." The extremely brief attention
given to the married lives of success heroes praised in both
Reader's Digest and *The Saturday Evening Post* suggested
that achievers were so wedded to their work that they either
paid little attention to or had to sacrifice many of the pleasures of family life.[10]

The celebration of material success almost devalued
human existence completely. One article portrayed baseball
star Sal Maglie as "an automatic vending machine . . . [who]
wheeled the ball up to the plate methodically and quickly."
Another described businessman Arnold Johnson as "a
human calculating machine, especially of capital-gains
situations."[11] In *Reader's Digest*, Robert L. Murray wrote
about five women who were given ten thousand dollars each
by a business firm after they had been exposed to a lethal
dose of radium on the job. At the conclusion of his article,
Murray stated that he was "almost inclined to believe that
deep down in their [the workers'] souls they almost believe
that the $10,000 they received for their lives was a good
bargain for them."[12]

Since our nation measures progress by material standards, the success ethic encourages the perspective that citizens are functional parts of organized society. This utilitarian
attitude has caused some success advocates to evaluate war
in callous commercial terms. Isaac Marcosson explained, in
1919, that "business lies—or should lie—at the root of everything." Praising General Pershing for personifying "the

application of the fundamental rules of trade to the thing called war," Marcosson contended that "war these days is simply colossal merchandising with men. Instead of converting raw steel into rails or girders it transforms the raw human being into a finished fighting man."[13]

War was thought of in terms of winning and losing just as the American dream spoke of success and failure. Just as the race for success was accepted as a self-evident good, so also was participation in a war for victory not to be questioned. The attitude which a soldier needed to fight efficiently, rather than the justifiability of such combat, became success adherents' prime concern. Thus, in accord with the tenets of positive thinking, writers became concerned with the morale of the troops during the Vietnamese war rather than the morality of American intervention in the Indochina conflict.

Success writers likewise urged politicians to manage domestic affairs according to commercial rather than democratic and humanitarian standards. While the dream of success has inspired reformers to extend opportunity to the less fortunate, conservatives have used the philosophy to demand that the government assist business enterprise but leave the impoverished and middle class to rise by their own efforts.

Bureaucratic metaphors abound in such conservative rhetoric. Describing the United States government's work as a "national business," Edward G. Lowry insisted that political matters "be conducted as efficiently and economically and on as modern scientific principles as any large private business." Marcosson similarly considered Herbert Hoover the head of a "vast national corporation" who studied public opinion "precisely like a manufacturer who analyzes the market for his sales distribution." Richard Child praised the corporate-minded Calvin Coolidge as a believer in "industry, sense, individual responsibility and self help. . . ." Similarly, in California Ronald Reagan ran on a platform likening government to business, boosting corporations, criticizing welfare recipients and promising budget cuts. Upon taking office, Reagan followed the usual corporate politician's practice of giving tax breaks to industry, raising middle class taxes and cutting aid to the poor.[14]

In effect, then, the success ethic promotes elite interests under the guise of boasting that the average citizen can advance as far as he wishes. Finding it a powerful ideology through which corporate America can justify its dominance and influence the public, 762 business firms in 1961 alone bought Norman Vincent Peale's *Guideposts* to inspire their workers to think positively, productively and obediently. Similarly, U.S. Steel spent $150,000 in 1953 to purchase Peale's magazine for its employees. On a much broader scale, magazines like *The Saturday Evening Post* and *Reader's Digest* promulgate the success ethic largely because they are corporations supported through advertising revenues paid by other corporations.[15]

Why do so many citizens fail to see the elitist orientation of success ideologists? At its root, the success ethic encourages supremacy, not equality. Articles in *Reader's Digest* and *The Saturday Evening Post* regularly praised successful figures who rose "to the top" or were "the best in the world." To be sure, Americans point with pride to their tendency to root for the underdog. In doing so, however, they reveal an interest in the struggling achiever rather than the downtrodden. If the underdog succeeds, he is praised; if he fails, he is soon forgotten.

In preferring successful individuals to those unable to advance, many adherents to the success ethic have indicated that they do not believe in the equality of men. College president John A. Logan, Jr., stated in *Reader's Digest* that Americans must "beware of the prevalent and pernicious misconception that democracy implies absolute equality and that any denial of equal worth is un-American. Democracy means equal rights before the law and equal opportunity for individual development to the limits of one's potential; democracy emphatically does not imply that everyone has the same potential, that knowledge and experience are not to be valued above ignorance and inexperience, and that every man's judgment is sovereign and that every opinion is as good as every other."[16]

Middle class Americans consequently have different attitudes towards the rich and the poor. In response to advertisements and articles praising businesses for providing jobs, goods and services to the public, citizens are led to consider business demands to correspond to their own interests. Since the poor need financial assistance, they have often been regarded as an irritating burden to middle class taxpayers.

The tension between equality and competition causes other middle class difficulties in understanding and caring about the problems of the impoverished. Because success advocates posit that America is the land of equal opportunity, many have believed that anyone can share in our nation's abundance if he so wishes. On the other hand, in stressing that an individual must be thrifty and competitive, success writers have led Americans to think in terms of conflict between individuals for a limited number of prizes. These conflicting assumptions of both abundance and scarcity have led many Americans to ignore the causes of poverty and sometimes consider the poor as a personal threat. Since it was assumed that any American could succeed, poverty was caused by laziness and lack of thrift. If all were competing for wealth, the elevation of the lower class would only add competitors to the race for riches and possibly lower the quality of middle class life. In *Reader's Digest*, Hanson Baldwin attacked welfare programs and integration by contending that the "20th century has been called in America 'the century of the common man'—and he is very common indeed. The leveling out process of the last 30 years has undoubtedly lifted some from the ruck but has pulled others down in the process."[17]

In sum, the success ethic fosters what Philip Slater has aptly called a "carrot-on-a-stick" mentality. Lured by the

promise of America's abundance, the average citizen represses
emotions, defers gratification and ignores his stress. And to
prevent the citizen from realizing that he is treated as a
functional instrument in our corporate economy, success
advocates scapegoat the poor, encourage respect for industrial
magnates and cause Americans to identify with economic
leaders wishing to profit from the average man's services
and vote.

Economic Opportunities: Dreams and Realities

Since the concepts of self-reliance and equal opportunity
and the admiration of corporate leaders' achievements have
influenced middle class values and politics greatly, it is
important to understand the extent to which the dream of
success adequately reflects social mobility in America. Much
of the support for the success ethic stems from the fact that
the middle class has been able to better itself financially to
some extent. Based on adjustments of 1929 incomes and
prices to those of 1960, the percentage of families living on
incomes from $7,500–$14,999 has risen from 9 percent in
1929 to 31 percent in 1960. The percentage of unskilled
laborers in America has dropped from 36 percent in 1910 to
19.7 percent in 1950, and in 1957 white collar workers
exceeded blue collar workers for the first time in our nation's
history.[18]
Nevertheless, the chances for success have not been as
great as self help philosophers would have Americans believe.
While 15.9 million businesses opened from 1900 to 1940,
14 million businesses failed in the same period. And while
many success advocates deny that extensive poverty exists in
America, the U.S. Government's Conference on Economic
Progress reported that 77 million citizens, or 40 percent of the
population, lived in poverty or deprivation in 1960. Four
out of five blacks live in such an economically depressed
state. As many people lived annually on $1000 or less in
1960 as lived on $7500 or more. Moreover, the fact that

four-fifths of all citizens over 65 years of age suffer poverty or deprivation especially indicates that a life of diligence and thrift does not necessarily result in the rewards promised by future-oriented success advocates.[19]

The contrast between statistics demonstrating the amount of overall upward mobility and the slight degree of movement among semiskilled, blue collar and poor occupational groups indicates that the American economy affords varying degrees of opportunity to different classes. The line between white collar and blue collar work is the hardest to cross over. Eighty percent of the urban labor force have either remained in their class or dropped in position in comparison to their fathers' economic rank. A professional's son has a 50 percent chance of receiving a college education while unskilled parents' children have only a 6 percent opportunity. And black Americans receiving a college education earn less than whites holding only high school diplomas.[20]

These statistics suggest that the success advocate's cliché that Americans can rise from rags to riches is a myth. In an extensive analysis of the presidents and board chairmen in the nation's largest railroad, public utility and industrial corporations from 1898 to 1953, Mabel Newcomer discovered that only 1.3 percent to 3.1 percent of the managerial elite have come from semiskilled or unskilled families. W. Lloyd Warner and James C. Abegglin determined that "the elite men of 1952 were recruited about eight times oftener than would have been expected under random placement. On the other hand . . . elite men were recruited only .16 as often as would occur in a fully open society."[21]

Thus, class background, inheritance and connections far more than the success ethic's formula of diligence, thrift and salesmanship affect the American's chances for advancement. Nevertheless, because the middle class assumes that most people belong to their economic class and consequently share equal opportunities, citizens generally do not recognize that the chances for success are uneven, uncertain and more dependent upon environmental circumstances than personal behavior.

Psychological Costs: A Life of Pretense

Since opportunities do not necessarily correspond to aspirations, the success ethic can encourage psychological stress within frustrated achievers. Being told that an individual can and must succeed through his own efforts, the would-be success may assume that he has control over his destiny. If such a person begins to sense that he may not reach his goals, he then may strive for superiority over either his environment or his fellow man to obliterate his feelings of helplessness and insignificance.

Of course, an individual could discard either difficult goals or an exaggerated belief in personal potentiality, but the highly moralistic character of the principle of self-reliance has provoked many Americans to feel obligated to succeed. The concept of self-reliance leads many to believe that personal deficiencies rather than societal limitations cause their failures. Moreover, if an individual devotes a large portion of his life to pursuing success, he may find it difficult to discard his dreams since such a change might suggest that he had heretofore wasted his life. Finally, if an individual begins to fear that he is unable to achieve his goals self-reliantly, he is often reluctant to drop earlier beliefs since his world would seem increasingly unintelligible as well as uncontrollable without such guides.

Out of helplessness, guilt and a need to retain the success ethic, an achiever unconsciously becomes concerned about the power of his will. To a considerable extent, the confusion over the concept of will and its resultant paralysis has been intrinsically connected to the crisis of contemporary middle class culture. Since much of this book is concerned with such confusion, only a brief outline of the consequences of success-oriented defense mechanisms is necessary here.

To retain a belief in complete personal control over his life by ignoring problems which challenge personal beliefs, an achiever is prone to use the devices of salesmanship, positive thinking, messianic self-description, fantasy, self-righteous absolutism, insistence on social conformity and possibly support of paranoid movements.[22]

Salesmanship techniques permit a person both to hide his stress and to gain influence over others. According to Dale Carnegie and other proponents of salesmanship, an achiever is required to affect humility while displaying a magnetic personality. He must appear interested in his customers or superiors so that they will grant him favors. By using a mask of confidence, a practicioner of salesmanship hopes to conceal feelings of uncertainty. Through praise, dynamism and modesty, he attempts to protect himself from disapproval while making customers sympathetic to his wishes.

An achiever also uses salesmanship techniques to manipulate his own mind and emotions to gain control and tranquility. Quoting William James's statement that "action seems to follow feeling, but really action and feeling go together; and by regulating the action, which is under the more direct control of the will, we can indirectly regulate the feeling which is not," self help writers such as Carnegie promised nervous Americans that by acting as if they were confident and happy, they would indeed become assured and content. In *Reader's Digest*, Bruce Bliven told Americans, "Control your emotions by your actions. The things you *do* help determine the way you *feel*. You are angry at least partly *because* you strike a blow; you are sad partly *because* you cry. . . ."[23]

Similarly, Dorothea Brande, in her highly popular *Wake Up and Live!*, grossly distorted Hans Vaihinger's and Alfred Adler's psychological theories to maintain that if Americans acted as if their beliefs were true, then their beliefs would be valid. Vaihinger had maintained that people acted as if their beliefs were true because such values, goals and self-conceptions could only be assumptions. If those assumptions were not realistic, Adler contended, an individual had to discard his fictions or become trapped in a neurotic and potentially psychotic self-defeating will to power. In direct contrast,

Brande used Vaihinger and Adler to argue that a person should continue to pretend that the success ethic was realistic even if he failed and assume that defeat was caused by an unconscious will to fail.[24]

In calling for a life of pretense success writers insisted that the individual should ignore frustrations and never blame others for his failings. Maxwell Maltz, author of several popular books on psycho-cybernetics, stipulated that "all our disturbed feelings—anger, hostility, fear, anxiety, insecurity— are caused by our own responses, not by any external stimuli." Maltz asked his readers to find a spot inside their minds in which they could forget personal problems for a certain period of time each day. Similarly, Norman Vincent Peale argued that "to a large extent by our thoughts and attitudes we distill out of the ingredients of life either happiness or unhappiness for ourselves." To end worry, Peale told his followers to say " 'With God's help I am now emptying my mind of all anxiety, all fear, all sense of insecurity.' Repeat this slowly five times, then add 'I believe that my mind is now emptied of all anxiety, all fear, all sense of insecurity.' "[25]

To further escape problems, positive thinkers advised their followers to rationalize away any difficulties they had. Trouble for Peale was the "Whetstone of Life" that "puts an edge on courage . . . [and may call] forth the latent nobility in man." If a person failed he should be happy in learning from his mistakes so that he could try again. And if a person continually failed, Gabriel Heatter maintained, he should content himself with having tried to succeed.[26]

Since recommendations to accept personal responsibility for failure, follow an out-of-sight-out-of-mind policy towards stress, and rationalize even defeat to be success essentially exonerated our cultural beliefs and corporate institutions from responsibility for the American worker's discontent, it is understandable why corporations have encouraged the proselytizing of the success ethic through men like Peale and Carnegie.

Unfortunately, rationalizations and escapist behavior usually fail to alleviate anxiety. But if an individual continues to retain an exaggerated belief in self-reliance and hope for unrealistic goals, he may resort to fantasizing that he is a god capable of magical powers. The tendency to assume godlike qualities is partly the result of the success ethic's emphasis on individualism. As de Tocqueville observed, Americans so exalt the individual that they begin to lose respect for the supernatural. Bruce Barton, in *The Man Nobody Knows*, called upon his readers to disregard Christ's title of "the Son of God" while they read his self help book and simply conceive of Jesus as the "founder of modern business." With the might of the Deity reduced, success writers often selected victors in the race for riches to fill His place. Henry Link claimed that "the business man, the employer, performs daily the miracle of converting water into wine. He converts raw materials into the means of a livelihood, and he converts undirected employees, individualists, into members of a team which has both direction and power."[27]

Welcoming challenges to succeed, writers spoke of magical qualities which helpless achievers hoped could augment the power of their wills. Frank Bettger spoke of the "Magic of Enthusiasm" in his book on salesmanship and A. H. Z. Carr deemed personal zest an "almost magical power."[28]

Success adherents also have tried to ignore dubious beliefs and societal deficiencies by dogmatically insisting that social critics stop publicizing national problems. Success advocates often accused critics of the achievement ethic of being motivated by personal failure or mental illness. Gilbert Seldes described the expatriate writer of the Twenties as "an American who . . . somehow failed in America—failed to understand it or to turn its tremendous opportunities to his purpose. . . ." In 1921, the editors of *The Saturday Evening Post* claimed that radicals were "characterized by abnormal mental and nervous states." Whereas "healthy-minded men manifest normality by joy of living, pleasure in their work,

willingness to face things as they are . . . and not by super-
normal idealism," radicals were motivated by "a shaming sense
of their own inadequacy." The editors recommended that
the radical "consult a wise physician. If none is at hand . . .
let him study and reflect upon Emerson's Essays . . . on
Self-Reliance and on Compensation."[29]

By attempting to enforce conformity to the dream of
success, confused achievers could reinforce their own doubted
beliefs. In demeaning social criticism, success adherents could
rationalize that they "realistically" had to be diligent even
if they did not attain or feel satisfied with the goals to which
they aspired.

Insistence upon power and conformity led some success
writers to demand an inordinate and often militaristic love of
order and discipline while contradictorily calling for self-
mastery. Link advocated the use of universal army training
to inculcate obedience in American youth. In *Reader's Digest*,
Hanson Baldwin demanded that young men be aggressive
and self-dependent so that they could become military leaders
who could discipline others into a victorious team willing to
die if necessary for their leaders' demands. By enforcing
discipline upon others, the frustrated achiever could hope to
attain the superiority and control so desperately desired.[30]

The desire for order, power and supremacy, when
coupled to messianic fantasies and an absolute reluctance to
change unsatisfactory beliefs predisposes success-oriented
individuals to support paranoid movements. Paranoia may
attack people who approach their goals but eventually are
prevented from achieving them. Guilty and ashamed of their
lack of success, such persons may attempt to conceal their
feelings of inadequacy from themselves and others by searching for imaginary villains to serve as scapegoats. They simplis-
tically imagine that obstacles to their advancement have
been caused by liberals, agitators, non-conformists and big
government. By elevating their opposition to the status of
witches and demons who hope to destroy the world, paranoids can imagine their struggle to be a sign of superhuman

ability. They proclaim the success ethic as an almost religious doctrine to convince themselves that demanding conformity to their values is a worthwhile and necessary moral crusade. Since paranoids engage in imaginary conflicts, however, they fail to resolve their real problems and thus remain anxious and frustrated.[31]

While self help writers were not paranoids, the extreme arguments they made after World Wars I and II offered strong ideological support to irrational reactionary politics. During the Red Scare and the McCarthy Era, the dream of success often was preached in highly religious terminology by writers apparently uncomfortable with but reluctant to change their beliefs. During both paranoid movements messianic descriptions of individual power and calls for conformity, order and discipline were popularized in success tracts. In the early Fifties especially, apocalyptic fears of the destruction of civilization by liberalism, welfare programs and Communism were regularly predicted by writers who desperately demanded the retention of the gospel of success. Both periods were marked by failure to confront societal inadequacies and serious inconsistencies within the success ethic. And at the end of both periods, many Americans seemed more lost than ever in the attempt to understand themselves and their society.

The Pleasure Ethic

To be sure, many Americans have not needed to retain faith in the dream of success through reactionary politics or the use of escapist defense mechanisms. For mildly success-oriented persons, the pleasure ethic has partially alleviated frustrations. Advocates of this philosophy, who appeared in the mid-Twenties and became highly popular during the depression, emphasized material consumption and friendships over thrift and manipulative relationships. Although often calling for Americans to be diligent and successful, advocates of the pleasure-oriented search for the self generally considered occupations secondary to enjoyment.[32]

Walter Pitkin's *Life Begins at Forty* contained most of the facets of the pleasure ethic. While Pitkin encouraged people over forty to rise to wealth, fame and importance, he mainly lamented that "AMERICANS DIE YOUNG LARGELY BECAUSE THEY NEVER START LIVING. Our silly dollar-chasing and our greasy grind of factory and our stupid philosophies of life all carry over into middle years the tempo and thrust of youth" and exhaust Americans. Unconvinced that future wealth was so enchanting, Pitkin urged Americans to carry "out successfully the dominant desires of the moment." Similarly, in *Orchids on Your Budget*, Marjorie Hillis told her readers to enjoy the present because "things to which you look forward too long are almost invariably disappointing when you get them, and you *might* die first anyway."[33]

Present-minded middle class philosophers considered the consumption of material products an important source of pleasure. Pitkin told his readers to concern themselves less with work and more with the pleasures of travel, reading and sports to find happiness. Hillis similarly maintained that thrift could make life dull unless people "invested in happiness."[34]

In addition, conventional pleasure-minded philosophers encouraged friendships to counteract the success ethic's emphasis on work and emotional repression. Katharine Anthony explained that "nobody can live wholly in a job. . . . How much better if we admit our need of love and affection and then try to build up these relationships in the full light of self-knowledge." Because Pitkin believed that professional specialization dulled the personality, he advocated personality development to acquire friends and make life more exciting. Hillis echoed the proponents of the personality cult and maintained that "companionship . . . is essential to happiness."[35]

The increasing demand for pleasure, consumption and

friendship has indicated a growing public dissatisfaction with our industrialized corporate society. The size of modern enterprises and mass production often have made individual efforts insignificant. Because the routinized efficiency of mass production has destroyed spontaneity in work, the individual has been left with a sense of boredom. The chain of command in modern economic structures has given few persons a sense of control. And the depersonalizing facets of our commercial, bureaucratic culture have led many to experience a profound sense of loneliness.

While the pleasure ethic allows Americans to vent frustrations and search for a more satisfying life than that prescribed by the success ethic, it does not motivate citizens to envision more radical transformations of their society to alleviate social discontent. Significantly, very few references have been made to politics in pleasure-oriented articles and books. Most pleasure seekers wish to find a comfortable place within the system rather than change the system itself. Their world consists of personal entertainment with their family and friends. Their political beliefs are more flexible than those of rigidly success-oriented reactionaries but do little to enhance an understanding of radical thought. Pleasure seeking consumers, especially in the 1960s, generally could not understand why rebellious youths were unsatisfied by material comforts and felt it necessary either to discard possessions or spread their affluence to others.

Of course, in some respects the growing popularity of the conventional pleasure-oriented approach to the search for the self did help to create the milieu necessary for the development of the youthful counterculture in the late Sixties. Pitkin's castigation of the "greasy grind of factory" life preceded the greater aversion to meaningless occupations which has characterized the loosely termed "hippie movement." The "get away from it all" dream of parents seeking escape from dreary and nerve-racking jobs in the 1950s anteceded the dropout ethic of the 1960s. The desire for friendship which grew in the 1940s and 1950s presaged modern youthful hopes for communality. The emphasis on consumption helped predispose countercultural youths to perceive a society of abundance which did not necessitate continual diligence. And pleasure-seekers' calls for living in the present foreshadowed the growth of freer forms of contemporary existentialism.

Most conventional pleasure seekers have been unable to notice the more radical countercultural extensions of their beliefs because of an ambivalent retention of the work ethic. While Pitkin deplored "our silly dollar-chasing," he still wrote articles for *Reader's Digest* encouraging young men to get ahead. Self help writer George Dorsey advocated entertainment and leisure, criticized people for becoming dull by accepting the routinization of work and yet promised his readers that a "steady drive at one thing, kept up long enough, will make you famous and possibly a genius." Similarly, Hillis told her readers both to live in the present and abide by the gospel of work.[36]

Unable to discard completely the compulsion to work, conventional pleasure seekers often appeared guilty in their leisure moments and needed to legitimize pleasureful activities through the facade of action. Alan Devoe acknowledged, in *Reader's Digest*, that Americans "live in a work-conscious era" and thus the "practice of idleness is not as easy as it sounds." Advertisements for pleasurable items regularly portrayed individuals driving automobiles through the countryside or running through fields while smoking cigarettes rather than simply resting in pastoral settings where they did nothing but enjoy nature.[37]

The inclusion of motion in pleasure-oriented philosophies revealed further similarities between the success and consumption ethics. Just as the achiever was to race for riches, the pleasure seeker was to search for enjoyment. As the Declaration of Independence prescribed, Americans were guaranteed only the pursuit of happiness, not happiness itself. The pleasure ethic sometimes has functioned to drive Americans towards unrealistic goals for the interests of business in a manner similar to unsatisfying achievement-oriented life styles. Conditioned to compulsive consumption just as much as they are compelled to work, bored housewives mill through department stores searching for excitement and something to do. Men, bored by the tedium of industrial jobs, buy gadgets to feel the power attached to technology. Because advertisements use the enticements of sex and popularity, we unconsciously buy products when we feel lonely and depressed even though the mere thought of attaining sexual gratification or friendship through the purchase of toothpaste suggests the absurdity of such inducements.[38]

The theme of movement in pleasure philosophies also reflected escapist tendencies similar to success-oriented defense mechanisms. The "let's get away from it all" variation of the pleasure ethic sometimes resembled the out-of-sight-out-of-mind fantasies of positive thinkers. Just as rationalizations failed to eradicate achievers' stress and occasionally led to authoritarian tendencies, so also could escapist pleasure seeking turn into aggressive behavior.

When the retreat to the mountains, seashores and suburbs after World War II failed to relieve frustration and boredom, many pleasure seekers turned to more dangerous entertainments such as skin diving and sky diving to escape the world without having to change their lives. Marion L. Boling told *Reader's Digest* subscribers that because he could not tolerate the lack of individuality and control his job offered, he had risked his life by flying nonstop from the Philippines to Oregon in a single engine airplane to regain his sense of self-reliance and self-respect. Even after such an extreme act, Boling concluded his article by saying that he still needed to return to the same unsatisfactory job.[39]

When escape still proved unsatisfying, many Americans in the 1960s turned to more violent interests such as James Bond fantasies and professional football. In *The Saturday Evening Post*, Bill Koman spoke both as a frustrated business-man and a professional football player for Americans who vented weekly occupational tensions through Sunday football.

"Football is a great outlet for me," Koman asserted. "I have to look at guys all week long who aren't performing for us, or whose bids are way out of line, and I want to annihilate them, but I can't. I have to be nice to them. On Sunday [when I play football], I don't have to be nice to anyone."[40]

To be sure, the pleasure seeking approach to living has led mainly to personal or vicarious forms of violent behavior and thus certainly has not been as socially threatening as repressive reactionary movements. Nevertheless, the increasingly desperate actions of contemporary pleasure seekers have indicated the incapability of escapist behavior to alleviate personal tensions or lessen the cultural climate of violence which has permeated our society and been too casually tolerated in modern times.

Moralistic and Humanistic Guides to Living

The beliefs which conventional middle class Americans have used to express more anti-materialistic, peaceful and humanitarian sentiments have been those associated with popular moralistic and humanistic guides to living. Both guides began with the assumption that the attainment of monetary success or material comfort could not be man's essential purpose. For the humanist, success aspirations threatened higher principles of life; for the moralist, money led the individual away from God. Thus, humanist Ernest Dimnet maintained in *What We Live By* that "the chief danger is that, frequently . . . the joy of success crowds out the remembrance of one's ideals." In a more moralistic tone, Billy Graham preached that one could not serve God and Mammon at the same time.[41]

Both philosophies called for rejection of the principle of self-reliance, although moralists believed the concept weakened devotion to God while humanists held that self-reliance limited human cooperation. Graham explained that the "philosophy of self-reliance and self-sufficiency [which] has caused many to believe that man can make the grade without God" led to a generation which "has produced more alcoholics, more dope addicts, more criminals, more wars . . . than any other generation which ever lived. . . . It is about time," Graham continued, that men place "less confidence in [them] selves and more trust and faith in God." Angered by the power drives of American success thought, Bishop Fulton Sheen demanded that men stop wanting to be God and instead humbly submit to the Deity. In a more humanistic spirit which could be shared by both churchgoers and agnostics, Rabbi Joshua Liebman preached that a person should acknowledge his inadequacies and cooperate with his fellow man.[42]

The ideals which both humanistic and moralistic philosophers advocated were individual and societal peace. Both groups assumed that world pacification would result from the spiritual development of the self. Rabbi Liebman asserted that *"social peace can never be permanently achieved so long as individuals engage in civil war with themselves."* Similarly, Bishop Sheen contended "there can be no world peace unless there is soul peace."[43]

Although moralists and humanists agreed upon goals, they differed on their definitions of peace and the means to attain it. Peace of soul, advocated by Bishop Sheen, connoted a calm self-assurance based upon firm religious beliefs, whereas peace of mind, promulgated by Rabbi Liebman, implied a tranquility acquired by the application of psychology to religion. Peace of soul was motivated by a sense of personal guilt and fear of God whereas peace of mind resulted from an idealistic acceptance of self and love of man.

Sheen admitted that psychology could be useful, but feared that it might become a philosophy of life justifying the release of man's repressed urges. He called upon his readers to suppress illicit desires, confess their guilt and acquiesce to the will of an omnipotent God. The individual then was to practice charity, tolerance and love towards others. Sheen feared that governmental authority might replace ecclesiastical direction, however, and thus placed strictures on the types of charity allowable. Individual actions based upon the Bible's dictates circumvented the need for national political reform. Persons should devote their lives to God's precepts of neighborly cooperation since, Sheen contended, "Social Christianity," or the effort to clear slums and promote international amity, could be inspired by the Devil.[44]

Liebman's advocacy of peace of mind similarly stressed the need for religious values, peace and cooperation but differed sharply from Sheen's attitude towards guilt, repression and political involvement. Liebman criticized religion for repressing individuals and fostering a sense of guilt. Only through love of self, Liebman believed, could the individual learn to love others.[45]

Liebman further urged his readers to become individualists, reject inhumane and inadequate social mores and guide their lives by universal principles which provided self-respect and tranquility. To express the ideals of love and tolerance, the individual should become involved in state and national reformist politics as well as perform charitable acts within his neighborhood.[46]

Both moralistic and humanistic philosophies did contain strong principles through which men were led to have concern for others. However, the different viewpoints of *both* philosophies also could ironically limit individuals' ability to correct societal deficiencies if the retention of moralistic values and humanistic principles was considered more important than actual care for others.

Acting out of guilt, the moralist might remain self-interested and submit to an authority mainly to gain favors or avoid pain. In religious actions, a fearful person might bow to an omnipotent God to reach heaven or, more likely, avoid the fires of hell. In politics, submission to God and skepticism of human potentiality led Sheen and his followers to demand trust in God's beneficence. As such, guilt-ridden philosophies tended to favor resignation to mankind's problems and stress personal rather than social concern.

While moralists did allow community social work, their assumption that religious dogma sufficiently analyzed social problems impaired their ability to empathize with and correct the plight of the less fortunate. This faith in absolutes together with a need to acquiesce to God's directives could lead an individual to think with Sheen that "a soul passes from a state of speculation to *submission*. It is no longer troubled with the *why* of religion, but with the *ought*. It wishes to please, not merely to parse [understand] Divinity." With such an attitude, persons seeing the difficulties of others might at first wish to understand and assist the suffering; but quickly, because of a disposition to act in accord with fixed moral principles, they would be redirected to judge social problems as products of degeneracy rather than as societal deficiencies. As Graham explained and Sheen agreed, "Unhappiness is an effect, and sin is the cause." With sin the basic world problem, social reform thus passed from the secular to the spiritual realm and in effect from the scope of human influence to the Almighty's power. The moralist could easily resort to demanding that his view of religion be accepted rather than hear the sufferers' pleas for political reform.[47]

Humanists found a greater role for political action since their respect for empathy and trust necessitated a search for socioeconomic and psychological causes of suffering rather than moral explanations. By relating problems to culture, institutions and the unconscious rather than to the soul or the devil, humanists thus could perceive issues in a more secular and humanly correctable fashion.

Even so, a dogmatic faith in humanistic ideals could limit a person's capacity for supporting social change as severely as moralistic guides. Unless carefully employed, psychology could become a substitute for religion. Rather than understanding human motivations, a humanist might judge individuals or America as neurotic or psychotic just as the moralist would categorize actions as venial or mortal sins.

If the idealistic assumption of human goodness and ability to progress became an absolute belief, a humanist

might find it difficult to confront social inequities for an
extended length of time. When first confronting social
suffering, a humanist might wish to help because of his faith
in man's essential goodness. However, if a social problem
suggested that all men were not by nature kind, a humanist
could begin to feel that his assumed view of human nature
was not necessarily valid. Thus, a social problem might turn
from being a circumstance in which someone needed assistance to a symbolic threat to the humanist's basic faith. If
the humanist was reluctant to modify his optimism, he
ironically might lose some of his interest in a societal problem and become more concerned with proving that his faith
in man was correct.

With such a redirected concern, some humanists would
then use their principles as inspirational guides for reassurance
rather than as motivational directives for reform. The insistence on care, which necessitates a decision to involve oneself
to lessen the sufferings of others, could be replaced by an
advocacy of universal love implying that an emotional force
could push men towards cooperation without the exertion of
anyone's will. The hope for love rather than the practice of
care ultimately could transform the sensitivity of an empa-
thetic humanism into the sentimentalism connected with
apathy.[48]

The reduction of humanistic ideals to modes of reassurance was evident in the rapid shift in popular tastes from
early post-World War II reformist humanistic literature to the
1950s inspirational books which seemed more concerned
with proving that people were kind than with encouraging
people to care for others. Departing from the humanistic
assertion that peace of mind necessitated participation in
reform movements, many beleaguered Americans in the Fifties
sought mind cure formulas whose sentimental reminiscences
of motherhood, the loyalty of dogs and small individual acts
of kindness gave solace to persons retreating from a terrifying
world where war and totalitarianism seemed to negate a faith
in human goodness.

While humanistic beliefs again became popular for a few years during the early Sixties, the mood of many conventional middle class Americans for the entire decade perhaps was characterized best by the cartoon figures in Charles Schultz's "Peanuts." Throughout his stories, Schultz advocated a humanistic hope that people would be kind to their fellow men. Sometimes, Schultz's humanism took on moralistic overtones. But at all times, it was apparent that Schultz's message was largely a sentimental desire for the retention of a faith in human decency which seemed to be absent in society. Charlie Brown basically believed in being kind, but he had little reformist spirit within him. Rather, he just tried to get along in a society of companions who cared little for his feelings. Surrounded by a success-fixated callous Lucy and a self-interested, pleasure seeking, fantasizing Snoopy, Charlie Brown could not even be reassured by the 1950s promise of feminine tenderness and canine loyalty. With the call for kindness embedded in a setting of social apathy, self interest and callousness, Schultz's message was founded less on a desire for cooperative effort to lessen suffering than on an ambivalent, weakened hope for human kindness and a passive response to aloneness and tragedy.

Thus, while the four conventional middle class guides to living have promised prosperity, enjoyment, spiritual meaning and social concern, an absolutist adherence to any one of these philosophies could instigate personal suffering or prevent an adequate response to discontent. There is nothing inherently detrimental in desires for success, happiness, morality and care. However, the manner in which our culture has defined these concepts leads to frustration.

The history of middle class America which follows illustrates how our guides to living have become so dysfunctional. Even though our beliefs clash, most Americans have not attempted to recognize these conflicts in a manner which would allow them to develop a more complex yet functional philosophy of life. Instead, they have embarked on a quest for reassurance which often attempts to fuse all four guides to living into a harmonious, vague and highly unstable culture. Through such behavior, Americans have become subject to a process in which personal philosophies of life have merged with ideological demands. Consequently, in assuming that they were working for their own interests, citizens were led to sublimate their emotional needs.

The disjunction between standards of behavior and assumed goals made us restrict our awareness, suffer needless stress on account of shame and guilt and find it difficult to satisfy our desires for individualism, community and a spirit of care.

Chapter 2

PASSIVITY AND FANTASY: The Impact of

Corporatism on the American Dream

How did our values become so distorted? While tensions always have existed between our culture and the search for the self, contemporary confusion dates mainly from when the rise of industrialism seriously challenged our basic values. During that period, the success ethic contributed to American development by bolstering the achievement orientation which many social scientists see as a crucial component in economic modernization. But the industrial system that emerged transformed the social reality that gave the success ethic whatever validity it ever had in giving meaning to American lives.

Refusing to recognize the growing unreality of their beliefs and the tensions between their concepts of achievement, pleasure, morality and care, Americans subjected the success ethic to increasingly bizarre rationalizations. Through these rationalizations, a process occurred in which the dream of success as a philosophy of life fused with corporate ideology to the extent that citizens, in seeking reassurance for their traditional values, accepted beliefs which were antithetical to their psychological needs but highly profitable to industrial interests.

What makes the period from the 1870s through the 1920s important for us today is that it demonstrates how our values were distorted, our personal desires were sublimated, and fantasy was made a substitute for thought. Specifically, the period exemplifies how individualism can turn into conformity, free will into passivity, care into self-interest, pleasure into profit and morality into materialism.

Harmony and Instability

To understand how these inversions occurred, we need to begin by looking briefly at preindustrial American history. In bringing the Protestant Ethic to the colonies, Puritans and Quakers had difficulty in integrating material, pleasurable, spiritual and humanitarian desires. Similarly, the Founding Fathers endorsed the spirit of capitalism but were concerned with its potentially disruptive effects on social order. In the early 1800s, farmers eager to amass profits feared that democracy and self-reliance would be eroded by a dependancy on the growth of an urban commercial culture.

Nevertheless, in the 1830s and 1840s, a majority of citizens put these problems aside to make the dream of success our dominant cultural paradigm. The Commissioner of Indian Affairs in 1832 insisted that private property "may not unjustly be considered the parent of all improvements." Secretary of War Crawford likewise maintained that "distinct ideas of separate property . . . must precede any considerable advance in the arts of civilization. . . ."[1]

Thus it was assumed that the success ethic did not conflict with our other values. One of the foremost spokesmen of the period, Ralph Waldo Emerson, argued in his essays on "Power," "Wealth" and "Self-Reliance" that the pursuit of riches did not impinge on moral behavior, social stability or democratic equality. To counteract the possible fear that the race for riches would destroy moral fiber, he contended that property would "not be in bad hands . . . but would [rush] from the idle and imbecile to the industrious, brave and persevering." Assuming that "wealth brings with it its own checks and balances," Emerson rejected the need for governmental restraints on economic competition to protect the public's welfare. Essentially, Emerson believed that each American should act in his self interest under the assumption that the fulfillment of the individual's interests contributed to the nation as a whole.[2]

Central to Emerson's assumptions was the concept of individualism. Claiming that "the appearance of character makes the state unnecessary," Emerson argued that "the wiseman is the State. He needs no army, fort, or navy—he loves men too well; no bribe, no feast or palace, to draw friends to him; no vantage ground, no favorable circumstances. He needs no library, for he has not done thinking; no church, for he is a prophet; no statute-book, for he is the law-giver; no money, for he is value; no road, for he is at home where he is; no experience, for the life of the creator shoots through him. . . . He has no personal friends."[3]

Underneath this bravado lay a dynamic but seriously disjointed social philosophy. The cultural foundation Emerson articulated paradoxically defined our society as a collection of happily lonely individuals disconnected from their government, God, home, tradition, knowledge and environment. Since the individual was in complete control of his life, the responsibilities of the government were few. Transferring God's and nature's power to man while suggesting that thought and religion were irrelevant, our culture unleashed a nonreflective, uninhibited will to power.

To be sure, not all Americans subscribed to these beliefs. But a sufficient number did to cause our nation to engage in a race for riches that became especially acute in the 1870s and 1880s. It became apparent that there was little justification for the mid-nineteenth century assumption that the success ethic insured harmony rather than chaos, moral improvement rather than self interest, and humanitarian sentiments rather than brutal competition. Industrial magnates fought competitors with a ferocity we find staggering today. Enough corruption entered business and politics that some historians have deemed the period the "Age of the Robber Barons" or "The Great Barbeque." And the suffering attending industrialism was so acute that urban centers burgeoned with slums and bloody labor strikes.

Even so, under the illusion that their conflicting ideals

could remain harmonious, most citizens remained determined to protect their success-oriented values. A few, such as the Social Darwinists, rationalized that chaos brought order by contending that competition was similar to the struggle for existence and thus in accord with natural law. Like Emerson, William Graham Sumner maintained that the government's only function was to guarantee equal opportunity. As Herbert Spencer explained, free enterprise allowed only the fittest to survive, insuring a "process of elimination by which society continually purifies itself." Eventually, Spencer predicted, this process would "end only in the establishment of the greatest perfection and the most complete happiness." Conversely, any governmental attempt to help the poor would only cause the unfit to survive and society to degenerate. Thus, Sumner postulated, the alternatives for Americans were clear and the choice simple: "[W]e cannot go outside of this alternative: liberty, inequality, survival of the fittest; non-liberty, equality, survival of the unfittest. The former carries society forward and favors all of its best members; the latter carries society downwards and favors all its worst members."[4]

Inasmuch as Social Darwinists admitted that liberty led to suffering, their theory appeared extremely harsh to the general public. To make the dream of success more palatable, Horatio Alger brought forth his moralistic achievement-oriented philosophy of life. Reflecting the individualistic temperament of his times, Alger discounted the difficulties industrialism posed for upward mobility by contending that the individual's greatest obstacle to achievement was himself. Any person, Alger maintained, could succeed if he were diligent, thrifty, ambitious and moral.[5]

Beneath his optimism, however, Alger implicitly conveyed a fear that moral behavior might become extinct in an age noted for corrupt and brutal economic activity. Consistently, his books were concerned with the plight of little boys whose rural morals were threatened by cities filled with both evil and promise. When his heroes succeeded through the aid of benevolent businessmen, Alger used their achievements to prove that virtue was worthwhile, kindness would prevail, and America continued to be the land of opportunity. While his characters generally succeeded by accident, Alger stressed that fortuitous opportunities were a natural reward for good behavior. In "Struggling Upward, or Luke Larkin's Luck," Alger admitted that his hero's success was caused in part by luck but emphasized that Luke was "indebted for most of his good fortune to his own good qualities." Theoretically, the American ideals of ambition, virtue and care could continue to be synthesized.[6]

The Sublimation of the American Dream

For all their reassurances, Alger's and Sumner's philosophies were seriously inconsistent in their advocacies of free will. Even though Alger asserted that self-disciplined virtue fostered success, the fact remained that his heroes succeeded by accident. Similarly, Sumner's distinctions between the unfit and the fittest suggested that all men did not possess equal talent or power.

In rationalizing these discrepancies, Sumner and Alger circumscribed Emerson's concept of opportunity and ambivalently advocated passivity as well as ambition. Sumner's justification of the survival of the fittest easily served to sanction subservience to corporate power and tolerance of poverty. Similarly, Alger's heroes rose from rags to respectability rather than from rags to riches. In recommending contentment with a middle class life style, Alger especially stressed the behavioral traits of obedience, respect and gratefulness towards one's employer. As a youth, Ragged Dick promised to serve his benefactor faithfully; when Dick became the successful Richard Hunter, he admonished Mark the Match Boy to "remember that I am your guardian and am to be obeyed as such."[7]

Industrial magnates, hoping to justify corporate power and encourage workers' obedience, began to make arguments which paralleled Alger's and Sumner's transformation of the dream of success. Andrew Carnegie argued that the consolidation of wealth and power in the hands of a few industrialists was an inevitable necessity for progress. Attempting to molify Americans who wondered if self-reliance could continue in an economic system of unequal power and wealth, Carnegie maintained that "individualism will continue, but the millionaire will be a trustee for the poor; entrusted . . . with a great part of the increased wealth of the community, but administering it for the community far better than it would or could have done for itself." Thus, Carnegie attempted to fuse care and ambition into the stewardship of wealth.[8]

While Carnegie defended upper class power, he insisted that average Americans retain the spirit of individualism to discipline themselves in working for the economic rewards offered by the industrial magnate. Individualism was not, however, to foster freedom of spirit or expression because such diversity could cause dissent or inefficient industrial production. Acting upon these beliefs, Carnegie demanded that workers preserve their fictions of individualism by rejecting unionism and working at twelve hour a day, seven day a week jobs in return for the 14–20 cents per hour salaries which he deemed adequate.

Similarly, John D. Rockefeller demanded that the corporation be considered an individual free from governmental regulation while asserting that for the common citizen "individualism has gone, never to return." In denouncing individualism, Rockefeller did not mean that Americans were no longer to be diligent and self-reliant. Instead, the worker was to abnegate his self-expression and self-control by submissively working for management's interests.[9]

The counterpoint between Alger's, Sumner's, Carnegie's and Rockefeller's principles indicated the beginning of a process whereby the public was attempting to preserve the success ethic as a philosophy of life while industrial leaders were transforming the dream of success into a corporate ideology deisgned to justify their power. The effect of this confluence was that Americans, in assuming that they were striving for success, were being acculturated to serve the goals of corporate society rather than their own self interests.

In this respect, Alger's encouragement of employee acquiescence helped facilitate the submissiveness which Carnegie and Rockefeller demanded. Since Alger, Carnegie and Rockefeller agreed that economic advancement was still attainable, business leaders could entice citizens to produce for them by offering the hope of achieving success. If citizens became disturbed that the rich were not controlled, the industrial magnate could argue that he wished to preserve the same freedom to control personal property for any man. At bottom, such equality of freedom was meaningless. The poor and middle classes' property did not provide the same degree of material benefit or power as the upper class's and the lower and middle class stood little chance of acquiring a commensurate amount of wealth. In effect, the bargain which Carnegie offered the American people was that in return for protecting his $400,000,000 estate, Carnegie would promise to defend similar achievements if they ever earned as much. Nevertheless, by assuming that the possession of property was more important than the amount of property possessed and that all could rise to riches, the public unwittingly was committed to defend the rich's interests rather than their own by demanding the protection rather than the more equitable distribution of wealth. While the success ethic for Emerson had been anti-institutional and democratic, for Carnegie and Rockefeller it had become just the opposite.

Many Americans were unaware of this co-option. Some workers made small economic advances. The acquisition of property made people feel that small dreams could actually be achieved. Though wages were low, they slightly increased for the average laborer.

For those who were economically frustrated, the confluence of corporate ideology and personal success philosophies was neither a very tranquil nor a readily apparent process. Labor unions held pitched battles with industries and farmers formed the Populist Party to combat railroads. Nevertheless, laborers and farmers rarely considered abandoning the dream of success. Instead, they merely wanted to attain their share of the nation's abundance without seriously redistributing the wealth corporations already possessed.

Similarly, the Progressive movement which burgeoned at the beginning of the twentieth century seemingly represented a serious middle class attack against the corporation. Elements of the success myth partially inspired such reformist sentiments. Concerned that morality and self-reliance as well as democracy and humanitarianism were being jeopardized, the public cheered Theodore Roosevelt's and Woodrow Wilson's denunciations of monopolies. Even so, the movement was oriented more towards preserving the dream of success than substantially changing the corporate structure.

In spirit, the Progressives wished to retain industrialism's benefits while preserving the opportunity for every American to succeed. Assuming that harmony and progress could be secured if individualism, morality and kindness prevailed, the Progressives instituted reforms to punish "bad" trusts and reinstate "good" government, protect citizens from the evils of drink so that they could strive to succeed, abolish child labor to insure humanitarianism in industry, and establish bureaucratic agencies to enhance the efficient use of national resources.

In practice, Progressivism accomplished little. The Clayton Anti-Trust Act generally was ineffective until the 1930s. Child labor laws were struck down quickly by business-minded courts. Prohibition was ignored by millions. And government agencies quickly became co-opted by corporate groups. Despite their rhetoric, Roosevelt and Wilson ideologically had much in common with corporations and often worked with rather than against modern industry. In gratitude to J. P. Morgan's efforts to stem the Panic of 1907, Roosevelt gave U.S. Steel control of the majority of iron deposits in America. Wilson respected business experience to the extent that after passing the Clayton Anti-Trust Act, he allowed businessmen to sit on the Federal Trade Commission and in effect regulate themselves. Thus, just as Alger's reaffirmation of self-reliance and virtue encouraged employee subservience, the Progressives in their quest to preserve the success ethic unwittingly aided the institutionalization of corporate dominance.

Progressivism failed because it was an attempt at reassurance rather than serious reform. Naively, the Progressives assumed like Alger that virtue and self-reliance provided adequate control in modern society even though the last quarter of the nineteenth century indicated the limited effectiveness of such standards of behavior. While the Progressives sensed that industrialism threatened their assumptions, they tried to celebrate rather than adjust their beliefs by telling the nation and each other that their values remained efficacious. Thus, the Progressive movement was in large part a public outcry asserting that man should be but was not in control of his life, that care should be but was not a significant motivating force in men and that morality should but did not protect men from each other. In this respect, the Clayton Anti-Trust Act represented more a symbolic expression of the Progressives' desire to be reassured of possessing power equal to that of the corporations than a serious attempt to counteract corporate strength. Even if industries acted morally, they already had amassed enough financial power to control and limit the mobility of the average American.

The outbreak of World War I further entrenched corporate power and encouraged the development of the organization man. Fearful of lower class unrest and the European conflict, the Progressives became increasingly concerned with the need for efficiency and conformity. Big businessmen were placed in governmental positions. Nativists demanded that individuals display patriotism by lauding the dream of success, refusing to strike and working efficiently for industries in the war effort.

In many respects, popular magazines published between 1897 and 1917, such as *Collier's*, *McClure's*, *Cosmopolitan* and *The Saturday Evening Post* reflected the integration of the success ethic with corporate ideology. In the 1890s, these magazines extolled businessmen resembling Emerson's man of power. By 1904, the same magazines lauded political reformers who exemplified man's continued ability to be self-reliant. After 1914, when magazines became more corporate-minded largely because of increased advertising revenues, the organization man was praised.[10]

While the integration of philosophical beliefs with corporate interests could facilitate an orderly economy, it limited the concept of self. Conformity restricted both self-expression and the psychological autonomy necessary for personal growth. In his concern for efficiency and accomplishment, the achiever could be prevented from appreciating the humane, imaginative and aesthetic qualities of life.

The Emergence of Fantasy

Between 1895 and 1915, a success-oriented social movement called the New Thought Alliance reflected the erosion of the self to an extreme extent. New Thought's basic premise was that the individual's mental efforts were emanations of God's power; it perpetuated Emerson's assumption that man possessed godlike qualities allowing complete control over one's destiny. As Frank Haddock contended in his Power Book Library, a series of books which were the best selling success tracts in the early 1900s, "The Will is God, the Will is Man / The Will is power loosed in Thought!" Through will power, the individual was to develop personal magnetism, manipulate emotions to be optimistic, and laugh to relieve tensions which interfered with work.[11]

Because of its devotion to power and the mind, New Thought represented an acquisitive transcendentalism in which mystery and fantasy functioned merely to achieve success. Desiring to tap unconscious powers rather than enhance piety or knowledge, New Thought devotees employed psychology rather than theology or philosophy in their search for the self.

For all its emphasis on psychology, however, New Thought ironically was based upon a messianic fantasy which psychiatrists have considered ultimately dysfunctional. In essence, New Thought's optimism was a mask for despair, its faith in the mind an excuse for mental manipulation and its promise of power an indication of the helplessness its followers experienced. As psychiatrists such as Alfred Adler have noted, individuals are most prone to fantasize godlike potentialities if they possess an exaggerated faith in their abilities to achieve their goals. Finding it difficult to discard dysfunctional beliefs out of fear that the world would seem even more uncontrollable, such persons manipulate their minds, ignore experiences which suggest the inefficacy of their beliefs, and optimistically fantasize that life is manageable. As a form of wish fulfillment, messianic fantasies develop as helplessness increases so that the frustrated achiever can retain a sense of significance and power.[12]

To be sure, New Thought advocates would not have agreed that the world they imagined was fantasy. Instead, they maintained that their beliefs met the needs of a corporate society. Inasmuch as their emphasis on optimism, personal magnetism and emotional manipulation corresponded with the boosterism, salesmanship and positive thinking which bureaucracies admired, they were correct. But the final irony of New Thought was that in attempting to elevate man to the supernatural by placing him in a corporate world, the movement stripped him of his very humanity. By requiring the individual to ignore unexplainable experiences, transform mystery into practicality, substitute rationalization for reason and control emotions, New Thought severely limited the individual's ability to explore, perceive, think or feel. Since the individual had to control himself to function efficiently, he came close to becoming a machine.

Ambivalence and Escapism in Postwar America

Although New Thought was an extreme extension of American culture, it presaged the rationalizations, fantasies and acquiescence to corporations which characterized the post-World War I era. In contrast to the Progressives' partial attempt to reform the socioeconomic structure, post-World War I Americans generally tried to obliterate their moral qualms and helplessness by changing their attitudes rather than their beliefs or society. They repeatedly resorted to mental manipulations, dogmatic defenses of untenable principles, political apathy and a pursuit of pleasure to ignore the anxiety caused by the retention of the dream of success.

Simultaneously, corporations became even more insistent on the need for conformity and harmonious employee relations. As selling became as important as producing and efficient plant management more necessary than individual effort, the need to influence the customer's and worker's behavior increased. And as salesmanship, advertising and management psychology fused with the public's need for rationalizations, the postwar period saw a series of bizarre fantasies which culminated in the triumph of the corporation.

The tensions which existed between success, pleasure, morality and care in the postwar era and the public's propensity for escapism both were reflected poignantly in Douglas Fairbanks' best-selling book of 1917, *Laugh and Live*. While Fairbanks confidently advocated a philosophy of life promising success and happiness, it was apparent that he had difficulty explaining how an American could conform and still retain his individuality, find friendship and yet be ambitious, care for others while remaining self-interested and be both moral and materialistic.

Fairbanks insisted that the individual find his identity by being true to himself, establishing his individuality and developing the inner qualities of honesty, self-reliance, will power, courage and ambition. At the same time, he contradictorily urged his reader to conform to the demands of others in dress and behavior because "Appearance counts for so much in this world."[13]

The advocacy of both inner- and other-directedness caused Fairbanks numerous problems. In developing his appearance, a person could ignore being moral since, as Fairbanks worried, an evil person could hide behind a seemingly kind personality. Moreover, inner- and other-directedness caused conflicts between friendship and achievement. Although stressing the need for friendship and recommending a "democratic" attitude at social gatherings, Fairbanks suggested disassociation with "inferiors" because "we are known by our companionships. We will be rated according to association— good or bad."[14]

With all of the restrictions Fairbanks placed on the individual to insure success, it was difficult to understand how a person could follow Fairbanks' suggestion "to let one's self go." While the individual was to be present-minded and discover "how successful the day will be," Fairbanks also told his reader to *"laugh and try again"* if he continually failed. Criticizing the spendthrift, advocating consumption and castigating Americans who lived beyond their means, Fairbanks confusedly recommended purchasing items which helped people succeed as a means to "save something for the 'rainy day' . . ." His remarks on care and self interest were also at variance. While stipulating that "consideration for others is man's noblest attitude," he abhorred assistance to the unsuccessful individual who "is forever whining . . . [and] contaminates our sense of justice."[15]

Fairbanks' ambivalent philosophy indicated the lack of direction and absence of vigorous intellectual effort of many Americans after World War I. Because Progressivism had failed to cope sufficiently with corporate power, traditional character-oriented guides for success seemed inappropriate and inadequate. Americans understandably were amenable to a variety of success formulas, even if they offered seriously conflicting tenets, in hopes of regaining a sense of control over their lives.

The apparent ease with which Fairbanks contradicted himself, moreover, reflected the propensity of other-directed individuals almost to take pride in not taking a stand on principles to appear moderate and pleasant to others. Through such indecisiveness, individuals could evade confronting the tensions posed by a seriously ambivalent and inadequate philosophy of life. Even so, the philosophy of being true to oneself was an empty one if the values to which one was true were highly questionable.[16]

To overcome contradictions, Fairbanks told his followers to conceal doubts behind a mask of optimism. Contending that fear "is the one thing we don't want along . . . [because it] plays a large part in the drama of failure," Fairbanks advised smiling so that a person *"needn't worry about the rest of the day."* Fairbanks repeatedly followed sections in his book where he discussed personal problems with the glib and exceptionally empty admonition just to laugh and live.[17]

Fairbanks' philosophy characterized the escapist attitudes of many Americans in the postwar era. The sophisticated socialite of the 1920s, whose characteristics were portrayed in *The Saturday Evening Post's* illustrations, appeared blasé as if to suggest that socioeconomic problems were unworthy of serious attention. Similarly, service clubs seeking to boost the image of American business supplanted Progressive organizations which had hoped to improve America's conscience.

The cult of Couéism carried forced optimism to its ultimate absurdity. Faced with problems, the individual was to chant the litany, "Day by day, in every way, I am getting better and better" on a knotted string which resembled a rosary. Advocates of this cult described their founder, Emile Coué, as God's ambassador and promised that his formula would make life "seem more worth living." Coué and his followers contended that the magical litany could "stop hemorrhages, cure constipation, cause fiberous tumors to disappear," give men occupational success and help pregnant women determine the sex of their future children. Endorsing these beliefs, Henry Ford announced: "I have read the phi-

losophy of Coué. . . . He has the right idea." Having conquered
failure and cured irregularity, the proponents of fantasy were
ready to take on Communism and God in their attempts to
preserve the American Dream.[18]

Power, Reassurance and Submissiveness

Underneath his exaggerated faith, Coué's rhetoric indicated far stronger doubts in the power of the individual's will
than had been implied by the passivity advocated by Alger,
the Social Darwinists and the New Thought Alliance. Coué
maintained that man's will was not sufficiently strong to
challenge life's problems because the will almost always turned
against the individual. Therefore he insisted that people
mechanically recite his litany and passively be directed and
given power through a form of auto-hypnosis.

Although Couéism actually was practiced by only a
small minority of Americans, the mind cure cult paralleled
many citizens' desires for power and reassurance in the efficacy of the dream of success. Throughout the postwar years,
many self help books made power one of the most important
goals in life. Similarly, from 1917 until 1926, power was the
goal most advocated in the sample issues studied in *The
Saturday Evening Post*. Power was equated with success fifteen times while wealth was considered in fourteen stories and
fame in only ten.[19]

Achievement-minded Americans often desired power to
force other citizens to conform to the dream of success. Such
conformity served as a reaffirmation to confused achievers
hoping to prove the necessity and merit of living in accord
with a frustrating philosophy of life. At times, this demand for
conformity stemmed from a sense of envy towards those who
did not share the confused customs of the success ethic. More
often, the dogmatic demand for conformity rose out of an
increased sensitivity to critics suggesting that material ambition diminished humanistic and moralistic sentiments. Intellec-

tuals such as Beard, Veblen and Dewey jolted the public's absolutist conceptions and socialist critiques insulted mainstream capitalist sentiment. Progressive accusations of immorality increasingly upset businessmen's consciences and the continuing influx of European immigrants, with their foreign values and customs, seemed to pose a threat to the middle class way of life.

The first group success advocates attacked were American radicals, perhaps the smallest and least influential of those deviating from middle class norms. The total number of Communists in America was between 25,000 and 40,000 out of a population of over one hundred million in 1919. Nevertheless, inspired by wartime patriotism, concerned with the Bolshevist Revolution, fearful of strikes and bombings which spotted America in 1919 and led by the demagogic Attorney General, A. Mitchell Palmer, the government began to arrest, imprison and deport political dissenters.

Success writers encouraged such anti-Communist activity. Corine Lowe was convinced that Bolshevism had become "a very real danger to our national life." Booth Tarkington worried that socialism would destroy human incentive. Judge Gary, Chairman of U.S. Steel, contended that "under a Bolshevist rule any nation must crumble and finally disappear because of the decrease in total national effort. Success could not come to a people where each individual has lost the incentive to labor through being robbed of all reward for earnest initiative."[20]

Thus, writers attempted to coerce political radicals to accept the gospel of success. Asking his readers, "Have you a little Bolshevist in your home?" Harry Wilson maintained, in *The Saturday Evening Post,* that radicals were children and should be treated as such. Angered because Bolshevists supposedly opposed hard work and business, he demanded that the "self-confessed 'intellectuals,' these pinks" be deported, sent to prison, or "ought to be spanked." George Kibbe Turner agreed "that this country may yet be saved by the confinement of all professional and semi-professional pacifists together

in wire compounds, where they will soon eliminate each other
from our national life by the free exercise of . . . [their]
habitual violence." *The Saturday Evening Post* praised A.
Mitchell Palmer, the leader of the Red Scare, and deemed radicals mentally ill.[21]

Immigrants also came under attack. *The Saturday Evening Post* urged passage of the National Origins Act of 1924,
believing that immigration restriction was needed to prevent
the infiltration of men who supposedly lacked diligence, thrift
and cleanliness. Edward Filene maintained that immigration
restriction was needed to limit the American labor force. With
fewer workers, employers would have to pay higher wages,
which in turn would allow workers to consume more and thus
increase American prosperity. For those who had already
migrated to America, Forrest Crissey advocated Americaniza-
tion courses to teach immigrants the value of self-reliance,
productivity and good citizenship.[22]

The remainder of Americans also were called upon to
conform to the success ethic. Anne Morgan lamented that
Americans had "gone mad in our schools and everywhere else
on individuality," demanded discipline and insisted that Americans retain their faith in a materialistic religion. *Nation's
Business* asked its readers to "Dare to Be a Babbitt" and most
of America seemed to take heed. In their quest for reassurance
from Alger to Babbitt, Americans preserved their faith that
the success ethic was a necessary philosophy of life. The triumph of corporate society was about to be assured as the
gospel of success became the religion of the 1920s.[23]

Materialism, Moralism and the Corporate Messiah

While late nineteenth century success advocates had been
the first major American spokesmen to begin the confluence
between a success-oriented philosophy of life and corporate
ideology, it remained for Bruce Barton to complete the relationship by blatantly merging religion, materialism and corpo-

rate behavior. The son of a Congregationalist minister, Barton became the head of one of the largest advertising firms in the Twenties. During the decade his words were quoted incessantly by politicians, magazines and the public alike. In later years he was to be a Republican congressman and a major advisor to President Eisenhower in the 1952 elections.

In 1925 and 1926, Barton dominated the best seller charts in the nonfiction class. In his first book, *The Man Nobody Knows*, Barton argued that Christ was the "founder of modern business" in his attempt to offer a success formula for a bureaucratic age. Maintaining that "great progress will be made in the world when we rid ourselves of the idea that there is a difference between *work* and *religious* work," Barton contended that "all work is worship; all useful service prayer." He asked his readers to "forget all creed for the time being" and consider Christ's life "the grandest achievement story of all [time]."[24]

Fascinated by Christ's ability to pick "up twelve men from the bottom ranks of business and forge them into an organization" that endured for two thousand years, Barton argued that Christ's behavior exemplified the traits of the organization man. He promised that individuals could find their identities and be successful if they "literally lost their lives in" the corporation.[25]

More other- than inner-directed, Barton contended that diligence, thrift and sobriety were insufficient in the pursuit of success in the corporate age. The achiever needed to possess an extroverted amiable personality like Christ, who was "the most popular dinner guest in Jerusalem!" Moreover, the individual was to acquire personal magnetism and practice "the 'principles of modern salesmanship' [which were] . . . brilliantly exemplified in Jesus' talk and work." Like Christ, the achiever was to possess self confidence, be energetic and yet not appear harassed and be sincerely interested in others to make them purchase his products.[26]

Barton continued to equate salesmanship with religion in his second best selling work, *The Book Nobody Knows*. As could be expected, the unknown book was the Bible, which

had become "the world's best seller." Barton disclosed that
"most of the Proverbs could hardly be called religious. They
are the shrewd guideposts to worldly wisdom, by which a man
may make his way through life with most profit to himself
and least discomfort to other people." Throughout the book,
Barton preached enthusiasm, extroversion and service, using
Biblical figures such as John the Baptist, Noah and Moses to
exemplify heroes who served others and became famous.[27]

The extreme attempts which Barton made to prove the
morality of materialism implied a conscience in the Twenties
filled with qualms of guilt about the pursuit of riches. In fact,
just before Barton's popularity, another book, Giovanni
Papini's The Life of Christ, had stayed on the best seller charts
for three years with the message that the sale of Christ for
thirty pieces of silver was "the first business done by the mer-
chant." From that time, Papini argued, the Devil had given
power to bankers and financiers so that they could "rule
nations, instigate wars . . . [and] starve nations." Maintaining
that "ye cannot serve God and mammon," Papini had asked
his readers to reject the selfish desire for riches and instead
follow a life exemplifying humility and love.[28]

To counteract these sentiments, Barton argued that success could only be attained by service to others. In a way, this
argument corresponded to Alger's attempt to fuse virtue and
success. But there was a difference between the two men's
positions. Alger's admiration for benevolence led to idealism
and sentimentality. Barton's enthusiasm for salesmanship
could lead to insincerity and manipulation.

Underneath Barton's religious analogies and celebration
of service was an intense preoccupation with power. Disturbed
that Christ's title of the Lamb of God "sounded like Mary's
little lamb" and was "something for girls—sissified," Barton
stressed that Christ's "muscles were so strong that when he
drove the money-changers out, nobody dared to oppose him!"
Strength in business seemed to give the individual his mascu-
linity. Rather than becoming a sissy, Christ established an
organization which "conquered the world."[29]

This fascination with power severely curtailed any

humanistic sentiments of care. While Barton attempted to prove that businessmen were Christlike in their selling of services, he described the stricken man at the pool of Betheseda as having a "whining voice" lacking in enthusiasm and thus not worthy of compassion. In an extremely callous tone, Barton contended that if the paralyzed individual were to be cured, he would no longer have the crutch of self-pity to lean on and would have to get a job.[30]

By offering a philosophy which channelled virtue and service into the pursuit of success and power, Barton gave escapist Americans and corporations alike the opportunity to ignore conflicts between materialism, morality, self interest and care. If corporations served the public, they should be admired rather than controlled. If individuals could be self-reliant, service could stop with the sale of goods rather than be extended to the poor.

But in gaining relief from the tensions that plagued citizens from the advent of industrialism through the Progressive Era, Americans paid a severe price. The Progressive concern to preserve democracy in an industrial nation was replaced by a trust in the ability of industrial leaders to manage America. In hoping to achieve progress and control over their destiny through identification with the organization, Americans became dependent upon corporate benevolence at the expense of losing part of themselves. And in accepting the success ethic so totally, serious questions remained as to how the individual could satisfy his spiritual desires and express a spirit of care.

The Triumph of the Corporation

American popular culture indicated that citizens were willing to accept Barton's rationalizations. In many cases, articles in *The Saturday Evening Post* and *Reader's Digest* seemed convinced that materialism and morality were compatible and almost identical. Angered by the "fallacy that being materially rich tends to [cause] spiritual poverty,"

Thomas Read maintained, in *Reader's Digest*, "I cannot see that it [oriental religion] produces any less crime and more happiness than the tenets of Rotary clubs, nor is it clear to me why meditating on the infinitude while sitting in rags on the ground should yield any clearer spiritual insight than doing so while sitting in a limousine." Bishop Charles Fiske anointed God as "a sort of Magnified Rotarian." Ministers gave sermons entitled "Solomon, a Six-Cylinder Sport" and labeled the Trinity "Three-in-One-Oil," presumably suggesting a substance which could lubricate the soul.[31]

Just as morality became subsumed under achievement, so also did self interest become synonymous with care. The editors of *The Saturday Evening Post* promised that "honesty pays . . . [and] the golden rule pays even better."[32]

As Christ was debased, businessmen took His place as the new American messiahs. Calvin Coolidge preached that "the man who builds a factory builds a temple . . . [and] the man who works there worships there." Judge Henry Neil worshiped Henry Ford for coming "closer to reconciling modern business with the ideals of Jesus than any manufacturer I know."[33]

Awed by the corporation, success writers reflected public sentiment by considering businessmen their favorite heroes in the sample issues analyzed in both *Reader's Digest* and *The Saturday Evening Post*. As indicated on Chart III, more big businessmen were praised in *Reader's Digest* success articles than entertainers, small businessmen, politicians, diplomats, white collar workers, blue collar workers and professionals combined. Similarly, in *The Saturday Evening Post* big businessmen were the most favored success heroes. Articles on both large and small businessmen equalled the number of success stories dealing with entertainers, politicians, diplomats, white collar workers and professionals.*

As the success ethic's standard bearers, businessmen reassured citizens that America was the land of opportunity

*See Appendix for content analysis charts on biographical heroes, success goals and standards of behavior reflected in *Reader's Digest* and *The Saturday Evening Post* sample issues analyzed for the period 1917–1969.

and demanded that government refrain from restricting the corporate pursuit of wealth. U.S. Steel's Judge Gary declared, in *The Saturday Evening Post*, that "there has never been any necessity in the United States for any healthy human being to remain in a condition of poverty and subordination. . . . Families poor in one decade loom leaders in the next, in proportion to their development of initiative and ability." Wanting freedom to enlarge his own utility empire, Samuel Insull maintained that "if there is not too much governmental interference this country will make greater progress in the use of electrical power in the next twenty-five years than in the past quarter century. . . . Here is something for citizens gifted with sound common sense to think about."[34]

Gary's and Insull's actions made the validity and sincerity of their remarks quite questionable. While Gary was proclaiming the opportunities of the working class, he was crushing a strike at U.S. Steel. Insull's aversion to governmental regulation probably was motivated by his fraudulent business activities which eventually caused his empire to collapse during the depression.

Nevertheless, many Americans were willing to accept businessmen's proclamations without doubts. Such faith in the success ethic was evident throughout both *The Saturday Evening Post* and *Reader's Digest*. As indicated in Chart I, out of one hundred fifty-five definitions of success given in *The Saturday Evening Post* sample articles and stories studied from 1917 to 1929, one hundred eighteen equated success with money, status or power. Forty-nine out of eighty-two definitions of success in *Reader's Digest* sample issues from 1926 to 1929 displayed a similar fascination with these goals. Moreover, the standards of material success were quite high. Only two articles in *The Saturday Evening Post* and one in *Reader's Digest* stipulated that success meant the acquisition of a job, whereas twenty-two articles in *The Saturday Evening Post* and ten in *Reader's Digest* contended that riches represented success. In both magazines, wealth was the symbol of success in more articles than promotions, upper middle class incomes, and attainment of a secure income combined.

Success writers were also confident that diligence, virtuous character, salesmanship and ambition were the major prerequisites for achievement. As detailed in Chart II, these four means to success were advocated one hundred two times in *The Saturday Evening Post* sample issues and forty-seven times in *Reader's Digest*. The combined minor requirements for success—imagination, luck, efficiency, positive thinking, talent, courage and prudence were mentioned seventy times in *The Saturday Evening Post* and twenty-four times in *Reader's Digest*.

The lack of attention given to talent and luck as important factors for success pointedly indicated both magazines' belief that it was the individual's responsibility to achieve his own success. Luck suggested that circumstances beyond one's control shaped a person's destiny while talent suggested that inbred ability, rather than character or personality development, assured attainment of one's goals. The combined factors of talent and luck were mentioned only twenty-two times in *The Saturday Evening Post* articles studied and only seven times in *Reader's Digest* sample issues. The fact that traits which the individual could develop himself were stressed one hundred seventy-six times in *The Saturday Evening Post* and sixty-five times in *Reader's Digest* displays how little attention success writers gave to uncontrollable causes of success or failure.

The propensity to forget Progressivism's partial attempt to reform corporations, accommodate to business interests and justify the pursuit of materialistic success led Americans to hope for a businessman or business-minded politician to assume the Presidency in the 1920s. In a 1919 editorial *The Saturday Evening Post* insisted that "We need a businessman for President" whose platform would be:

"Work or starve.

Save or want.

Play together or you'll play hell.

Be a good American or get out."[35]

The ascension of Harding, Coolidge and Hoover to the Presidency fulfilled all of the success advocates' hopes. Hard-

ing's easygoing friendliness conformed to the cult of personality development. His membership in the Elks, Hoo Hoos,
Odd Fellows and Moose Lodge, and his claim, "If I could
plant a Rotary club in every city and hamlet in this country I
would then rest assured that our ideals of freedom would be
safe and civilization would progress," typified the urge to join
booster clubs and place American prosperity in the hands of
optimistic businessmen.[36]

Writers were quick to praise Harding's allegiance to the
dream of success. Samuel Blythe told readers in *The Saturday
Evening Post* that Harding had "a philosophy that has not
worked out so badly." Praising the President's amiable personality and ability to use recreation to work diligently, Blythe
maintained that Harding brought prosperity to America by
"putting the country, governmentally, on a business, self-
supporting basis." The progress Harding brought to America
"isn't a millennium by any means," Blythe admitted, "but it
is somewhat millennial" in that it would allow tax reductions
and greater prosperity in later years.[37]

Perhaps the President most devoted to the success ethic
in the Twenties was Calvin Coolidge. Believing that "wealth is
the chief end of man," Coolidge sought to convert Washington
into a "businessman's government." With Andrew Mellon, the
head of the aluminum monopoly, as his Secretary of the
Treasury, he succeeded. Continuing the quest for the millennium, Coolidge cut government costs, granted favors to
corporations and refused to assist the less fortunate.[38]

Herbert Hoover's administration further promoted the
gospel of success. The fact that Hoover was both a millionaire
believing strongly in scientific management and an adminis-
trator who fed ten million Belgians during World War I seemed
to prove that wealth, efficiency and humanitarianism were
compatible. Moreover, Hoover's rise from an orphaned childhood to riches and power seemed to justify the belief that
any diligent person could achieve wealth and even the Presidency.

Hoover's respect for his own achievements led him to

encourage others to compete for riches. He proclaimed that
the government "shall safeguard to every individual an equality of opportunity to take that position in the community to
which his intelligence, character, ability, and ambition entitle
him." Hoping to "stimulate [the] effort of each individual
to achievement," Hoover explained that the government would
"set a race . . . [and be] the umpire of fairness in the race."[39]

Pleased by the rate of material progress in the Twenties,
Hoover prophesied the millennium in 1928 by saying that "we
shall soon, with the help of God, be in sight of the day when
poverty will be banished from this nation." In Middletown,
"men were talking of the arrival of 'permanent prosperity'"
and in June, 1929, Bernard Baruch told Bruce Barton that
"the economic condition of the world seems on the verge of a
great forward movement."[40]

Ironically, while the economic policies of Harding,
Coolidge and Hoover were intended to bring prosperity, in
fact they accounted in large part for the crash of 1929. Dedicated to increasing production rather than consumption, the
politics of normalcy practiced assistance to corporations and
the rich while preaching self help to the poor. Little attention
was paid to the eighteen million Americans living in abject
poverty before the depression in 1929. While five percent of
the population possessed one-third of the total national
personal income, seventy-one percent had incomes under
$2500, an amount considered to be the minimum standard
for a decent living. Forty-two percent earned less than $1500
annually. Yet rather than help the lower class, Harding and
Coolidge increased the unequal distribution of wealth by the
tax reform bill of 1921 and the partial refund of income tax
revenues to the upper class. Hoover displayed his preference
for manufacturers over consumers by allowing four hundred
trade associations to be formed with the help of the government to enable businesses to stabilize their prices and eliminate competition. By 1929, almost half of the national
corporate wealth was in the hands of the two hundred largest
non-financial corporations.[41]

This unequal distribution of wealth left the upper class
with more money than it could use for consumptive purposes.
Consequently, the rich were inclined to speculate heavily
in the stock market, precipitating the 1929 crash. More
importantly, the low incomes of forty-two percent of the
population prevented them from purchasing enough goods to
equal America's productive capacity. This lack of consumptive
power was by far the most significant reason for economic
stagnation after 1925 and the magnitude of the depression
which occurred after the stock market crash.[42]

The Rise of the Consumptive Pleasure Ethic

The fact that industrial production almost doubled during the 1920s seemed to prove success advocates' assumptions
and thus helped blind Americans to the inadequacies of their
economic beliefs. Still, the growth of production transformed
the American economy from one of scarcity to one of potential abundance. While industrialists thought in terms of
production, they were forced to encourage consumption by
advertising to increase their markets.

Motivated by mass advertisements, Americans began to
purchase radios, automobiles and other luxuries with increasing frequency. The growth of consumption tastes was reflected
in the mass media as well. During the Progressive Era and
World War I, pleasure and consumption were made distinctly
secondary to work and thrift in most popular magazines. From
1917 to 1925, articles advocating consumption appeared spo-
radically in The Saturday Evening Post and Reader's Digest.
After 1925, the number of such articles greatly increased
when the public's consumptive power reached its maximum
but far from economically satisfactory capacity. In the period
from 1925 to 1929, entertainers whose biographies reflected
consumer aspirations replaced productive businessmen as
the most popular success figures in The Saturday Evening Post.
Thirteen articles were written about entertainers in the 1925-

1929 sample issues compared to eleven stories published about businessmen. Similarly, in *Reader's Digest* sample issues from 1926 to 1929, frugality was advocated only once while five articles promoted consumption.

In part, the desire to find happiness through the purchase of luxury items was a natural outgrowth of the pursuit of riches. Having scrambled to make money, many Americans were eager to enjoy their rewards. Reflecting the escapist mood of the Twenties, many frantically pursued the world of the Charleston, speakeasies, flappers and luxury to forget their problems. The result, as the President's Research Committee on Social Trends stated, was a "new attitude towards hardship as a thing to be avoided by living in the here and now, utilizing installment credit and other devices to telescope the future into the present."[43]

Significantly, the development of an escapist pursuit of pleasure reflected many Americans' discontent with a life devoted to work and achievement, indicating the inability of the success ethic to satisfy adequately citizens' needs in the mid-Twenties. Complaining that the United States was "a nation of passionate industry," Cornelia James Cannon observed in *Reader's Digest* that "it is not without reason that the generations have reiterated that 'all work and no play makes Jack a dull boy.' Though we are a feverish nation and make a great deal of noise, must we not admit that we are somewhat like Jack at his worst?" Cannon envisioned increased leisure as the source of American salvation and hoped citizens would develop hobbies and devote their interests to play. Raymond Essen similarly maintained that leisure was important to "our true standard of living" because "Americans have become a hard, restless, over-energetic people."[44]

The development of the consumptive pleasure ethic in the mid-Twenties marked two developments in American culture. On the one hand, the pleasure ethic enlarged the scope of American life which until the post-World War I period was based largely on future-oriented productive behavior. On the other hand, the fact that corporations began in the mid-

Twenties to encourage consumption to sustain their profits indicated another confluence between business ideology and public desires. The ability of advertisers to profit quickly from a desire to release tension through the consumption of material products made the pleasure ethic another means by which industry could capitalize on the public's stress. Moreover, through offering luxury goods, industry found an extremely persuasive symbol by which to justify its benevolent paternalism and consequential power.

Moralists and humanists were quick to point out the barrenness of pleasure and success ethics as substitutes for a viable philosophy of life. While such writers did acknowledge the need for enjoyment, they contended that the retreat to entertainment could not satisfy the individual's spirit. James Truslow Adams, in *Reader's Digest*, complained that Americans were so devoted to wealth, status, conformity and consumption that they were making civilization monotonous by "the mere living of standardized lives and keeping up with the Joneses." Worried that the American was becoming a materialistic "barbarian," Adams called for people to discover a worthwhile existence based upon "the abiding values in life." Albert J. Nock also was concerned by the materialistic mood of the Twenties because he believed that "without intellect, without beauty, without religion and morals, and with but the most rudimentary social life and manners . . ." it was difficult "to live a full and satisfying life . . . ."[45]

Two self help books in the late Twenties, George Dorsey's *Why We Behave Like Human Beings* and Ernest Dimnet's *The Art of Thinking* similarly rejected the pursuit of riches, found pleasure seeking unsatisfying and advocated idealism and cultural development. Dorsey postulated that "man is not by nature a beast of burden or fitted by nature to keep his nose to a grindstone" and admitted that individuals did suffer from repression. However, Dorsey rejected contemporary pleasure seeking philosophies which he believed were based upon popularized versions of Freudian psychology. The cult of "Freudism," he maintained, was "a disease and should be put out of its misery." To attain peace and happiness, Dorsey urged individuals to develop themselves culturally and "practice the Golden Rule . . . [because] humanity must be the goal of human endeavor."[46]

Likewise, Dimnet concluded that the "person whose mind is filled with the images of petty pleasure, comfort . . . [and] in short, material well-being" closed himself to opportunities for finding his identity by seriously thinking about values. Dimnet called for nonconformity, progressive education and the study of writers and artists to give the individual his "salvation."[47]

Such humanistic and moralistic denunciations of the pursuit of either money or materialistic enjoyment, however, did not characterize the attitudes of most Americans in the Dollar Decade. Almost all of the advocates of nonmaterialistic principles and tastes were intellectuals. Their opposition to commercialism suggested more an ideological conflict between intellectuals and businessmen than a serious ambivalence within the mind of the average citizen. Thus, success and pleasure seeking devotees continued to rationalize or run from their problems rather than struggle towards a better understanding of themselves and their society. As they approached 1929, they were filled with gaiety and unprepared for the depression.

Strangely enough, the increase in consumption made advocates of success fearful of a depression before the crash of 1929 even while they were preaching prosperity. Although it was a lack of adequate consumption rather than an over-abundance of purchasing which caused the depression, some success writers were concerned that Americans would be punished for immoral and frivolous spending. Since consumption implied taking from others rather than sacrificing oneself to serve others, and because leisure and the purchase of luxuries were the antitheses of the virtues of diligence and frugality, the trend towards pleasure seeking and installment buying seemed sinful. The increase in Wall Street speculation, ironically inspired by success advocates' demands for the attainment of wealth, similarly worried the apostles of industry and thrift. Speculation seemed like gambling and thus incompatible with the doctrine of saving. *The Saturday Evening Post* was concerned that Americans were discarding diligence in hopes that their money magically would work for them in the stock market.

According to the success creed, production, thrift, work and the continual pursuit of wealth were necessary to make life worthwhile and cleanse the individual of guilt. In a 1919 issue of *The Saturday Evening Post*, Forrest Crissey preached that the production of goods for the world would give "industrial salvation" while an excessive amount of consumption would bring about a depression. When a recession did occur in 1921, James Collins suggested immorality and a lack of the virtue of thrift as its cause.[48]

By 1929, however, success writers found it difficult to discuss production and consumption in such dichotomous terms. Even if consumption were sinful, it was needed to insure continued production. Bruce Barton searched the Bible to justify businessmen's encouragement of spending, discovered that Christ used advertising to enlarge His corporation, and concluded that the "parable of the Good Samaritan is the greatest advertisement of all time."[49]

Barton's rationalizations, however, did not seem convincing enough. The moral dilemma of the apostles of success was well illustrated in an article by Garet Garrett in *The Saturday Evening Post* just six months before the crash of 1929. Garrett contended that the "old problem of production . . . has been solved . . . by machine power. The problem is suddenly upside down. It is how to dispose of the product, how to get people to consume it." But alongside Garrett's article appeared a foreboding cartoon. In the illustration, an airplane entitled "Mass Production" fed gasoline while in flight to another airplane named "Seven Years of Prosperity" through a hose marked "Mass Consumption." Disturbed by the proceedings, a man labeled "Old-Fashioned Economist" warned a smiling person representing the public "WE ARE DEFYING NATUR-

AL LAW! WE'LL NEVER GET BACK TO EARTH WITHOUT
A SMASH-UP."[50]

Garrett's forebodings were significant not only because
of their prophetic quality and expression of the conflict
between production and consumption but also because his
fears were embedded in another dilemma surrounding the
problems of helplessness and power into which postwar Americans had gotten themselves. In his article, Garrett displayed
an intense admiration for technological strength. He praised
industry for creating a sound wave which could destroy life
and raved that the power of machines increased man's wealth.
If the industrial environment was so strong, however, could
it be controlled? Garrett had misgivings. He admitted that
"the worker lost control of the means of production" to the
machine and that "private ownership [was] passing from
the control of industry" to an impersonal corporate management. While he optimistically spoke of fiscal growth, he
warned of the inevitability of economic change which might
result in irrational speculation and widespread unemployment.
Unwittingly, Garrett's rhetoric revealed that in identifying
with corporate industrial power to achieve their dreams of success, Americans had lost control of their economic destiny.[51]

In becoming so susceptible to industrial power through
Alger's philosophy of reassurance, the Progressives' politics
of symbolism, New Thought's organizational mysticism,
Barton's corporate morality and the insistence on conformity
and political apathy, the American quest for control ironically
ended in the increase of fantasy and passivity. While the mask
of confidence which many wore to conceal their qualms for a
time gave way to a sincere belief in American progress, by
1929 the inability to resolve the inadequacies of the success
ethic severely reduced the quality of American life.

In essence, the period between 1870 and 1929 had
merged all four guides to living into modern corporate success-
oriented thought. Care was restricted to the self-interested
service businesses provided to the public. The pursuit of

success became a religion in itself. And if rationalizations which Americans constructed to justify the validity of the success ethic failed to alleviate stress, the American was quickly becoming conditioned further to escape doubts through the purchase of products which increased corporate profits.

The 1920s represented the extreme extent to which corporations ruled our culture and society. The depression and World War II forced Americans to reconsider the issues they generally avoided since mid-nineteenth century. Still, the effects of the rise of industrialism and corporatism have continued to be felt. The fantasies which grew with the American quest for reassurance warped our values and created an irrational cultural web from which Americans, from the depression to the present, have not been able to disentangle themselves.

Chapter 3

THE DEPRESSION: Shame, Guilt, and the

Search for the Self

The depression seriously challenged the American Dream by leaving fifteen million citizens unemployed. Even for the three-quarters of the population who retained their jobs, such as the readers of *The Saturday Evening Post* and *Reader's Digest*, the economic disaster caused fears of unemployment and lessening chances for promotion. Thus, Americans began to wonder if their values were functional, their self-conceptions of potential power accurate and their goals attainable or worthwhile. Caught between wanting to protect traditional values and sensing the need to alter their beliefs, Americans stumbled and vacillated throughout the Thirties in their attempts to find workable guides for living.

From our present perspective, the Thirties offers a striking example of how Americans could change their beliefs and still feel restricted by cultural mores. Many people were able to recognize the need for economic regulation, governmental assistance to the poor, and a more pleasurable and cooperative view of life. Nevertheless, their retention of the concept of individualism jaded these insights. In everyday life, our love of individualism helps account for our embarrassment when we fail, discomfiture in accepting assistance from others and inability to perceive external sources of our stress. During the Thirties, the emotional consequences of individualism were exceptionally severe. Citizens deeply suffered from what Dixon Wecter described as a "mood of lost self-esteem.'' Assuming that personal merit was defined by work and achievement, people who aspired to be gods only a few years before were forced to sell apples or go on relief. Even with one out of four citizens out of work, the unemployed often blamed themselves for their economic problems. Faced with starvation, many still felt uncomfortable in having to need governmental assistance. The American response to the depression reflects how strongly shame and guilt affect the imagination in the search for the self.[1]

The Consequences of Shame and Guilt

While all of us experience guilt and shame at different times in our lives, we rarely consider what these feelings are and how they influence our ability to think. Most Americans equate shame with embarrassment. While shame does connote such discomfort, it can be a far more sweeping and complex emotion, capable of altering a person's beliefs. Shame represents the stress engendered by the inability to reach a goal. It does not necessarily reflect blame on an individual. An American disturbed by his inability to succeed in the Thirties could contend that *"it's* a shame [not *I'm* ashamed] that my beliefs do not work and I may not achieve success, so perhaps I should question my values and goals. Perhaps money is not so important. Perhaps hard work and thrift cannot give me the security I desire. Perhaps an individual cannot make it on his own.'' Such an emotional response would allow the individual to see that his cultural beliefs were simply assumptions. If the individual did not feel morally compelled to retain unworkable assumptions, then he could avoid blaming himself, look for the external causes of his stress and seek possible solutions. By not taking beliefs personally and by recognizing that others similarly might not be to blame for their failings, individuals could cooperatively explore alternatives instead of finding scapegoats for their problems. Shame can thus soften individualism to the point of encouraging a sense of community.[2]

In addition, Americans often feel the simpler emotion of embarrassment, especially when they fear disapproval in moments of failure. This emotion limits imagination and co-operation by directing the person's concerns towards himself rather than his values. Many Americans hid behind masks of pseudo-confidence during the depression to protect their images and prevent the questioning of their inadequate values.

Guilt, or the stress engendered by the transgression of a moral rule, similarly can prevent an individual from looking beyond himself for the causes of his problems. Feeling guilty, an individual usually confesses personal inadequacies rather than question his morals. Even if he attempts to evade guilt by rationalizing that the supposed sin never occurred, he does not question a moral rule but simply contends that it was never disobeyed.

While a recognition of guilt based on respect for oneself, the rights of others and principles of universal justice can enhance one's autonomy, morals which simply are culturally induced may encourage a compulsive obedience to questionable values. Acculturated to accept individual responsibility for economic success *and* failure, Americans often erroneously blamed themselves for causing the depression. This response also allowed them to simplify their problems. Rather than attempt difficult social reforms, Americans could believe that they only had to change themselves to realize their aspirations. Thus, citizens could continue believing that their values had meaning and avoid the conclusion that their environment was impossible to control.

Since in moments of crisis individuals often experience shame, embarrassment and guilt simultaneously, Americans acted ambivalently during the Thirties. In part they modified or rejected the success-oriented values which had been used to find meaning in their lives. Often, they continued to accept those values, confessed that they had not lived up to the gospel of success or pretended that conflicts did not exist between their beliefs and reality. By the end of the decade, it was difficult to determine just what Americans consistently believed. The success ethic was shaken badly but not des-

troyed. Pleasure seeking consumption philosophies had grown
in popularity. And moralistic and humanistic self help books
were practically non-existent even though the New Deal had
been based on an increased spirit of cooperation.

Guilt as a Means of Escape

The first response of Americans to the depression was to
reaffirm their traditional values. It seemed logical to cling to
the dream of success in the first year or so after the crash
because the absence of a major depression from 1896 to 1929
suggested that economic growth was the normal course of
America's history. Without being able to foresee that the
depression would continue well into the Thirties, many simply
considered the crash a temporary setback to their material
ambitions.

As the depression dragged on, however, the efficacy of
the dream of success became questionable. Still, many Americans condemned themselves for the depression rather than
question the values or workings of their socioeconomic system. Just as Horatio Alger had contended that an achiever's
greatest obstacle was himself, the public sentiment, as expressed by the population of Middletown, continued to
emphasize that "if a man doesn't make good it's his own
fault. . . ." In the South, Wilbur Cash observed that parish-
oners "heard from the pulpit that it [the depression] was
a punishment visited upon the people from the hand of God
as a penalty of their sins . . . [and] accepted it in some fashion, and, as always, without demur." Similarly, E. Wight
Bakke discovered that the jobless New England worker considered his unemployment the result of personal inadequacies.[3]

What exactly were the sins that Americans supposedly
committed? The shady practices on the New York Exchange
as well as the frivolous talk of sex and drinking in the Twenties
suggested that immorality pervaded our culture. Garet Garrett's
forebodings in the late Twenties began to haunt Americans.

Many felt that as our economy became more consumption- and pleasure-minded Americans had transgressed the virtue of thrift. Stock market speculation came to be seen as gambling. Both trends seemed to imply a sinful abandonment of diligence.

Self help writers encouraged these guilt-ridden sentiments by arguing that it was the American soul rather than the nation's institutions and values which were responsible for the depression. In his introduction to Vash Young's *A Fortune to Share*, Earnest Elmo Calkings argued that "the cure for our economic ills" rested on the realization that "the only way to reorganize the world is for each of us to reorganize himself." Similarly, Marjorie Hillis told her readers that "it's time you did some serious self-investigating" for the causes of failure.[4]

Diligence was the major requirement for success stressed in *The Saturday Evening Post* and *Reader's Digest*, being advocated fifteen and seventeen times in the respective magazines. Often, self help apostles insisted that work was necessary for individual regeneration. Ernest Dimnet explained that action "revealed to idleness the virtues of pressure," thus increasing one's "moral strength." Similarly, Henry Link asked the individual to select a "vocation" as part of his return to religion.[5]

Virtuous character itself was stipulated as a major factor in the gospel of success. Ten articles in *The Saturday Evening Post* and nine in *Reader's Digest* preached that success was contingent upon morality. Henry Link professed his allegiance to the Protestant Ethic by preaching that God gave abundance to those who were good. Dale Carnegie similarly averred that "if we are so contemptibly selfish . . . [and] if our souls are no bigger than sour crab apples, we shall meet with the failure we so richly deserve."[6]

If guilt was used by average citizens to avoid recognizing the causes of their depression, it similarly was used by self help writers and corporations as a defensive tactic. Both success advocates and corporate leaders had promised the millennium in the Twenties and claimed that corporations were fully

capable of leading America. As the depression expanded, such
assurances were in danger of losing their credibility. Thus,
by placing blame on the individual worker, business leaders
hoped to preserve their social status.

While some businessmen humanely tried to protect their
employees, the actions of most were deplorable. John E.
Edgerton, President of the National Association of Manufacturers, preached that the laborer's moral weaknesses had
caused unemployment and demanded confidence in the business community. One wealthy family announced that it had
solved its personal financial difficulties by firing fifteen
servants.[7]

Most jarring of all were the statements of Henry Ford.
In the Twenties, Ford had spoken for most businessmen
in claiming that corporations mainly wished to serve the nation. During the depression, Ford's actions revealed how
quickly the desire for service could dwindle when confronted
with the essential business goal of making money. Between
1930 and 1931, Ford laid off 45,000 workers. Nevertheless,
Ford argued that "the very poor are recruited almost solely
from the people who refuse to think and therefore refuse to
work diligently." A few months later he preached, "It's a
good thing the recovery is prolonged. Otherwise the people
wouldn't profit by the illness." The following year, Ford's
elitist sentiments came out when he contended that "the
average man won't really do a day's work unless he is caught
and cannot get out of it."[8]

Besides demanding the acknowledgment of personal guilt,
success advocates and corporate leaders insisted that Americans remain optimistic and passive. Garet Garrett argued that
Americans had been seduced by the temptation of riches without work in the Twenties, were paying for their "folly" and
could only retain faith in the success ethic while waiting for
the economic system to stabilize itself. Hillis offered a "sermon" suggesting that an optimistic belief in success was almost
a prayer. Calling upon Americans to emulate people who
"don't cringe or get an inferiority complex, even though

they're to blame for the whole situation [lack of success] and
know it," she maintained that "clear and honest thinking is
one form of worship" as she told her readers to have faith
in the possibility of achievement. Vash Young similarly called
for Americans to be motivated by positive thinking or a
"belief in God" and *The Saturday Evening Post's* readers were
assured that banker Frank Vanderlip began his rise to fortune
by "just thinking and wishing fervently."[9]

Having made optimism a spiritual necessity, American
businessmen continued the fantasies of the 1920s by spreading
wishful thinking throughout the land. In Muncie, Indiana,
local business leaders convinced General Motors not to put
boards on the windows of its abandoned automobile plant to
prevent passengers on nearby railroads from seeing the indications of economic decline. On Wall Street, an executive gave
white carnations to his managers to keep up their spirits. In
Cincinnati, people concealed doubts by wearing buttons
announcing "I'm sold on America. I won't talk depression."
And industrialist Charles Schwab asked Americans to "just
grin . . . [and] keep on working."[10]

As businessmen struggled to maintain their position as
the nation's financial experts, their rhetoric became steadily
more dubious. U. S. Steel's Myron C. Taylor confidently
proclaimed that "out of the depression we have been going
through we shall have learned something of high importance."
Unmasking the breathtaking discovery, Taylor concluded, "It
is too soon to say just what we are learning." Will Rogers
retorted, "It's almost been worth this depression to find out
how little our big men knew."[11]

The Politics of Guilt

Not all defenders of the dream of success were as pomp-
ous as Ford and Taylor of course, but the insistence on a
confident and moralistic retention of traditional values
blunted the imaginations of men who normally were far more

humane than their actions indicated in the 1930s. Although Herbert Hoover's humanitarian credentials were well documented in his earlier years, his desire to regenerate America by reaffirming the success ethic caused him to hurt rather than help the average citizen.

Consistent with his 1920s philosophy, the President continued to help businessmen rather than increase public consumption. Hoover chartered the RFC to lend money to banks, building and loan associations and railroads in hopes that businesses would give jobs to the citizen as they had promised in the Twenties. Unwilling to attribute the nation's problems to our values and institutions, he blamed the economic decline on a world depression. Moreover, Hoover refused to acknowledge that there was a severe maldistribution of national wealth even though the Brookings Institution disclosed that sixteen million American families were unable to purchase even basic necessities.[12]

Hoover's reluctance to recognize the extent of national suffering stemmed partially from his fear that relief would damage "the spiritual responses of the American people" by lessening the desire for diligence. In addition, since he was compulsively faithful to the virtue of thrift, he refused relief expenditures which might unbalance the budget and cause the "squandering [of] ourselves into prosperity." Hoover maintained that only local and voluntary organizations should help the poor. Above all, the President attempted to lift spirits through a monotonous call for confidence.[13]

Since Hoover's pro-business, anti-consumption tactics were strikingly similar to the Twenties fiscal policies which helped precipitate the depression, his programs actually accentuated the nation's problems. Economist William T. Foster lamented that "M. Coué seemed to have become our Minister of Finance." Businesses cut payrolls rather than prices. Local and voluntary relief agencies were unable to compensate for Hoover's inadequate programs. Relief payments amounted to $2.39 a week per family in New York, while in Dallas and Houston minority groups were given no assistance. Detroit had to cut one-third of the families on relief as Ford refused to assist the poor adequately. Over one hundred cities did not provide relief in 1932 and few states did much to help the unemployed.[14]

Trapped by his beliefs, the President found it difficult to recognize the inadequacies of his programs. To the claims of state agencies that national aid was needed Hoover responded that "Nobody is actually starving." But some citizens were: in Chicago fifty men started a riot by fighting for a garbage can left behind a restaurant. Towards the end of his administration, Hoover finally began to approve small appropriations for relief. Nevertheless, his actions were too little too late as one-quarter of the population became unemployed by 1932.[15]

As the depression dragged on, the public became angry with Hoover's policies. Shanty towns were named "Hoovervilles," empty pockets turned inside out were called "Hoover flags," and newspapers used for night covers on park benches became known as "Hoover blankets." Like the service station attendant in Steinbeck's *The Grapes of Wrath*, people asked, "what's the country comin' to? That's what I wanta know. . . . Fella can't make a livin' no more. . . . I ask you, what's it comin' to? I can't figure her out." An eighty-year-old Californian had the answer: "Years ago Horace Greeley made a statement, 'Young man, go West and grow up with the country.' Were he living today, he would make the statement, 'Go West, young man, and drown yourself in the Pacific Ocean.'"[16]

Even Charles Schwab stopped grinning and admitted ". . . I'm afraid, every man is afraid. I don't know, we don't know, whether the values we have are going to be real next month or not." As the gospel of success became increasingly insufficient, people were ready to question their beliefs instead of themselves.[17]

Values in Doubt

The most significant value shaken by the depression was thrift. As early as 1930, even Calvin Coolidge urged citizens to consume more to reinvigorate the businesses he loved so much. The ex-President's statement, however, confused rather than converted most Americans. Will Rogers wrote that Coolidge's position "is absolutely going against all the laws we have been brought up to. . . . Imagine telling the working man to spend, that if he doesn't put his money into circulation why he won't have a job. . . . [It's] hard to tell what to believe nowadays."[18]

As the depression grew worse, however, Rogers and many other Americans reversed their opinion. Although eight articles in *The Saturday Evening Post* encouraged frugality, five articles disagreed. In *Reader's Digest*, only three articles praised thrift while five suggested its obsolescence. Quoting the *New York Sun*, *Reader's Digest* reflected the growing sentiment that *"there are times when we would like to change Macy's famous slogan, 'It's Smart to Be Thrifty' to 'It Smarts to Be Thrifty.'"*[19]

The aversion to thrift and subsequent drift to consumerism was displayed poignantly in three best-selling books of the mid-Thirties, Marjorie Hillis's *Orchids on Your Budget* and *Live Alone and Like It* and Walter Pitkin's *Life Begins at Forty*. All three books indicated that their authors were torn between success and pleasure seeking concepts. Although Hillis and Pitkin contended that diligence and future-oriented achievement were necessary to give life meaning, both emphasized the desirability of living in the present. Life was to be enjoyed by travel, entertainment and the consumption of goods.

Hillis explained that the depression itself was a major cause of the rejection of thrift. She reminded her readers that some people had saved in the Twenties in expectation of a fuller life in the future. But, Hillis went on, the depression obliterated people's savings, making thrift far less meaningful.

Pitkin's pleasure-oriented view stemmed more from an irritation with the senseless devotion to work which he believed Americans possessed. In a statement which was all the more striking because he often stressed diligence in his book and other articles during the Twenties and Thirties, Pitkin

angrily contended that "for the past million years 99.999 percent of all who have been born have spent most of their time
and energy in making a living. . . . Is it to be marvelled at,
then, that so few of us know how to live?"[20]

The types of heroes admired in the 1930s also reflected
the transition from a devotion to thrift and production to
the desire for consumption and leisure. On radio, Jack Benny
became famous for portraying a ridiculous tightwad. Both as
a song and a Broadway play, "You Can't Take It with You"
became an American hit. In *The Saturday Evening Post*, the
shifting admiration from productive businessmen to pleasure
seeking entertainers which occurred after 1926 was magnified
greatly during the depression. *Reader's Digest* reflected a
similar change in the early Thirties.

Other elements of the success ethic also began to change.
While *Reader's Digest* conservatively maintained that the
individual controlled his destiny, *The Saturday Evening Post*
was more ambivalent. Luck had been the seventh most
important cause of success in *The Saturday Evening Post*
sample issues from 1917 to 1929, but in the 1930s it was the
third most important. While ability ranked tenth in *The
Saturday Evening Post*'s list from 1917 to 1929, during the
Thirties talent became the fifth most important success
requirement.

The emphasis on talent often took on a Darwinian
character. Emil Ludwig argued that French Premier Briand
was an influential diplomat because he "inherited a peculiar blend of blood in his veins from two parents." Walter Pitkin maintained that because of a "natural selection of
workers" the "intellectually superior people live longer than
inferior" individuals. For Pitkin, the depression "marked
the beginning of a new era in which the nit-wits steadily lose
ground to the Best Minds."[21]

The re-emergence of Darwinism often possessed a racist
orientation. Magazine heroes with immigrant backgrounds
generally did not make as much money as subjects of stories
who possessed Anglo-Saxon surnames. With the exception of
criminal types, Caucasians always succeeded. In contrast,

blacks almost always failed. In the few stories and articles
written about blacks in *The Saturday Evening Post*, Octavus
Roy Cohen described them as stupid and lazy. In *Reader's
Digest*, only one black success figure, Joe Louis, was mentioned in one hundred sixty-seven articles. The author
attributed Louis's success to destiny and the fact that he "was
a truly savage person . . . a wild animal."[22]

It is important to note that the shift away from diligence
and thrift, devotion to the pleasures of the moment and
implicit recognition of fatalistic forces in life did not supplant
the tenets of the dream of success. Rather, these changes indicated a growing ambivalence in American popular culture.
While fan magazines may have suggested that movie stars
succeeded by luck and lived in the present, the public went to
the theater to see Disney productions in which Practical Pig
found security through diligence and Snow White sang the hit
song "Someday My Prince Will Come."

Moreover, many of the books and articles leaning heavily
toward pleasure seeking and consumption still contained
contradictory advocacies of traditional success principles. Pitkin criticized people for working too hard for future wealth,
but he devoted much of his book to demonstrating that
people over forty could succeed if they tried. And while Hillis
advocated consumption, she admonished readers not to live
beyond their means. Hillis' method for attaining luxuries on a
limited income was by saving on certain items to spend on
others. Budgeting, rather than installment buying, was her
solution.

Conservative success writers often avoided accepting the
ramifications that inherited talent had upon the gospel of
success by maintaining that the average man possessed special
abilities which could be cultivated through diligence. Dale
Carnegie emphasized that every man had untapped talents and
promised that his book would help readers "discover, develop,
and profit by those dormant and unused assets." Helena H.
Smith noted, in *Reader's Digest*, that Paderewski "was a
musical child, but he was no prodigy; he had the genius which
takes time and grueling work to mature." While Pavlova's

feet were "tipped with magic," Saul Hurok told *The Saturday Evening Post*'s readers that the ballerina was successful because she worked "religiously." Luck similarly was made secondary to effort. David Lawrence maintained that although luck often was present in attaining success, it usually was less important than common sense, diligence and salesmanship.[23]

Liberals were less dogmatic. In *Reader's Digest*, Paul Hutchinson wrote, "Of course it is not true that the Puritan virtues which Mr. Coolidge both preached and embodied—industry, thrift, personal integrity—have been wholly cast into discard. But," he went on, "those virtues are under such scrutiny as they have never been subjected to in the past. They must change—they *are* changing—because Western civilization itself is changing."[24]

Hutchinson pointed out that the old belief in laissez-faire "has now run its course" and that "'rugged individualism' is just about the sorriest looking slogan left over from the boom era." With so many men unemployed, Hutchinson maintained, it was impossible to emphasize the virtue of diligence. Thrift appeared just as meaningless "when the wastrels are no more broke today than those who scrimped and slaved to 'put something by.'" Hutchinson concluded that new programs resulting in "a rapid and widespread redistribution of wealth" were necessary if America were to prosper again.[25]

Thus, as people began to question their beliefs instead of themselves, they allowed themselves the opportunity to change. But the tenacity with which the success ethic lingered in our culture suggested that it would influence American politics and thought as the depression continued. Americans were ready to suspend but not reject their traditional values.

Imagination and Ambivalence: Franklin Roosevelt and the American Dream

Perhaps more than any other figure of the period, Franklin D. Roosevelt reflected the public's ambivalent attitudes towards the success ethic in the mid-Thirties. Speaking to

a nation dissatisfied with Hoover's programs yet uncertain
what should be done, Roosevelt vacillated between demanding
that the government be curtailed and expanded, the budget
be balanced and yet inflationary, and aid be given to citizens
while expenditures not be increased. On the whole, however,
it was apparent that Roosevelt was willing to let his humanitarian sentiments override an allegiance to the success ethic
if people continued to suffer.

Roosevelt's political success also resulted from his
ability to symbolize the aspirations of the voters. A man who
had combated polio successfully and now was running for
the Presidency, Roosevelt appeared well suited to help the
public end their economic paralysis and strive again for
success. And through his famous assertion that "the only
thing we have to fear is fear itself" and his jaunty grin, FDR
gained the attention of voters who desperately wanted
confidence.

Roosevelt's mission, then, was both to transcend and
reactivate the dream of success. After describing his inauguration as a "day of consecration," the President entered the
White House and proceeded to illustrate how great were the
ambivalences within his personal mission. Early New Deal
programs, such as the NRA and the President's decision to
slaughter pigs rather than give them to the poor, suggested
that Roosevelt was going to worry more about overproduc-
tion than underconsumption. Concurrently, FDR's endorse-
ment of relief legislation indicated his recognition of the need
for increased consumption.

Throughout his administration, the tension between
humanistic sentiments and an allegiance to the dream of
success troubled Roosevelt profoundly. Because of his respect
for diligence, he often hoped to end the need for welfare
checks. In a letter to Colonel House in 1934, Roosevelt wrote,
"What I am seeking is the abolition of relief altogether. I cannot say so out loud yet but I hope to substitute work for
relief." Roosevelt also was disturbed that large expenditures
would unbalance the budget and was hesitantly dragged

along by a more liberal Congress wanting larger appropriations for the unemployed.[26]

Roosevelt's actions in 1934 and 1937 best illustrated his vacillation between recognizing the inadequacies of the self help tradition and feeling guilt over transgressing the commandments of thrift and diligence. By January, 1934, Roosevelt was providing 4.23 million Americans with relief checks; but four months later, he felt so guilty toward sponsoring what he feared to be a dole that he fired four million Americans to balance the budget. Again, in 1937, he was disturbed by the size of relief roles even though it was largely through such aid that the depression had not gotten worse. Roosevelt's stress became so great that against the advice of his consumer-minded advisors he drastically cut the relief roles, causing a severe recession.

While he continued relief for many years, Roosevelt made certain that projects such as the CCC, WPA, PWA and CWA required work in return for a government check as often as possible. And since Roosevelt deliberately made relief payments less than prevailing wages to prevent a preference for relief over employment, he indicated that the function of relief was only to rehabilitate the individual to the point where he could rejoin the race for success.

The dream of success, then, while slightly encouraging Roosevelt's reformist sentiments, seriously impeded his programs. Because he wanted to reinvigorate the success ethic, he was willing to help many of the unemployed get back on their feet. Still, his programs failed to go far enough. Relief rarely was extended to those who needed the most help, such as sharecroppers, migrant farmers and other severely impoverished groups.

It was when Roosevelt was partially able to release himself from the success ideology which shackled Hoover that he prevented increased unemployment and reduced the number of jobless citizens. Since he was willing to look at America's socioeconomic structure for the causes of the depression, Roosevelt corrected many of the circumstances which led to

the economic disaster. Wealth was redistributed to some extent
and consumption increased. Speculation was curbed by the
inauguration of the Securities and Exchange Commission. The
Banking Act of 1935 shored up our financial institutions and
the prohibition of holding companies strengthened the
corporate structure. While the New Deal definitely was not
radical, it was able to put aside the tenets of the success ethic
sufficiently to be the most effective reform movement of
the twentieth century.

Cooperation and Individualism

During the early New Deal years, Americans exhibited a
spirit of cooperation which contrasted strongly with the
individualistic tradition of earlier periods. Citizens lent their
support to the NRA by proudly displaying the Blue Eagle
emblem which symbolized the common cause. Workers unable
to unionize in former decades built a strong labor movement.
The President's fireside chats seemed to bring unity to the
nation and Americans felt an attachment to their government
which was similar to the patriotism displayed in World War II.

It would be a mistake, however, to envision the New
Deal years as being marked simply by a spirit of community.
Americans generally united into interest groups. While they
realized that cooperative ventures could be more effective than
rugged individualism, most citizens acted cooperatively to
protect as much of the concept of individualism as possible.

In this spirit, conservatives generally supported the New
Deal in its earliest years. While *The Saturday Evening Post*
was hostile to Roosevelt, the equally conservative *Reader's
Digest* endorsed FDR's program. The latter magazine's David
Cushman Coyle insisted that the unemployed be given
governmental assistance through appropriations financed by
taxing the upper income brackets. George Milton even wrote
an article praising the TVA.

Nevertheless, *Reader's Digest* generally supported New

Deal programs which seemed to protect corporate interests and the concept of individualism. Often they used articles written by New Dealers to advocate this position. A. A. Berle, Jr., contended that businessmen had to become more responsible to save traditional values from the threat of collectivism. Thus, Berle maintained, "Commerce has now to think in terms not of a customer who can be parted from his money but of a need which has to be satisfied." Cooperation and service, Berle concluded, allowed a "middle course" between outdated individualism and collectivism to preserve America's "way of life."[27]

The NRA's attempt to persuade businesses to reform themselves with the government's assistance seemed the best "middle course" for many *Reader's Digest* writers. Henry Leach blessed the NRA as an "application of the commandment 'Love thy neighbor as thyself.'" Leach believed the NRA would revive prosperity while at "the same time, we are to maintain self respect and initiative. American individualism is to be made socially helpful." Donald Richberg, General Counsel of the NRA, similarly believed his project would allow "self-government in industry . . . in order that its values may be preserved" against either socialism or "a return to the gold plated anarchy that masqueraded as 'rugged individualism.'"[28]

Even though such writers endorsed governmental economic regulation, their sentiments of service, individualism and anti-Communism were often similar to the rhetoric of business-minded politicians in the 1920s. Thus, while success advocates could condone business-government cooperation, they quickly became skeptical of public relief. By 1935, *Reader's Digest* consistently began to criticize the New Deal. Former Secretary of War Newton Baker maintained in *Reader's Digest* that "of the various forms of relief, governmental relief is the most dangerous and debilitating." "I am concerned because as individuals we are apparently becoming less self-reliant—willing to surrender the adventure of striving, willing to be content with a sort of secure equality in a State which

does all our planning and thinking and providing for us."
Marc Rose complained that "the dole was sapping the character of those who lived upon it" and praised Morman church
leaders who believed that "independence, industry, thrift and
self-respect should once more be established among our
people."[29]

Rose's faith in the relationship between individualism
and self respect indicated that conservative Americans still considered governmental assistance to the average citizen shame-
ful. At the same time, businessmen embarrassed by their
loss of status in the mid-Thirties tried to resurrect the need
for an individualistic and corporate-minded culture. Jealous of
the New Dealers' popularity, many accused Roosevelt of
Communist tendencies. J. P. Morgan warned a Senate committee that "if you destroy the leisure class you destroy civilization."[30]

The position of corporate-minded individualists was
stated clearly by Harold Gray, the creator of "Little Orphan
Annie." Throughout the cartoon strip, Gray portrayed people
who felt humiliated as a result of personal problems. Annie's
friends were afraid of losing community respect and Daddy
Warbucks often felt his image had been tarnished by liberals
and social critics. To cope with such embarrassment, Gray
offered a philosophy which carried the confluence between
Alger, Sumner and Andrew Carnegie to its logical conclusion.

On the one hand, Annie used a Shirley Temple rhetoric to
reassure Americans that honesty, diligence, perseverence and
confidence were rewarded even during the depression. Between
exclamations like "AW GEE" and "LEAPIN' LIZARDS,"
Annie managed to slip in pithy words of wisdom like "'YOU
CAN IF YOU WILL.'" An expert on economic theory, Annie
proclaimed: "'FREE'! HUH—NOTHIN' IS FREE—IT ALL
COSTS SOMEBODY—TOO MANY PEOPLE ARE LIVIN'
'FREE' OFF O' OTHER PEOPLE—I'LL KEEP TRYIN' TO
EARN MY WAY—" Admiring her effort, a grocer remarked
"HARD WORK AND LONG HOURS DON'T SCARE HER—
SHE'S THE KIND DEPRESSIONS CAN'T LICK."[31]

If Annie was the feminine counterpart of Mark, the
Match Boy, Daddy Warbucks was a blend of Andrew Carnegie
and William Graham Sumner. The industrial magnate had
an insatiable lust for power and wealth. Significantly, he suffered as much as the struggling Annie. Daddy Warbucks
consistently felt badgered by liberal reformers and anarchistic
labor leaders. He could not understand why he did not
command sufficient respect. An elitist who used democratic
rhetoric, Warbucks lamented that the public was being misled
but confidently asserted that soon the people would use
their common sense to come around to his way of thinking.
Benevolently, he considered his wealth to be a gift which was
to be distributed to the working class for the benefit of civilization. His employees refused to unionize because Warbucks
gave them jobs, homes and free entertainment. In return for
loyalty, the industrial leader promised that he would not
allow another depression to occur.

Underneath this rhetoric, Annie's and Warbucks' statements contained serious deficiencies. Annie was diligent
and moral, but like Alger's heroes she usually succeeded by
luck and was dependent on her guardian's benevolence. Warbucks seemed to live by a different code. While claiming to
be honest and kind, he ultimately maintained that "FORCE
IS THE ONLY REAL LAW."[32]

It was difficult to understand why Warbucks and Annie
were so ambitious. The beleaguered capitalist constantly felt
threatened by competitors who often wished to murder or
kidnap Annie. Moreover, Warbucks once lost $10 billion and
admitted that he was greatly relieved. Similarly, Annie
happily gave up the fame and fortune of Hollywood after her
cinema debut to prevent any notoriety from giving her
enemies a clue to her whereabouts.

The most touching scenes in the comic strip were Annie's
acts of kindness and the occasions when she sat on Daddy
Warbucks' knee and told him how much she loved him. On the
latter occasions, however, Warbucks usually announced that
he had to leave on another business trip and felt saddened that

he could not be with the one person who meant so much to him. As he battled for wealth, Annie devoted herself to serving others.

Put together, the various and disconnected themes in "Little Orphan Annie" conveyed the limitations of the American dream. The different roles of Warbucks and Annie suggested that a father could be ruthless while his child performed the good deeds which gave life dignity. If Annie had been a boy and had been allowed to mature, one wonders if she would have had to sacrifice her innocence in the pursuit of success. With its emphasis on shame and achievement, the comic strip indicated that the avoidance of humiliation through ambitious behavior could easily result in loneliness. Moreover, the comic strip implied a confusion over means and ends which had authoritarian consequences. Above all, "Little Orphan Annie" indicated how incompatible the concept of rugged individualism was with a spirit of community, unless one considered community to represent a conformist allegiance to the corporation. The sense of cooperation which emerged during the New Deal was soon to be jeopardized by self help philosophers attempting to convince embarrassed Americans to conform to an empty corporate dream of success.

Myths, Masks and Submission: The Defense of a Faltering Dream

Success writers, put on the defensive by the depression and the New Deal, resorted to shame-oriented, contradictory and authoritarian rationalizations. Like Gray's little waif, success writers used positive thinking to attack Roosevelt's policies. Stanley High told citizens in both *The Saturday Evening Post* and *Reader's Digest* to put an "end to defeatism" by opposing relief and having faith in the possibility of employment. Incredibly, Priscilla Pennypacker told *Reader's Digest* subscribers, "For the most part, I do not mind poverty.

It is amusing in its way. There is a certain zest and excitement in nickel-stretching." The editors of *Reader's Digest* expressed similar sentiments in their praise of a family who supposedly found that "$40 a month spells happiness. . . ." The editors made only passing reference to the fact that the family they described had to hunt for their food and could not afford a bathtub.[33]

To reinvigorate faith in the American dream, success advocates increasingly appealed to feelings of embarrassment which might afflict beleaguered achievers. Accordingly, they advocated defense mechanisms which could alleviate doubt and shame. Positive thinking was recommended to compensate for uncertainty. The flattery of salesmanship was advocated as a means to neutralize potential criticism. Achievers were promised that conformity would encourage respect.

Three very popular self help books, Dorothea Brande's *Wake Up and Live!*, Dale Carnegie's *How to Win Friends and Influence People* and Henry Link's *The Return to Religion* emphasized these defensive techniques. Brande, who was the past circulation manager of H. L. Menken's *American Mercury*, offered a formula so intriguing to citizens that her book was reprinted twenty-four times between 1936 and 1941. Promising the opportunity to have a controllable and purposeful life, Brande warned her readers against having the *"Will to Fail."* To *"escape from futility,"* Brande told them to *"act as if it were impossible to fail."* To facilitate living this life of pretense, Brande urged Americans to be future-oriented and forget the difficulties of the present depression. Americans were to be "constant workers" who limited the periods they spent with friends or on entertainment so that they would not be distracted from the goals they were to achieve.[34]

The popularity of Dale Carnegie's *How to Win Friends and Influence People* was by far the greatest manifestation of millions of Americans' desires to continue believing in the possibility of success. Carnegie's book went through twenty-two printings in its first nine months. In 1937, 729,000 copies of the book were sold and Carnegie's doctrines were preached on radio, taught in success courses and published in newspapers throughout America. At a New York meeting, thousands of citizens listened to speakers who testified that Carnegie's method had changed their lives. Men who had failed in the past because of a lack of self confidence told an appreciative audience that through Carnegie's formula they had developed courage and become successful. The entire ceremony was reminiscent of religious revivals in which the regenerated rose to tell a congregation of their return to the faith and resultant salvation.[35]

Like Brande, Carnegie insisted that if the individual acted as if he would succeed, he would eventually become a success. Carnegie told his readers that they should control their thoughts to develop confidence and a dynamic personality. Since people liked optimism, his protégés were to smile even when they were depressed. Carnegie further instructed his followers to praise customers and employers and talk about other people's interests even when their own problems made them feel antisocial. Thus, while Carnegie offered his followers influence, his formula contradictorily required them to conform to the demands of others.

Link's book echoed Carnegie's sentiments so closely that Carnegie urged his readers to purchase *The Return to Religion* and study it closely. Just as Carnegie contended that salesmanship was a reassertion of "the Golden Rule," Link argued that salesmanship was a "religion" to which Americans had to conform. Link told his readers to be extroverts, accommodate their personalities to the tastes of others and continue believing in the possibility of success.[36]

Underneath this rhetoric, it was evident that all three writers found it difficult to give clear reasons for believing in the dream of success. Carnegie's assertion that people should pretend that they were successful made individuals mechanically subscribe to doubted beliefs. Brande told her readers to accept her "as if" philosophy on faith simply because "if we insisted on proving the reality or efficacy or even probability of most of the conceptions on which we base our practical procedures, we should have no time left to act." Having disposed of reality, Brande promised her formula would *"seem like magic."*[37]

To substantiate her claims, Brande demanded that "we accept the premises for action which are presented to us on good authority." Link went even further. "What you need," he explained, ". . . is not *under*standing but *over*activity, a minimum of thinking, and a maximum of doing in company with others; a situation in short where other people do the thinking and give the orders, and you do the work."[38] At bottom, then, Carnegie, Brande and especially Link were advocates of subservience. In effect they advised the American to use his free will to obey either mechanical formulas or the demands of superiors.

The lessening faith in will power, which was indicated by Alger, Coué, Barton and others and developed further by self help writers during the depression, represented a major transition in the dream of success. Traditionally, the success ethic was based upon the premise that man, by his own will, had within him the power to shape his life. The power of the will, then, was the basis for success advocates' faith in self-reliance. But with the growth of corporate power and the depression, success writers revealed doubts regarding the strength of the individual's will. The use of salesmanship, fantasy and auto-hypnosis made the individual subject to organizational power or self-delusion. If the individual could not will his own destiny, it seemed senseless to demand self-reliance. Without self-reliance the individualistic dream of success had no substance. Direction by others who had the power to assist the individual's upward mobility was necessary to compensate for the lessened power of the will. Because of this dependancy, a conformist other-directedness became central to the dream of success.

To what goals, however, was the individual to conform? Success writers in the late Thirties did not seem to be sure. While Carnegie stressed the need for future achievement, he

maintained that happiness in the present represented success
in life. While he showed people how to manipulate their peers,
Carnegie also emphasized the need for friendship as an end
in itself. While using materialistic standards to gauge success,
he chose as one example of achievement a person who
claimed to be "a happier man, a richer man, richer in friendships and happiness—the only things that matter much after
all."[39]

Brande also revealed ambivalent goals, remarking that
success "may, [and] . . . often does, include some recognition
from one's fellows, and greater financial rewards; on the
other hand, it may not." Link maintained that only by being
moral could the individual attain a worthwhile existence,
but his book was mainly devoted to developing the reader's
external personality rather than his internal character. Although Link preached that unselfish service made life meaningful, he criticized New Deal attempts to help the poor
and offered methods for individuals to advance their economic
self interests.[40]

If their advice was nebulous, Carnegie, Brande and Link
clearly expressed a fascination with power. The title of
Carnegie's book explicitly promised a method to influence
people. Brande and Link went further, implying that their
formulas provided superhuman powers. Brande promised readers a "talisman" which would help them achieve success.
Link's book closely resembled Barton's sentiments in contending that while "Jesus is not commonly thought of as a
social light . . . the story of his life is a story of winning friends
of all kinds in all kinds of situations." Having made salesmanship a religion and Jesus a booster, Link proceeded to conclude that businessmen possessed Christlike powers and
accordingly were to be obeyed.[41]

The confusion over means and ends, the inordinate interest in power and the demand for blind acceptance of cultural
beliefs and messianic leaders were traits ominously similar
to totalitarian characteristics. In both his book and an article
in *Reader's Digest*, Link revealed how easily the success

ethic could acquire an authoritarian tone. Angered by "malcontents, parlor communists and social theorists who, because they will not change themselves, talk about changing the entire system," Link proposed in *Reader's Digest* that "we may yet have to put one half of our population into CCC camps in order to cure the fears which trouble a nation." Link further recommended that children enter the military to learn to take orders.[42]

For a while, it appeared that sentiments similar to Link's might divert America from the New Deal towards a paranoid political movement. In 1938, the House Committee on Un-American Activities was formed. In its first days the committee heard testimony that 483 newspapers, 280 labor unions and 640 organizations including Roman Catholic groups, the Boy Scouts and the Camp Fire Girls supposedly were infiltrated by Communists. In large part, the committee attempted to discredit the New Deal as a Communist conspiracy. However, its plans eventually were thwarted when one witness contended that Shirley Temple had lent her name in support of Communist causes. Secretary of the Interior Ickes' sarcastic retort that HUAC's exposés necessitated "a raid upon Shirley Temple's nursery to collect her dolls as evidence of her implication in a Red Plot" was echoed across the nation. The paranoia caused in part by many Americans' inability to acknowledge the emptiness of the dream of success was postponed until the McCarthy witch hunts of the early Fifties.[43]

Although many Americans were confused, they continued to cling to the dream of success. The emphasis given material success in *The Saturday Evening Post* and *Reader's Digest*, plus the popularity of Carnegie's book, which overshadowed all other self help books of the decade, suggested that a large segment of the population continued to believe in the success ethic. Although writers like Hillis and Pitkin indicated the growing movement towards pleasure-oriented consumptive philosophies, they still advocated achievement and individual responsibility in their books.

As indicated on Chart IV, the vast majority of success

articles and stories studied in *The Saturday Evening Post*
and *Reader's Digest* suggested that money was still the most
important measure of success in the depression years. Out of
one hundred eleven sample articles in *The Saturday Evening
Post* between 1930 and 1939, seventy-seven praised monetary
attainment, sixteen considered status the equivalent of success, eight praised power and only thirteen considered
non-material items such as love and happiness to equal
success. Likewise, in one hundred sixty-seven sample articles
in *Reader's Digest*, fifty-four articles defined success material-
istically, fourteen considered status an essential goal, eleven
admired power and twenty-nine called for love, happiness and
kindness to others.

The standards of material achievement, in fact, remained
quite high. While thirteen articles in *The Saturday Evening
Post* sample issues considered employment or security to
represent success during the depression years, twenty-seven
articles continued to stress that success was equated with
great wealth. In *Reader's Digest*, nine articles deemed a job or
security to be adequate attainment while twenty-one exalted
the acquisition of riches.

In addition, with the exception of the tenet of thrift,
there was little explicit denunciation of formulas for success
in *The Saturday Evening Post* and *Reader's Digest*. The
criticism that did appear was confined generally to the middle
Thirties. Only four articles suggested that hard work did not
lead to fame and fortune while thirty-two stories maintained
that diligence was rewarded. One article contended that
morality was not important for success, but nineteen stressed
the necessity of virtue. Two articles advocated caution to
insure success, but forty-eight urged readers to be confident,
ambitious and adventurous. Only one article attacked salesmanship while thirty stories stressed the need for conformity.
All but two of the best-selling self help books accepted
every principle except thrift in the gospel of success. Even
Pitkin, who denounced diligence, still posited that perseverance and salesmanship were necessary for achievement.

Implicitly, however, the six major methods advocated in *The Saturday Evening Post* and *Reader's Digest* indicated the contradictory and confused nature of success formulas. The emphasis given to diligence, will power and morality—the first, fourth and sixth most advocated requirements for success in both magazines—suggested that individual character traits still allowed the American to shape his destiny. But the second most promulgated means to success, salesmanship, emphasized that personality enhancement rather than character development insured attainment of one's goals. The conformity implicit in the doctrine of salesmanship, plus the increased attention given to luck and talent in the Thirties, made it even more questionable whether self-determination or acquiescence to power or circumstance was most important in the individual's future.

While the American dream of success remained a powerful cultural force throughout the Thirties, it was increasingly threatened by the consumption ethic's precepts, the depression and the New Deal. The advent of World War II was to bring an even more serious challenge to a philosophy which had become nebulous and highly unstable. While our individualistic tradition was able to counteract the cooperative efforts of the New Deal and thus forestall the growth of a spirit of community, Americans brought together during the war years were to have far greater difficulty in understanding the relationships between the individual and his society.

Chapter 4

INDIVIDUALISM AND COMMUNITY

The experience of World War II, coming immediately after a decade of depression, severely weakened an already faltering success ethic. While the war did eliminate unemployment, it made people unsure of the future. Consequently, World War II guides to living differed markedly from those offered in the Twenties and Thirties. Criticisms of the success ethic received much more attention than in previous years. Reflecting strong desires for security, power and purpose, self help books were oriented to problems much more basic to the search for the self than the mere attainment of success.

To be sure, success advocates remained vocal during the war, but their admonitions became even more defensive than they had been in the Thirties. The significance of success advocates' remarks lay less in their impact on American thought during the war than in their preservation of values which were to distort many of the insights gained from 1940 to 1945 after the global conflict subsided.

Because of the non-materialistic orientation of most wartime self help literature, authors began to discuss the possibilities of self-actualization, the importance of the concept of community and, above all, the problem of how much power the individual possessed in modern society. To cope with these issues, popular philosophers used religious and psychological concepts to a greater degree than they had in the past.

In their soul searching, a number of problems began to

emerge. How could a person preserve his individuality and yet attain a sense of community? If war indicated the lack of power which nations had over their destinies, what degree of control could individuals expect in their personal lives? If the degree of power a person could possess was in doubt, to what extent was an individual responsible for exerting himself to improve personal and societal conditions?

The War Attacks the American Dream

While these questions were troublesome, on the surface the war effort seemed to be, as John Kenneth Galbraith noted, "an almost casual and pleasant experience" for the majority of Americans. A sense of community partially replaced the individualistic spirit which traditionally pervaded our atomized society. Civic organizations, churches and schools forgot petty antagonisms to carry on the business of helping end the war. In *The Saturday Evening Post*'s photographs, Americans stood together smiling and with arms around each other in stark contrast to the affected poses of the 1920s and the determined grins of the Thirties.[1]

Part of the happiness Americans felt stemmed from the fact that war production allowed millions of victims of the depression the opportunity to find jobs again. The belief that every item produced in industrial plants would help destroy Fascism gave many a sense of significance in their work. Participation in the war effort was made all the more meaningful because of the sacrifices it entailed. On the homefront, rationing and blood donations were considered important acts which could save the lives of soldiers and bring the war to a swifter conclusion. In battle, the average soldier, who formerly had been a laborer, shopkeeper or relief recipient became a national hero willing to risk his life for the perpetuation of freedom. In *The Saturday Evening Post*, Harry Paxton praised Navy firemen for their efforts in saving ships from serious damage. *Reader's Digest*'s David Woodbury lauded

shipyard engineers who "don't get medals or newspaper head-
lines, but they get something else—the certain knowledge that
without them many a ship would never meet the enemy."[2]

Wartime ceremonies reinforced such sentiments. Memorial services became almost religious events in which Americans
were made to feel important by the sanctification of their
sacrifices. Ceremonies devoted to the Unknown Soldier and
"the vacant chair" served to emphasize the importance of the
average fighting man who, while away on a distant mission,
remained present symbolically in civilian rites devoted to the
cause of victory.[3]

The acceptance of sacrifice, the new-found sense of
importance and the enjoyment of cooperation predisposed
Americans to ignore pleasure seeking. With the need to
ration, it became implausible for writers to advocate materialistic consumption. As the war dragged on, industries endorsed the slogan "use it up, wear it out, make it do or do
without" and had it reprinted in over 400 magazines and
periodicals with a total circulation of 90 million readers. Articles also stressed that because Americans felt their work to
be worthwhile, they were far less interested in escapist
entertainments.[4]

More significantly, the war experience led citizens to
question the dream of success. Freed from the boredom of
everyday middle class work which Americans had tried to ignore in the Twenties but had begun to acknowledge with
Pitkin during the depression, many started to compare their
present significant undertakings to former occupations. In
their comparisons, writers revealed the dissatisfaction citizens
sensed with their peacetime jobs. T. E. Murphy wrote of white
collar workers who wanted "to be useful," worked in war
production lines and thus found "a new joy in life in the extension of their work week." Peggy McEvoy was more
explicit, speaking of a worker who happily became involved
in the war effort "fresh from 15 years of boredom behind
a counter of the Perryville, Md., general store."[5]

The satisfaction stemming from significant occupations

was to have an extremely important effect on heightening the alienation from work which Americans experienced after World War II. Dissatisfaction with trivial occupations became increasingly evident during the war years as the definitions of success became transformed. Materialism still remained the basic standard of success, but many writers began to question the need for striving. As indicated on Chart VII, while nineteen articles in *The Saturday Evening Post* and *Reader's Digest* still stipulated that wealth indicated success, an equal number contended that happiness, satisfaction or significance derived from work gave life meaning. Beginning in 1941, Richard Thruelsen wrote a series of articles for *The Saturday Evening Post* which its editors maintained would not be the usual success stories. Instead, Thruelsen's articles were to be "factual" accounts about *"typical"* Americans in different occupations designed to offer examples for readers searching for satisfying jobs. His articles described occupations such as transport piloting and truck driving rather than big business pursuits. Moreover, he stressed that training was important to find a pleasurable job.[6]

The success figures admired in the two magazines also indicated a diminished fascination with monetary achievement and an increased admiration for the common man content with his work. Blue collar workers were the subject of thirteen success stories while big businessmen were praised in only eight.

Understandably, the emphasis on the importance of the common man stemmed from the desire of the mass media to inspire the home front in the war effort. Nevertheless, the diminution of the need for achievement was not entirely a consciously willed decision. The lessened emphasis on the goal of wealth also was caused by a change in many American's attitudes towards the possibility of control over their lives. The surprise attack at Pearl Harbor, the development of the atomic bomb and the possibility of being drafted, crippled or killed made it difficult to plan optimistically for future success.

As a result, biographical articles on entertainers, who remained the most popular success heroes from 1941 through 1945, reflected a recognition of the power that uncontrollable forces exerted on individuals' lives. Although writers implicitly stressed accidental factors in success stories in the Thirties, it was not until the war that writers directly acknowledged the role of fate in the outcome of a person's life. Gretta Palmer noted, in *Reader's Digest*, that actors and actresses only rarely succeeded and that their fame was only the result of luck and inherent ability.[7]

In essence, then, the lessened emphasis on personal success was forced upon Americans and mainly served to enlarge the gap between dreams and possibilities. Similarly, the war not only heightened desires for community but also emphasized the sense of aloneness which Americans experienced. An advertisement portrayed a woman saying, "My husband's in the Army. I'm in a shipyard. . . . We're in the war together." At the same time, popular songs of the period were entitled "Long Ago and Far Away," "I'll Walk Alone" and "I'll Be Seeing You." The desire for unity and sense of separation produced a sentimental, often melancholy feeling such as that conveyed by Bing Crosby's hit "White Christmas."[8]

In a Christmas radio program during the war, Jack Benny conveyed this ambivalence perfectly. Gathered at a yuletide party was the entire gang which Benny played with—Don Wilson, Rochester, Mary Livingston and Phil Harris. As the group rollicked together they radiated a chumminess which symbolized the closeness Americans desired. Andy Devine dropped by to offer a toast. Calling each member of the gang by name, Devine happily noted that they had been friends for years and hoped that their friendship would continue for a long time. Then Benny was asked to give a toast and the mood suddenly became more serious. As he raised his glass, Benny apologized for not being able to meet all the individual soldiers on the Atlantic and Pacific fronts but said reassuringly that citizens were with their fighting brethren in spirit.

As he admitted that the war dampened the happiness and good fellowship of Christmas, the band began to play melancholy Christmas carols. Over the airwaves of Armed Forces Radio, the world confrontation seemed only to amplify the gap between the dreams of community and significance and the experience of isolation and tragedy.

Superman, Willie and Joe

The wartime ambivalence also was illustrated in the difference between two of the most popular cartoon strips of the period. In late 1938, a new hero rose in popular culture who reflected both the desire for significance and community and the extreme extent to which Horatio Alger's beliefs had been transformed into fantasy. In their search for the self, Americans became captivated by a man possessing a split personality. Mild mannered, diligent and almost anonymous Clark Kent, whose conventional behavior failed to earn him the respect of his girl friend Lois Lane, had within him the power to be Superman. The relationships between Alger's heroes and Superman were many. Superman, like Mark the Match Boy, was an orphan. In fact, he lost his parents twice, both in the holocaust on Krypton and when his adopted earthly parents passed away. On his deathbed, Superman's father warned him to remember that the world was filled with evil forces which victimized innocent citizens. His father's last request was for Superman to dedicate his life to stopping these forces and upholding the law. Always civic-minded, Superman used his enormous power to perform acts of kindness for others just as Alger's heroes were marked by their beneficence. An individualist who fought on his own, Superman earned the respect of elites and average citizens alike. As the force of goodness in a world of evil, he began conquering munitions makers and saboteurs even before America entered the war. In short, Superman reassured citizens that even in a world threatened by Fascism, life's problems could be remedied easily by the fusion of individual power, a sense of community, a respect for morality and the practice of care.[9]

The question remained, however, whether or not the average person could ever become the "MAN OF TOMOR-ROW." The comic strip creators seemed to imply he could even though Superman usually had to come to the aid of mere mortals. During the Forties, Superman failed only twice. Once, in taking his physical for induction into the Army, Superman's X-ray vision caused him to read the eye chart behind the one he was supposed to. Consequently, he was declared 4-F. On another occasion, Superman participated in war games but was defeated by the common American soldier. The lesson was clear. While Superman possessed extraordinary powers, he was no match for the average citizen caught in the fervor of World War II. On the cover of an Action comic book, a girl looked to a sailor, marine and army man and gushed "YOU'RE MY SUPERMEN!"[10]

If Superman was a national dream, he contrasted poorly with the American experience. Another cartoonist, Bill Mauldin, said, "The only way I can try to be a little funny is to make something out of the humorous situations which come up even when you don't think life could be any more miserable." As he travelled with the 45th Army division for three years, Mauldin created a series of cartoons entitled "Up Front" to express his feelings. The cartoons were immensely popular both on the battlefield and at home and earned Mauldin the Pulitzer Prize.[11]

The central figures in "Up Front" were two soldiers, Willie and Joe. In contrast to the energetic and glamorous Superman, the two GIs were weary, resigned to the possibility of death and anxious to forget everything and simply go home. Lacking Superman's power over destiny, Willie and Joe represented for Mauldin the "normal people who have been put where they are, and whose actions and feelings have been molded by their circumstances." In an age celebrating individual significance, Willie and Joe were scarcely distinguishable from each other except for the size of their noses. Unable to transcend humanity in their defense of justice, Willie and Joe were far from gentlemen. As Mauldin explained, it was impossible to act in a dignified fashion when survival necessitated shooting the enemy in the back.[12]

Still, Mauldin considered the American soldier unselfish, courageous and definitely noble. A spirit of comraderie pervaded his cartoons. Nevertheless, Mauldin sensed inadequacies in the wartime rhetoric of unity and individual merit. In essence, community necessitates empathy as much as idealism. But Mauldin felt the average citizen understood little of the soldier's experience, especially because of the distorted heroic image portrayed in Hollywood movies. Even in a period when citizens eulogized the boys overseas, Mauldin admitted that he felt compelled to publish his cartoons because he felt that the soldier was not being remembered.

New Directions in the Search for the Self

Caught between their dreams and experience, Americans searched for guides to living which promised power, significance, community and care. Although only five out of one hundred twenty articles in *Reader's Digest* noted that the attainment of power marked an individual's success, fourteen out of seventy-five articles (or almost 20 percent) in *The Saturday Evening Post* made power the most important goal for people assaulted by the blows of depression and war.

The need for encouragement and control inclined many towards religion. Fear of death on the battlefield or anxiety over a relative's safety inspired many to ask God to intervene in fate. The editors of *Reader's Digest* explained that "to men facing death in combat, God is very near and personal." Thus, Americans were receptive to the words of Rev. Peter Marshall, pastor of the New York Avenue Presbyterian Church, chaplain of the United States Senate, and soon to become the hero of Hollywood's "A Man Called Peter." As

Marshall explained, "There *can* be life, liberty, and the pursuit of happiness available to all men" if Americans "learn to let God guide and control our hearts."[13]

As religious fervor increased, materialistic ambitions waned. In a period when death was possible at any moment, money seemed less important than the preservation of life and preparation for the hereafter. Marshall insisted that Americans "must decide between God and materialism." A. F. Cronin wrote in *Reader's Digest* that "Times are changing; values are in the melting pot. Amid the desolation of this war-torn world, let us remember that God fulfills himself in many ways." Cronin admonished readers to respond to the transformation of values by "cast[ing] out all self-interest. . . . Today a man's best assets are his health, a stout heart, confidence in his own integrity. His only true capital is, was, and always will be his soul."[14]

Psychology became the companion rather than the adversary of religion in the search for the self and community. In *The Saturday Evening Post*, Jack Alexander attributed Marshall Field's conversion from pleasure seeking to philanthropy in large part to consultations with a psychiatrist. "It was after . . . [Field's emergence] from the medical confessional that this instinct for public service . . . began first to lope, then to charge."[15]

Spiritual, psychological and social concerns clearly were beginning to counter traditional materialistic perspectives. The search for the self was ready to address itself directly to the concept of identity and launch an attack on the dream of success.

The Limitations of Idealism

The confluence of desires for power, religious solace, psychological insight and the attainment of self through service to others was most pronounced in the best-selling self help books of the early Forties. The first of these books to appear was Harry Emerson Fosdick's *On Being a Real Person*. As one of America's foremost liberal Protestant ministers, Fosdick offered a philosophy which advocated courage, integrity and social kindness. He implied that the dream of success stemmed from man's baser motives.

The importance of Fosdick's book did not lie merely in its liberal orientation. The vague and contradictory principles he advocated reflected the difficulty of developing a philosophy which allowed individuality and power as well as community and care.

Fosdick began his book by asking how much control an individual possessed in modern society. Admitting that "one cannot lightly talk about being the master of one's fate," he still maintained that "life consists not simply in what heredity and environment do to us but in what we make out of what they do to us." He asked Americans to accept their limitations and do the best they could with their abilities.[16]

Fosdick's concern for effective self-improvement stemmed from his assumption that many Americans had become so internally divided by ambivalent desires and unrealistic beliefs that they found it difficult to act. By acknowledging the existence of ambivalence, Fosdick's assessment of the average citizen's condition was far more incisive than that of previous self help writers. In contrast to popular philosophers who talked loosely of power, morality, self interest and service and then proceeded to advocate escapism and unrealistic goals, Fosdick demanded that the individual encounter reality and recognize that "conflict is an inescapable element in human experience. . . ."[17]

Ironically, after recognizing the existence of tension Fosdick tried to subvert it. The goal of his philosophy was to give the citizen "a high degree of unity within himself." Americans were to develop organized lives by the internal "harmonizing of conflicts . . . [and] the subjugation of revolts." This repression was to be accomplished by adhering to a "scale of values" based on unselfishness and trust in God. The answer to tension was a positive faith in religion, he asserted, because "the complex nature of the world's problems, beyond the competence of common men even to grasp, makes a leader seem a godsend, and devotion to him a privilege." Personal desires for power and individuality were to be sublimated into a "one-directional" life style oriented towards service to mankind. Ultimately, he contradicted his emphasis on power by demanding "self-surrender" to God and ironically argued that self-integration was accomplished by an effort to "get ourselves off our hands" by acts of kindness to others.[18]

Fosdick's philosophy thus lay somewhere between morals and ethics. Criticizing conservative theologians, he contended that absolute morals and an emphasis on guilt stifled understanding and inclined people to rationalize responsibility. Still, Fosdick admonished readers to live up to ideals on the basis that "we . . . accept responsibility when we succeed; we may not slough it off when we fail."[19]

While Fosdick's theology encouraged people to be active, kind and liberal, its emphasis on community limited the possibility of self-actualization. The Protestant minister was not an existentialist philosopher who envisioned possibilities stemming from the creative use of ambivalence. Instead, he was an idealist in the pragmatic American tradition. While he called for a unified identity, his emphasis on living up to ideals defined by God rather than acting in accord with self-defined principles suggested that the self and its ideals were separate rather than integrated. Actions were based on performing duty out of respect for the rights of others rather than upon universal ideals applicable to both the idealist and his peers. Without equal emphasis on individual and community needs, Fosdick understandably called for sacrifice, diminishing the idealist's right to power and care himself.

Since self-sacrifice connotes a loss of identity, Fosdick's idealism could foster a sense of frustration, making it difficult for liberals to sustain a spirit of care. Community, in the absence of individual significance and power, turns to conformity. The ultimate consequence is apathetic sentimentalism rather than active reform.

Autonomy and Care

Much of the confusion within Fosdick's philosophy was avoided in another self help book, *Peace of Mind*, written by Rabbi Joshua Liebman. Liebman agreed with Fosdick on the need for community and faith but he also insisted upon the development of individuality and self confidence. Liebman's book was the second best seller in the non-fiction class in 1946, the top seller in 1947 and the third best seller in 1948. In 1946 alone, the book went through forty printings, was selected by the book of the month club and was condensed in *Reader's Digest*.

The popularity of *Peace of Mind* was all the more dramatic because it stood in marked contrast to the typical best-selling self help tracts. Rather than offer the usual array of trite clichés and personal anecdotes to demonstrate the possibility of achievement, Liebman firmly repudiated the dream of success. In place of a materialistic philosophy, Liebman thoughtfully integrated the teachings of Freud and theology to offer beliefs with which the citizen could find himself and cope with the world. Americans were to use psychology to understand the causes of their failures, hates and fears. However, self-awareness was only the means and not the end of the individual's search for identity. Since consciousness had to be coupled to responsible action, Liebman contended that psychology "must be supplemented by religion" which alone could give "a sense of our purpose in the world, a feeling of relatedness to God, the shared warmth of group fellowship, and the subordination of our little egos to great moral and spiritual ends."[20]

Liebman believed that inner tranquility "has always been the true goal of the considered life. I know now that the sum of all other possessions does not necessarily add up to peace of mind; yet, on the other hand, I have seen this inner tranquility flourish without the material supports of property. . . ."[21]

To attain a calm self-assurance, Liebman recommended the rejection of the dream of success. Because of the success ethic, Americans aspired to unrealistic goals, became neurotic devotees of competition, acquired a fallacious sense of their own power and developed selfish rather than charitable attitudes. As a result, Liebman explained, Americans were continuously frustrated when they failed to achieve absolute victory. Because of their frustration, they lost trust in themselves, sought reassurance rather than insight and forced others to subscribe to their ideals in the hope that such conformity would be a sign of the righteousness of their beliefs.

Such intolerance prevented Americans from looking objectively at either their personal difficulties or the problems of others. In their self-interestedness and lack of empathy, Americans failed to understand the plight of the poor, misunderstood the workings of the economy, attributed all problems to individual failings and thus became fearful when societal problems arose which individuals were unable to resolve. With these fears, it was impossible for Americans to attain peace of mind, which alone would assure social harmony and the prevention of war.

Liebman also criticized religions which were preoccupied with fostering a personal sense of guilt for preventing Americans from attaining an inner tranquility. Religious beliefs which stressed submission to God and repression of personal desires forced people to worry about their individual sins instead of acting with God out of love for one's fellow man.

To cope with their fears, said Liebman, Americans had to modify their sense of individualism. On the one hand, because the success ethic and stern religions produced self-hatred by encouraging the individual to blame himself for his failings, Liebman urged the American to lower his aspirations and accept the fact that no individual is the complete master of his destiny. Americans could gain self respect by accepting the fact that they had imperfections as well as talents. On the other hand, irritated by religions that demanded kindness to others at the expense of self respect, Liebman suggested that the Golden Rule be reinterpreted to read, "'Thou shalt love thyself properly, and *then* thou wilt love thy neighbor.'"[22]

Though Liebman asserted that individuals were not as powerful as success advocates had assumed, he admonished his readers not to become hedonistic, fatalistic or submissive. Americans must learn, he insisted, "to live not for the fleeting and perishable ecstasy of the moment, but for the eternal and abiding values which alone are the sources of self respect and peace of mind." Rather than be resigned to his inability to change the world, the American was to accept the responsibility for changing society and simply reject the belief that any man alone could effect the reformation. Instead of striving as individual messiahs to conquer the world, men had to learn to cooperate to end poverty, racism and war.[23]

The Return of Submission and Success

Tradition-minded supporters of the success ethic agreed with Liebman that Americans should resist any fatalistic sentiments. However, success writers were disturbed by the standards and goals advocated in the best-selling self help books in the 1940s. Liebman's emphasis on individuality and the rejection of materialistic goals and Fosdick's preference for community attacked vital elements in the dream of success. Consequently, success writers attempted to channel the desire for power into the pursuit of success rather than the alleviation of personal stress and social problems.

In an article in *The Saturday Evening Post* entitled "What's the Matter with the U. S. A.?" S/Sgt Jameson G. Campaigne expressed the discontent which success advocates had with many Americans' wartime attitudes. "Why is it," Campaigne asked, "that we, the people of the greatest nation in the world, are acting confused and indecisive?" Answering his own question, Campaigne blamed cynics, cautious individuals and "liberals . . . [who] hold up as their ideal a regimented system of 'security'" for threatening the traditional system of "initiative and ingenuity that find their best expression in a free competitive society under law."[24]

To counteract the declining interest in achievement, success writers set out to rejuvenate the American spirit and to halt social legislation considered antithetical to their beliefs. Positive thinking, will power and courage were advocated sixty-one times in one hundred ninety-five articles in *The Saturday Evening Post* and *Reader's Digest*. Success heroes were praised for their optimistic determination. Inventor Simon Lake was admired by Harland Manchester in *Reader's Digest* for never understanding the meaning of the word "impossible." Ernest O. Hauser lauded Lloyd's of London in *The Saturday Evening Post* for being "The World's Most Famous Optimists."[25]

By emphasizing these characteristics, success writers continued the trend of increasingly stressing mental control to encourage doubting Americans to believe in the possibility of achievement. Will power, which was the fourth most popular requirement for success in the 1917–1929 and 1930–1939 period, became the third most advocated prerequisite for achievement during World War II. Similarly, courage rose from being the eleventh most advocated requirement for achievement in the 1917–1929 period to eighth during the depression and fourth during World War II. Positive thinking, which was the sixth most promulgated method of achievement in the 1917–1929 period and had dropped to ninth during the depression and war years, began in 1947 to be the second most popular means for achievement.

Although they were forced to concede the necessity of economic regulation in the early war years, success advocates kept a wary eye on governmental activities and became increasingly hostile to social legislation as the war progressed. In 1941, the editors of *The Saturday Evening Post* admitted the need for rationing and price controls to end the war: "Much more than the necessity to embrace it [government controls], we hate the one word that defines it. Nevertheless, the sooner we make up our minds to accept it . . . just so much sooner we shall come to the end" of the war. By 1943, success writers grew increasingly fearful of government involvement in industry. *Reader's Digest* reprinted an article from *The United States News* to warn the public about the government's $14 billion investment in industries to stimulate the war effort.[26]

The government also came under attack for making Americans dependent on social welfare legislation. J. P. McEvoy criticized the relocation of Japanese Americans during World War II because he feared that they would abandon ambition and diligence and become permanent wards of the state. Joseph Livingston wrote, in *The Saturday Evening Post*, that "the real danger the country faces today is not that Government officials will do nothing about unemployment, but that they will do too much. . . . This is a period," Livingston asserted, "in which the economic self-interest of the individual must be permitted to exert itself, a period in which he who helps himself helps the country. . . ."[27]

By 1945, success writers accused the Democrats of breeding Fascism in America while fighting Germany. The source which writers often used to substantiate their assertions was Friedrich Hayek's *The Road to Serfdom*. In a condensed form, Hayek's book was reprinted in *Reader's Digest*. Although Hayek had assumed that his book would be read only by economists, he discovered with surprise and some discomfiture that it quickly became popular with economic reactionaries.

Hayek warned that "the forces which destroyed freedom in Germany are also at work here." Governmental economic planning, he believed, was eroding "the system of private property . . . [which was] the most important guarantee of freedom." Thus, he urged that "if we are not to destroy individual freedom, competition must be left to function unobstructed." With control of the means of production divided among independent individuals, Hayek theorized that each American could have the power to choose his own occupation and leisure. Without individualism, Americans would

be subjected to a totalitarian government which could force
the individual to accept unpleasant work and direct his daily
life.[28]

To counteract the supposed threat of totalitarianism,
success proponents began to advocate the substitution of
grass roots politics for national governmental legislation.
Reader's Digest found "reassuring" W. M. Kiplinger's predic-
tion of the *"trend . . . toward conservative ways of thinking
and doing."* Kiplinger believed that many Americans were
becoming dissatisfied with governmental economic regulation
and wished to reassert individualistic private enterprise. "It
is a phenomenon of the grass roots," Kiplinger observed, "and
it will leave its mark on the policies of *any* postwar administration, regardless of party labels."[29]

Success writers encouraged this conservative sentiment.
Marc Rose praised the town of Cripple Creek, Colorado, for
coping with its own economic problems without relying on
the WPA's assistance. Paul de Kruif extolled the efforts of Elk
City, Oklahoma, in building a hospital without receiving a
"government handout." David Lilienthal, former chairman of
the TVA, criticized "apologists of Big Government" and
recommended that governmental agencies such as the TVA
"be placed in the hands of local agencies." Through community self help, success adherents hoped to retain at least part
of their cherished principle of self reliance rather than accept
Liebman's insistence on the need for government involvement
in social problems.[30]

Thus, by 1946, American attitudes towards success were
becoming polarized. Seventeen years of depression and war
had severely increased the tensions caused by the growth of
industrialism, bureaucracy and the ambivalences of success
thought itself. For some, the economic and global chaos
increased their need for security, tranquility, love and cooperation. For others the growth of government posed a threat to
their traditional values and life styles. Many Americans, like
Liebman, were willing to reject the individualistic pursuit of
wealth for cooperation in the task to end the social problems

of poverty, discrimination and war. Others, admiring Hayek, were just as determined to retain an atomized, competitive, materialistic society in which people were concerned more with their economic self interest than with the problems of the underprivileged.

Amidst this dispute, Willie and Joe returned from the war in 1946 and began working in a gasoline station. Mauldin was disillusioned by what he saw. Having been deprived of luxury goods for so long, Americans began consuming material products at such a furious pace that they quickly forgot the war. Willie's wife greeted her national hero by complaining that Willie hadn't taken time from the war to buy her stockings in Paris or Rome. As business returned to usual, Mauldin portrayed ex-soldiers being exploited by real estate brokers, used car salesmen and even veterans' organizations.

The significance of the average American was dwindling fast. In one cartoon, Mauldin drew his version of the statue of the Unknown Soldier. The forgotten warrior was enshrined in marble sleeping face down on a park bench. In another cartoon, reminiscent of the Thirties, a soldier resting in a park used a banner with the inscription "WELCOME HOME OUR HERO" as a blanket. A fellow veteran remarked, *"Yer lucky it's cloth. Mine was paper an' it wore out."* As conservatives complained of government aid, a GI in a hospital asked two visitors, *"How's things outside, boys? Am I still a war hero or a drain on th' taxpayer?"*[31]

In commenting on his cartoons, Mauldin admitted that he was something of an egalitarian rebel. He preferred to side with the common soldier rather than his superiors and said that he found himself "more often in sympathy with people who opposed the 'elite' than not." What distressed Mauldin particularly at the beginning of the postwar era was the emergence of anti-Communist sentiment. As he drew cartoons advocating free speech and denouncing witch hunts, some newspapers stopped publishing his work.[32]

Superman, however, was becoming more popular. Unfortunately, the Superman who was the civic-minded law

and order American was only a step away from being a dangerous messiah. In meeting his responsibilities to the community,
Superman had no qualms about violence as he sought to
protect truth, justice and the American way. Because his
enemies were bigger than life, terrifyingly evil and often
sought to manipulate men's minds, Superman could justify
his abnormal ethics. In short, the fantasies which bred and
justified Superman were strikingly similar to those which
fostered paranoia.

Mauldin had noted that the sense of community which
arose in the Army was somewhat authoritarian by necessity.
On the homefront, patriotism extended to imprisoning Japanese Americans who did not seem to fit the American
way. Soon, the imaginary Superman was to be replaced by a
Congressional demagogue who insisted that conformity
equaled community. As care diminished in the quest for
significance, Americans were soon to forget Liebman's insight
that autonomy and social progress necessitated a spirit of
both individuality and community. The insights of World War
II were about to be replaced by the fantasies of the Fifties.

Chapter 5

FANTASY AS REALITY: The Desperate
Retention of Doubted Beliefs

In the beginning of the postwar era, comedian Henry
Morgan became popular for his melancholy humor and self-
portrayal as "a nice enough fellow . . . but all screwed up, like
you are." Morgan's assessment of Americans was terse and
accurate. The depression, war, governmental growth and postwar inflation made many persons doubt that they could
control their lives. Norman Vincent Peale observed that Americans had "become so keyed up and nervous that it is almost
impossible to put people to sleep with a sermon. I haven't
seen anyone sleeping in church in years—and I tell you that's
a bad situation."[1]

In this milieu, success-oriented, pleasure seeking and
moralistic philosophers encouraged an escapist attitude to
attain peace of mind. Many sought reassurance through the
paranoid fantasies of McCarthyism, the political inaction
of the Eisenhower-Nixon years, and the growth of a pseudo-
religious revival. As a result, the polarization of viewpoints
and growth towards alternatives which emerged during World
War II were reduced to an apathetic and unrealistic consensus
filled with rationalizatons and sentimental platitudes.

The success ethic survived only to become a philosophy
without substance. Even the most prominent success advocates
expressed doubts concerning their assertions and hoped to
convince themselves as well as their followers of the efficacy
of their beliefs. Conformity became a substitute for com-

munity and individuality, passivity became preferable to reform, care was reduced to sentimental do-goodism and fantasy replaced reality in much of American society. As an era devoted to positive thinking, the Fifties illustrated how optimism can be one of the most dysfunctional traits in the search for the self.

The Growth of Ambivalence

A comparison of the methods for success preached in *The Saturday Evening Post* and *Reader's Digest* from 1917 through 1929 to those advocated from 1947 through 1955 indicates the confusion about achievement which had developed by mid-century.* In the post-World War I era, there was a clear distinction between major and minor requirements for success. Diligence, morality, salesmanship and will power were advocated twice as many times as positive thinking, efficiency, luck, talent and imagination. In the post-World War II period, the spread between the second most advocated requirement, positive thinking, and the ninth, luck, was far closer. As Chart XIX on page 189 of the Appendix indicates, in the combined sample issues of both magazines the inherited factor of talent was recognized in only one less article than the controllable requirement of courage, and the fatalistic role of luck was acknowledged in only four fewer articles than the potentially developable influence of virtue.

In *Reader's Digest* sample issues, will power and virtue were advocated twenty-four times between 1926 and 1929 while luck and talent were recognized on only seven occasions in success articles; between 1947 and 1955, will power and virtue were preached thirty-six times while luck and talent received thirty-three references. In *The Saturday Evening Post* sample issues from 1917 through 1929, virtue and will power

---

*Reader's Digest statistics for the pre-depression period are from 1926 through 1929 only.

were advocated forty-seven times while luck and talent
received twenty-two acknowledgements; from 1947 through
1955, virtue and will power were recommended twenty-one
times while talent and luck accounted for success on eighteen
occasions. In short, success formulas from 1947 through 1955
were more contradictory and diffuse than those preached
before the depression.

Chart XIX on page 189 of the Appendix indicates a significant shift in the relative positions of certain behavioral
traits advocated in the two periods. Although diligence consistently remained the most advocated method of achievement, positive thinking moved from a distant sixth in the
1917–1929 era to a strong second in the post World War II
years. Similarly, courage rose from eleventh to fifth.

These statistics suggested that success advocates' conceptions of existence and purpose changed drastically between
the two periods. Life was no longer understood as a clear-cut
challenge in which the individual could succeed by the application of a few simple rules. Rather, life had become a
confusing burden which had to be endured. The different
dedications of Bruce Barton's *The Man Nobody Knows* and
Dr. John Schindler's *How To Live 365 Days a Year* demon-
strated this change. Barton began his book with the Biblical
quotation, "Wist ye not that I must be about my Father's
business?" implying that commercial pursuit was an obvious
goal of Christ and, by inference, Christ's followers. Barton
went on to extol Christ's efforts to challenge and conquer the
world. In contrast, Schindler dedicated his popular 1950s
book "TO THE UNSUNG MAGNIFICENCE OF ORDINARY
PEOPLE who, from paleolithic caves to modern assembly
lines, have shown the *courage to endure* and the *determination
to make the best of it.*"[2]

Success goals were as diffuse as success formulas. The
most popularized goals indicated a lack of direction and a
desire for comfort and escape. While Dale Carnegie's *How To
Stop Worrying and Start Living* promised a formula to help
Americans succeed, the book essentially was designed to

protect the individual against stress. Of the seventeen best-selling self help books published between 1948 and 1955, only one, Frank Bettger's *How I Raised Myself from Failure to Success in Selling*, was specifically devoted to materialistic advancement. The vast majority of postwar self help literature was of an "inspirational" rather than a success-minded character. The popularity of Joshua Liebman's *Peace of Mind*, Fulton Sheen's *Peace of Soul* and Billy Graham's *The Secret of Happiness* indicated many Americans' desire for tranquility. Peale's *The Power of Positive Thinking* and *A Guide to Confident Living*, along with H. A. Overstreet's *The Mature Mind*, offered the hope of finding certainty in a perplexing world. Other books, such as Dale Evans Rogers' *Angel Unaware*, Catherine Marshall's *The Prayers of Peter Marshall*, Lillian Roth's *I'll Cry Tomorrow* and Thomas Merton's *The Seven Story Mountain* reflected the desire to find solace through religion.

Often, these inspirational books testified that material success could not provide inner satisfaction. Peter Marshall asserted "that no business contract [,] no order or commercial consideration can ever be worth the happiness of one's home or the peace of one's mind." Bishop Sheen criticized the individual for gratifying limitless desires for riches "when he impoverished himself from within." Dale Evans Rogers contended "that real success was *spiritual*" rather than commercial and Billy Graham cited a Texas millionaire who admitted, "I thought money could buy happiness—I have been miserably disillusioned."[3]

The success goals advocated in *The Saturday Evening Post* and *Reader's Digest* definitely reflected ambivalences concerning achievement. While wealth and money remained the most often mentioned goals in both magazines, their relative emphasis compared to non-material attainments was greatly reduced. Although the number of articles praising material and non-material goals were almost equal in the 1926–1929 period, *Reader's Digest* consistently published almost twice as many articles praising material success as articles dealing with non-material goals from 1930 through

1945. In contrast, as Chart XX on page 190 of the Appendix indicates, from 1947 through 1955 only nine more articles defined success in material rather than non-material terms. Similarly, in *The Saturday Evening Post*, the spread between financial and non-pecuniary goals was lessened severely. In that magazine, materialistic standards had been advocated seventy-four times, compared to thirty-five references to non-material desires in the 1917–1929 era. From 1947 through 1955, materialistic achievements were praised in fifty-five articles, while non-material goals were stipulated in thirty-one stories.

Writers who continued to admire fame and fortune from 1947 through 1955 often found it difficult to demonstrate a causal relationship between effort and achievement in biographies of success heroes. The lives of entertainers, who remained the most popular subjects of success biographies, were increasingly discussed in deterministic terms. Eckert Goodman concluded that "the high spots in [composer Richard] Rodgers' life dovetail so logically as almost to suggest a predestined design," and Eleanor Ruggles deemed actor Edwin Booth "Destiny's Child."[4]

The difficulty of success writers in relating effort to goals also was suggested by the odd assortment of success figures praised. Jacob Hay praised a model ship builder, Robert Wilcox wrote about a goldfish breeder's success, and George Perry devoted four pages in *The Saturday Evening Post* to Andy Mulrain, "world's champion garbage man." While success writers selected businessmen as the second most popular heroes in *The Saturday Evening Post* and *Reader's Digest* from 1947 to 1955, the appearance of hobbyists, fish breeders and garbage men indicated how far writers were willing to search to prove that success was attainable.[5]

Anomie and Paranoia

The confusion regarding values and goals and the apparent disunity between means and ends suggested a condition of anomie, which Robert K. Merton has described as a "disassociation between culturally prescribed aspirations and socially structured avenues for realizing these aspirations." Experiencing anomie, the individual finds his beliefs incapable of helping him manage his environment. The resultant confusion can have paranoiac overtones. The potentiality for support of or participation in paranoiac activity increases after an individual experiences a degree of fulfillment in his quest for significance and then is stymied before attaining complete superiority. Frustrated, he desires power to regain control of his destiny. However, because such a person is morbidly afraid of failure, he prefers to stage his battle for superiority in a world of fantasy to prevent a confrontation between his dreams and reality. To compensate for his sense of inferiority, he sometimes has delusions of grandeur and exaggerates his personal problems. He develops a messianic self-conception, determines that he, more than his contemporaries, understands the distinction between good and evil, believes that his problems are shared by a world which is about to be destroyed, and attempts to destroy imaginary villains whom he believes are persecuting him to prove his supremacy and save the world.[6]

Paranoid movements, and the ultraconservative politics which generally accompany them, are endorsed mostly by persons who, though confused about the workability of their values, are determined to hold on to them. Such individuals defend their values with absolutist arguments and demand conformity on the rationalization that values differing from their own challenge the moral foundations of civilization.[7]

Such paranoid traits were clearly evident in many Americans' rhetoric and behavior after World War II. During the early Forties, many had achieved a sense of significance through involvement in the national struggle against Fascism. But after having enjoyed a feeling of worth and affording themselves the luxury of admitting dissatisfaction with peacetime occupations, Americans were forced again into mundane activities after the war. James Gardner, an official in the Veterans Administration, observed the pervasiveness of this quest for importance in hundreds of interviews with returning soldiers. "[Y]ou get the same story over and over again," Gardner remarked. "They like the idea of making more money but they like even more the idea—as they keep putting it—of 'getting to be somebody.'"[8]

To compensate for their lack of importance, many Americans supplanted the battle against Fascism with a fight against Communism. In so doing, they often sympathized with McCarthyism, imagining that Communists had infiltrated the government and liberals were destroying the dream of success. Although relatively few Communists had reached the higher echelons of government and had exerted little political influence, the arrest of Klaus Fuchs for transmitting atomic secrets to Russia, the fall of China and the Russian testing of the atomic bomb inspired the fear that Communism pervaded America and was about to destroy the world.

Not all citizens who supported McCarthyism were paranoid, of course. Many condoned McCarthyism because of their desire to retain the dream of success. In using anti-Communist and positive thinking arguments to preserve the success ethic, many self help writers who were not paranoid themselves offered strong ideological support for the McCarthy movement, which was fed largely by the public's anomic confusion.

Many Americans became captivated by George Orwell's anti-utopian *Nineteen Eighty-Four*, which predicted a society of indistinguishable persons subjected to a totalitarian government. James Hilton wrote, in *Reader's Digest*, that the book was "As timely as the label on a poison bottle" and William Hard predicted that governmental development of electric companies would lead "toward authoritarian government." The editors of *The Saturday Evening Post* also were quick to suggest similarities between Orwell's novel and political liberals, contending that "there is a considerable amount of 1984 in the so-called Truman program. . . ."[9]

Arnold Toynbee's *Study of History*, a massive analysis of the rise and fall of twenty-six civilizations, led many readers to theorize that America suffered from thoughts and

behavior which had obliterated former dominant nations.
E. T. Leech was disturbed that "THIS COUNTRY—indeed,
the whole world—is being swept by an epidemic of the
gimmees." Leech asserted, in *Reader's Digest*, that unless
Americans forgot their love of security, stopped social welfare
legislation and again strove individually to succeed, America
would deteriorate as quickly as the Roman Empire which
had declined on a diet of bread and circuses.[10]

To stop the supposed Communist threat, witch hunts
which reflected the irrationality of the McCarthy era occurred
across the nation. In Wheeling, West Virginia, a policeman
discovered that penny candy machines were dispensing little
geography lessons with the candy wrappers which stated that
Russia was the largest nation in the world. When City Manager
Robert L. Plummer bellowed, "This is a terrible thing to
expose our children to," Wheeling took quick measures, as
Eric Goldman sarcastically observed, "to protect the candy-
store set from the knowledge that the Soviet Union existed
and that it was the biggest country in the world."[11]

The citizens of Vandalia, Missouri, became so preoccupied with the threat of socialism that they sent postman
Abraham Kilby to England to study the subversive ideology.
Kilby was somewhat bewildered by the excitement his scout-
ing mission caused, explaining that "my trip came to be
played up in the news until you would have thought I had
made the first successful flight to the Planet Jupiter instead
of just a flight to England. . . ." Upon his return, Kilby assured
his community and the nation, through a story in *The Saturday Evening Post*, that socialism was detrimental to individual
initiative and suggested that England change its economy to
the free enterprise system.[12]

Reader's Digest published a condensed version of *The
Soviet Spies*, a book which purported to reveal the existence
of Russian spies in North America. John T. Flynn accused
teachers of spreading socialism by teaching "that our American system of private enterprise is a failure . . . [and] that our
way of life must give way to a collectivist society. . . ." The

anti-intellectual character of the McCarthy movement was epitomized by Mrs. Thomas J. White, a member of the Indiana State Textbook Commission, who attempted to remove the story of Robin Hood from library shelves. "[T] here is a Communist directive in education now to stress the story of Robin Hood," White asserted. "They want to stress it because he robbed the rich and gave it to the poor. That's the Communist line. It's just a smearing of law and order."[13]

The most prominent leader of the witch hunts, Senator Joseph McCarthy, typified the successful yet insecure American of the cold war era to an extreme extent. As a child, McCarthy had been eager to succeed to remove the shame of his awkward appearance and low financial status. Encouraged by his mother's promise that he would "be somebody," McCarthy continually tried to succeed in school and at play. His ambition had led him to break promises, buy votes to win a school election and play so seriously that his associates found him a bore. Upon reaching the Senate, he bragged that he had done well "for a Mick from the backwoods. . . ." But McCarthy's insecurity still plagued him and he desperately desired recognition.[14]

McCarthy blindly lashed out in Senate investigations at the army, the diplomatic corps, liberals, clergymen, teachers and lawyers in hopes of finding the imaginary villains he needed to conquer. In *Reader's Digest*, H. I. Phillips defended Congressional investigations, asserting, "You may not relish so many Senatorial inquiries. . . . But even at their worst they can't come close to making the picture look as bad as the defiant witnesses themselves make it. These witnesses are the ones who are really alarming the American people."[15]

In his frenzy, McCarthy could never be certain of the number of Communists he promised to uncover, On one occasion he stated that he knew of 205 agents, but when pressed to reveal his adversaries, he reduced the number to 57 without giving any names. Eventually, the lack of substance in his accusations and his attack on the army caused the demise of his movement, but not until thousands unfortunately had had their reputations smeared by his paranoid investigations.

One of the most significant characteristics of the witch hunts was that the beliefs which McCarthy and some of his followers claimed to defend against Communism were values they rejected to some extent. Claiming to preserve democracy, McCarthyites acted in a totalitarian manner. While claiming to reinvigorate individualism, they demanded conformity. Criticizing liberals for being dogmatic, they blindly followed their own fixed values. Praising law and order, they were undisturbed by the fact that they ignored the Constitutional rights of the average citizen.

Such discrepancies between statements and behavior suggested that anti-Communism was largely a symbolic action. In effect, the reactionary McCarthyites were "pseudo-conservatives" as Theodore Adorno noted. The "pseudo-conservative is a man who, in the name of upholding traditional American values and institutions and defending them against more or less fictitious dangers, consciously or unconsciously aims at their abolition." Frustrated in their desire for power and significance, the McCarthyites were just as authoritarian as the Communists they condemned.[16]

The Uncertainties of Optimism

Positive thinking, like paranoid politics, was another method by which Americans attempted to escape questioning the failure of the dream of success.

The broadcasts of Gabriel Heatter, a popular news commentator in the Forties and Fifties, vividly exemplified this desperate optimism. Jack Alexander estimated, in *The Saturday Evening Post*, that Heatter's audiences numbered as many as eight million Americans and were middle-aged, lonely, worried and frustrated. To comfort his listeners, Heatter would begin his newscasts with the positive assertion, "Ah, there's good news tonight. . . ." While World War II was rag-

ing, the atomic bomb being dropped and the cost of living
spiraling, Heatter relayed "stories of heroism, unselfishness,
mother love, optimism, prayer, the faithfulness of dogs,
and so on."[17]

Heatter's celebration of the success ethic was even more
tenuous than his wartime optimism. The saddest epitaph for
a man, according to Heatter, was not that he failed but that
"he might have been." Success was not necessarily achievement but was instead "the thrill of trying." With inverted
logic, Heatter offered the ultimate contradiction in success
thought. "[D]efeat," he concluded, "is an honorable enterprise, is victory enough."[18]

Although Heatter was a positive thinker, *The Saturday
Evening Post* characterized him as "an optimist with a sense
of impending doom." Heatter acknowledged that he felt
unhappy, frustrated and "very inadequate." Once he had
considered suicide when he saw continual tragedy in international war. To alleviate his despair, Heatter preached
optimism in his daily radio programs. After the armistice he
began a Sunday show entitled "A Brighter Tomorrow." The
theme of the Sunday program was, "We've survived the war,
but there's a real war ahead to keep our way of life."
Heatter's purpose thus became the battle to preserve his
vacuous dream of success.[19]

He explained that "those spiritual overtones that people
notice in my broadcasts come from my own personal need
for a lift, a need to do something for my own inadequacy and
anxiety. When I talk about conquering fear, for instance, I
am talking at myself primarily."[20]

Even so, Heatter's anxiety remained deeply intense.
While preaching tranquility on the radio, he perspired so much
that he had to change his clothing after each program and
take frequent rest periods. Whenever he went to parties, he
lived in anguish, hating to be "subjected to persons with
positive views on everything." Such exposure, according to
Alexander, gave him "a feeling of inferiority."[21]

The strong contrast between his stress and expressions of

reassurance suggested that Heatter might have great difficulty in understanding himself through the retention of a success-oriented philosophy which was ultimately empty. Three weeks after the appearance of Heatter's biography, the newscaster acknowledged as much in a letter to the editors of *The Saturday Evening Post*. Heatter explained in the letter that he was grateful for the article which had "HELPED ME TO KNOW MYSELF BETTER THAN I HAVE AT ANY OTHER TIME IN MY LIFE. . . ."[22]

Hope Versus Optimism

Clearly, Heatter's optimism was a defense against despair rather than an authentic expression of hope. Hope represents a recognition of tragedy and a willingness to confront problems in order to improve the condition of life for both oneself and one's contemporaries. In contrast, optimism attempts to ignore the existence of suffering to permit the retention of beliefs through wistful dreams of a better tomorrow. In short, hope is present-minded, active, compassionate and realistic. Optimism is future-oriented, passive, sentimental and escapist.[23]

During World War II, the closeness of tragedy to everyday life had been a major influence on the growth of a spirit of community and the questioning of our cultural beliefs. As super-patriotism replaced a cooperative national spirit in the Fifties, the recognition of tragedy gave way to an insistence on the retention of the American Dream. But even with their optimistic rhetoric, most self help writers found it difficult to justify the retention of the dream of success.

Like Heatter, William Campbell Gault contended, "They won't kill the dream in my game. And how about yours?" in an article which complained about "*the Universal Rat Race.*" In *Reader's Digest*, Bernice Fitz-Gibbon quoted the adage,
>"Not the quarry *but the chase*,
>Not the trophy *but the race*."

Thus the success ethic was reduced to an advocacy of unquestioned striving without the desire for any particular goal.[24]

The most noted exponent of positive thinking, Norman Vincent Peale, exhibited an inclination towards far right politics and doubts in the optimistic philosophy he espoused. Peale had belonged to the reactionary Committee for Constitutional Government during the depression and even endorsed a book implying that Franklin Roosevelt was a dictator. After the growth of his popularity in 1948, Peale was warned to refrain from publicizing his admiration for the Republican Right to prevent potential buyers of his books from being disturbed by his political beliefs. Until 1960, when he supported an organization which advised against John F. Kennedy's election on the grounds that a Catholic was unfit for the Presidency, Peale adhered to a self-imposed censorship.[25]

Peale had conducted a positive thinking clinic in New York since the depression, preached optimism in his Marble Collegiate Church, and advocated his philosophy to an estimated 30 million Americans through weekly newspaper columns, national radio broadcasts and his own magazine, *Guideposts*. His book, *The Power of Positive Thinking*, became the best-selling nonfiction book of modern times and ranked second only to the Bible in sales during the Fifties.

Peale directed his advice towards confused, nervous Americans who were exhausted by the race for success. Chapter titles in *The Power of Positive Thinking* and *A Guide to Confident Living* included "Believe in Yourself," "How to Break the Worry Habit," "How to Get Rid of Your Inferiority Complex," "How to Achieve a Calm Center for Your Life" and "Forget Failures and Go Ahead."[26]

While admitting that social conditions caused some problems, Peale in general held that the individual was responsible for his success and happiness. Rather than advocate social change to alleviate suffering, Peale demanded that the individual adjust his attitudes to ignore difficulties. One of man's greatest problems, Peale contended, was a defeatist attitude. If Americans had doubts about their ability to succeed, Peale recommended a mental catharsis "at least twice a day, more often if necessary" to empty the mind of "fears, hates, insecurities, regrets, and guilt feelings." After adopting an out-of-sight-out-of-mind attitude, the individual was to overcome exhaustion and try to succeed.[27]

Ironically, the contradictions in Peale's books suggested that America's foremost optimist was uncertain of the power positive thinking gave. Although he contended that effort and a positive attitude could "overcome any obstacle" and give the reader "any high place" he desired, he warned his followers, "This does not mean that by believing you are necessarily going to get everything you want or think you want."[28]

Moreover, Peale's words indicated that he questioned the power of positive thinking in his own attempts to succeed. He often used the rhetorical device of recalling how his own problems caused despair and then attempting to show how optimism came to his rescue. At times these personal anecdotes suggested that Peale had doubts about his own formulas. He noted that when he was writing *A Guide to Confident Living* he became so discouraged with the manuscript that he "literally threw it away." His wife saved the manuscript and bolstered Peale's spirits, and of course the book became a success. On another occasion, while publishing *Guideposts*, he became despondent about the future of his magazine. When an associate recommended that Peale think positively to bring success to his venture, Peale admitted "I wasn't convinced as yet" until he considered the idea and asked friends for more advice. In the early Sixties, he recounted another occasion when a faithful admirer tried to lift Peale's spirits by reading a booklet which contended that a person could control his fate and conquer fear. Peale remarked, "I was not very impressed," and asked the reader who wrote the inspirational piece. The admirer responded, "You did. . . . This is one of your printed sermons."[29]

To overcome the potential inadequacies of his formula, Peale promised that positive thinking would inspire God to give the individual adequate power to succeed. Peale bolstered his contention by recounting an instance when he placed his hands on a beleaguered businessman and seemed to feel the power of God flow through him.

While Peale's association of God to other-directedness and the dream of success seemed similar to Barton's analogy between Christ and the ambitious businessman, the two authors differed in their basic assumptions concerning the relationship between Christianity and power. For Barton, Christ was a symbol of power which justified the use of strength and the goal of influence in commercial contests. For Peale, God had become more than a symbol which justified power; God was the source of power itself.

Peale theorized that the power of Christianity could be transmitted to the individual through prayer. Paralleling Coué, Peale asked his readers to repeat ten times daily, "If God be *for* us, who can be *against* us?" to become confident. To influence others, Peale recommended transmitting "flash prayers" into the "two billion little storage batteries" of another person's brain to magnetically influence such a person to smile and be interested in the positive thinker's suggestions.[30]

Peale's use of Christianity to bolster the staggering success philosophy led some ministers to question how religious his beliefs actually were. Rarely did Peale refer to salvation as man's purpose. While he did refer to religious devotion to God and Christian kindness to others, Peale seemed more concerned with making God a partner in man's self-interested desires. The secular characteristics in Peale's philosophy eventually caused Peale to speak of Christianity less as a source of mystery than as "a simple yet scientific system of practical techniques of successful living that works."[31]

The inadequacies in Peale's philosophy were also evident in Dale Carnegie's *How to Stop Worrying and Start Living*. Maintaining that optimism encouraged security and happiness, Carnegie asserted that if the individual acted as if there were no problems, he could make his life what he desired it to be.

Carnegie also demanded that the individual continue to devote himself to work to avoid a sense of meaninglessness.

The justification for this position was somewhat lame. Carnegie praised a man who worked sixteen hours a day and became so fatigued that he did not have the energy to worry. If Heatter had encouraged work without the need of a goal, Carnegie had gone a step further by making diligence the means to obliterate consciousness itself.

Like Peale, Carnegie also recommended religion as a source of strength. But the religion he preached lacked substance and was mainly a self-interested instrument. "I no longer have the faintest interest in the differences in creeds that divide the churches," Carnegie announced. "But I am tremendously interested in what religion does for me." Carnegie believed that religion would give him solace, increase his happiness and give him spiritual values. He tended to view religion more as a method of reassurance than a philosophy of life.[32]

Without searching deeply into religion for the purpose of existence, and by merely reaffirming the need for work to prevent Americans from thinking, Carnegie made it clear that he was determined to preserve the success ethic without clarifying how such a philosophy could help the citizen comprehend his identity. Quoting Santayana, Carnegie announced, "Man is not made to understand life, but to live it."[32]

Religion, Retreat and Resignation

Peale's and Carnegie's use of religion as a device for success drew a receptive audience because mid-century America experienced what church historian Martin Marty had described as "a revival of *interest* in religion." " 'Interest,' "Marty noted, "is a rather limp and non-committal word to be using about discussion of ultimates. It carries overtones of self-advantage and self-concern more than other-advantage and God-concern."[34]

While church membership rose from 49 percent of the population in 1940 to 60.3 percent in 1954, the substance of religion was greatly diminished. God's majesty was lessened to the point that a Hollywood starlet described Him as "a livin' Doll." Many Americans believed that they were paying respect to the Deity by attending movies like *The Robe* and *Quo Vadis*. Popular songs humanized God as the "Man Upstairs" and canted the cult of reassurance in songs like "I Believe".[35]

Such sentiments contrasted strongly with the World War II moralistic and humanistic philosophers' beliefs. Whereas Liebman and Fosdick urged sensitivity to the problems of others and cooperative action based on a spirit of care, postwar moralists offered platitudes which contributed to the apathy of the Fifties.

On the surface, it seemed that mid-century religious writers had more in common with their moralistic predecessors than the success advocates of their day. Billy Graham, Peter Marshall and Fulton Sheen were quite critical of the success ethic, preaching that neither comfort nor wealth could give the individual a sense of purpose. Moreover, Sheen insisted that self-reliance was impossible and Graham considered it a concept detrimental to moral growth.

While moralistic and humanistic writers in the Forties also had criticized the success ethic and self-reliance, they had used such a position to justify their insistence upon cooperative reformist behavior based on a spirit of care. In contrast, Graham, Sheen and other moralists in the Fifties urged passivity. Sheen urged the individual to surrender himself to God's will. Similarly, Marshall asserted, "It is true that we cannot change human nature. But God can." And Graham reassured his followers that if an individual trusted in Christ, then happiness, food, clothing and shelter "would be automatically supplied."[36]

In taking this position, Graham and Sheen saw little need for understanding social problems from a political perspective. Suffering was caused by sin rather than a maldistribution of power and wealth. With such an assumption, Graham and Sheen completely reversed Liebman's liberal

positions on guilt and social reform. Whereas Liebman criticized religions for being repressive and promoting a sense of
guilt, Graham and Sheen insisted that men confess their sins
and obey God's laws. They emphasized neighborly kindness
more than involvement in national struggles for civil rights
or anti-poverty programs. Moreover, Sheen warned of the
dangers of Communism and suggested that support for
national welfare projects was almost sinful.

By condoning political conservatism, maintaining that
stress was caused by personal inadequacies, and reassuring
Americans that faith was a sufficient answer to uncertainty,
moralistic philosophers offered a position similar to that of
the positive thinkers. By demanding that people act in accord
with established morals rather than search for new beliefs,
moralists supported the anti-intellectual temperament of the
Fifties.

Finally, by urging neighborly acts of kindness and yet
demanding moral self help with regard to national problems,
Graham and Sheen placed peculiar geographical limits on the
spirit of care which helped perpetuate the success ethic.
Moralists, in denouncing communism and liberalism, assisted
the anti-Communist defense of the success ethic which was
based on a fear that if care required community, then a liberal
concept of national community was only a step removed from
communism. Such logic was questionable. Since care is by
nature a spirit to be universally applied, recommendations to
restrict the practice of care to community projects lead to
the ludicrous conclusion that care was not to extend beyond
the boundaries of Main Street and Fifth Avenue. And the
affinity between liberalism and communism certainly was not
proven by mid-century paranoids.

In contributing to a cultural milieu which urged escape
from the tensions within American values, moralists and
success advocates gained support from devotees of the consumptive pleasure ethic. Many tried to retreat from their
problems by turning to activities where they could "get away

from it all." *The Saturday Evening Post* observed that millions
of Americans were buying boats and traveling to natural
resorts to relax from the tensions of work. At times, the attempt to escape commercial anxieties became desperate.
Robert Froman wrote that there were a million North
American islands which could be bought and that they were
being purchased at a frantic rate. Photographer John Cloud
explained that he bought an island because he "figured that an
island was the only place where I would ever get any peace
of mind." An Ohio businessman predicted, "If everyone in the
world had an island he could get away to once in a while, I
wouldn't be surprised to find most of our problems solved."[37]

Positive thinkers endorsed the idea of finding a retreat.
Margaret Blair Johnstone wrote in Peale's *Guideposts* and
Reader's Digest that an escape to a sanctuary was a "flight *to*
reality." By relaxing, the individual would find "the power
to face life on lifted wings." For Peale, relaxation energized
the American to continue striving for success.[38]

Together, the confluent tendencies of positive-thinking
success advocates, moralistic philosophers and pleasure
seekers transformed the tensions between these different
guides to living into a bland consensus. Much of religion had
lost its mystery, becoming what Arthur Link and Bruce Catton
have called a "bargain-counter operation in which God, in
exchange for prayer, doled out peace of mind, worldly happiness, and worldly success." Businessmen built prayer rooms
in their office buildings and uttered sentimental platitudes
while they pursued their self interests. "In God We Trust," as
Marty observed, "had to be stamped also on the folding symbols of America's bow to Mammon." And throughout
America, conformity was so rampant that students worried
about trivia like wearing a new formal to a prom instead
of being disturbed with the emptiness of their society.[39]

In such a cultural setting, Americans understandably
voted for an Eisenhower-Nixon administration which displayed
little interest in alleviating America's cultural and societal

deficiencies. Eisenhower's grandfatherly image reassured Americans exhausted by war and domestic reform. In his inaugural address, Eisenhower asked God to bestow His blessing on America. Sheen praised the President for issuing a proclamation calling for the Fourth of July to be a day of penance and prayer to help the nation.

What Eisenhower hoped to reform in the American soul, however, was unclear. In the "get away from it all" Fifties, Eisenhower achieved more respect for his golf scores than his political imagination. In general, his selection of businessmen for the Cabinet indicated that he sympathized with supporters of the success ethic. One of his appointments, Treasury Secretary Humphrey, was so captivated by success stories that when asked by a reporter if he had read Hemingway's *The Old Man and the Sea*, Humphrey responded, "Why would anybody be interested in some old man who was a failure and never amounted to anything anyway?" Sinclair Weeks hoped to use his position as Secretary of Commerce to "create a 'business climate' " in America and Secretary of Defense Wilson asserted that "what was good for our country was good for General Motors, and vice versa."[40]

Even with the preponderance of business leaders in the Eisenhower administration, the politics of the Fifties were noted more for their inaction than for a government-business entente like that of the Harding-Coolidge-Hoover years. Often the political lethargy was praised as positive action. Eisenhower explained that he refused to criticize McCarthy's investigations because such criticism would have been a "negative," rather than a "positive" act. When opponents of Eisenhower called for concern over the possibility of an atomic war, they were criticized for not thinking optimistically. During the Eisenhower-Nixon years, New Deal legislation was preserved, but so little action was taken to help the poor that poverty was not reduced. The celebration of positive thinking was only a complimentary rubric for our social paralysis.

The Crisis of American Culture

America had reached a cultural breaking point. Many Americans displayed misgivings towards the success ethic by listening to Sheen's and Graham's attacks against materialism. Even so, they tried to obliterate the tensions between morality and materialism through cults of reassurance. In so doing, they destroyed the essence of religion. Still others attempted to convince themselves that the success ethic was worthwhile, even though Heatter's, Carnegie's and Peale's rationalizations were seriously deficient.

The crisis Americans faced, however, was not suddenly thrust upon them. History rarely is distinguished by watersheds marking the transition from one era to another. The confusion apparent in mid-century success tracts was a culmination of the doubts implicit in the earlier writings of Brande, Carnegie and Link. The pleasure- and consumption-oriented books of the Twenties and Thirties had already observed the difficulty in justifying diligence. The escapist attitudes of the Twenties and implicit acknowledgement of fate in entertainers' biographies during the depression and war presaged the sense of helplessness and desire for retreat of later citizens.

Finally, the abnegation of the will, denied and yet so obvious in success books, was evident in the mind cure and salesmanship literature of the Twenties and Thirties. Coué's lack of faith in the will and advocacy of self-hypnosis, and Brande's belief in the magical talismatic powers of her "as if" formula revealed a mystical faith shielding doubts about self-reliance which were similar to Peale's assertion that mental manipulations could supplant the individual's control over his destiny. Barton's and Carnegie's doctrines encouraged accommodating personal desires to those of the organization. And Link's admiration of powerful messiahs who directed confused Americans anticipated the propensity of Americans to follow McCarthy's demands for submission.

By mid-century, these trends brought the crisis of identity to a peak. Americans had stumbled into a culture of contradictions as bewildering as the backwards world of Alice in Wonderland. Positive thinkers were plagued by doubt. McCarthyites criticized others for attacking values from which they themselves had strayed. Affirmative action meant apathy. After trying to preserve outdated values through an avoidance of thought, Americans had proven only that the dream of success was a highly inadequate guide in the search for the self.

Chapter 6

THE RHETORIC OF CARE

Because the success ethic failed to provide direction during a period when middle class frustrations and the problems of poverty, racism and war seemed unmanageable, many Americans felt increasingly lost in the late Fifties and Sixties. Consequently, they began to grope for new goals to alleviate their stress. The goals which began to emerge were happiness, influence, a sense of usefulness and love. Underlying this trend was a growing recognition of the need for care in American society.

Although an awareness of the emotional needs related to the search for the self was developing, the period from 1957 to 1970 was more significant in illustrating the obstacles people encountered in their attempts to sustain a spirit of care. While middle class goals changed, the means for attaining these ends remained the same. Americans coupled their pleas for care with an insistence that the concept of individualism be retained. While calling for sensitivity towards human suffering, they remained blindly optimistic in their faith in American progress. And while urging cooperation, many insisted upon the retention of the competitive dream of success. The tension arising from searching for emotional satisfactions through traditional standards of behavior in large part accounted for the bewilderment of the late Fifties and the paradoxes and ironies which made living through the Sixties such a disillusioning experience.

Charlie Brown and the Changing American Dream

To be sure, Americans had been concerned with fulfilling emotional needs prior to the late Fifties. Nevertheless, the distractions of depression, war and paranoid politics overrode those concerns. As the waning paranoid craze failed to compensate for significance and community, Americans became sensitive to the more basic desires in their lives.

By 1957, both *The Saturday Evening Post* and *Reader's Digest* began to display a decided preference for discussing non-material forms of success. As indicated on Chart XIII, in *The Saturday Evening Post* issues studied for the period 1957–1959, non-material ideals were advocated in fifty-eight articles while only nineteen stories discussed monetary goals. Happiness derived from one's work was admired twice as often as the attainment of wealth. The goals of love and leisure were advocated more often than all types of material success combined. Similarly, in the *Reader's Digest* sample issues for the same period, non-material goals were espoused seventy-seven times while monetary achievements were praised in only thirty-two articles and criticized in three. Thirty-four articles discussed the desirability of possessing a sense of usefulness by serving others while only fourteen articles admired wealth.

The types of heroes each magazine admired also indicated a heightened interest in pleasure, significance, and service. Entertainers who enjoyed life were the people most respected in *The Saturday Evening Post*. Professionals who served others through their work were the favorite subjects for biographies in *Reader's Digest*. It is important to note, however, that neither magazine consciously attempted to abandon its faith in the success ethic by admiring life styles based on the pursuit of happiness or care for others. In *The Saturday Evening Post*, entertainers often found happiness and love while they were striving for riches. While nineteen *Reader's Digest* stories praised professionals usually devoted to service, seventeen articles continued to admire big businessmen who generally were distinguished by their attainment of wealth. Nevertheless, considering the total content of both magazines, it was apparent that they had shifted their standards for goals which made life worthwhile.

Although both magazines sensed the goals which would enhance Americans' lives, they implied that these goals were difficult to attain. The most popularized standards of behavior in both magazines indicated an ambivalent admiration of effort and a need for reassurance. As indicated on Chart XIV, in the *Reader's Digest* issues studied for 1957 to 1959, diligence and will, concepts which necessitated action, were advocated in only two more articles than courage and positive thinking, means by which troubled persons sought strength and solace. Similarly, in *The Saturday Evening Post* sample issues, diligence and will were called for only seven more times than positive thinking and courage. And virtuous character, a value suited both for service-minded actions and the need for spiritual comfort, was the first and second most popular standard of behavior in *The Saturday Evening Post* and *Reader's Digest*, respectively.

By placing so much emphasis on the need for confidence, self help philosophers often unwittingly suggested that the precepts of diligence, kindness, virtue, will power and individualism were incapable of providing the control which Americans desired over their lives. Still, such writers and their audiences attempted to retain faith in these inadequate standards of behavior out of fear that they would feel even more lost if they discarded values which formerly had given them direction. As a result, many desired security even more than the satisfaction of their newly articulated emotional needs.

Indicative of the changing and confused attitudes of middle class Americans towards the quality and manageability of their lives was the emergence of Charles Schultz's cartoon strip "Peanuts" in the Fifties. The characters in "Peanuts" began their lives in a middle class neighborhood where they were well provided for but definitely unhappy. Lucy, the leading female character in "Peanuts", was a shrewish child incapable of feeling or expressing love. Linus wandered through life compelled to carry a security blanket wherever he went. And Snoopy, the canine counterpart of Walter Mitty, continually searched for happiness through fantasies.

The central figure in "Peanuts," of course, was Charlie Brown, an anti-hero destined to fail. In *The Saturday Evening Post*, Hugh Morrow described Charlie Brown as "the epitome of non-achievement, the boy who strikes out at the crucial moment of the crucial baseball game. His chief claim to distinction is that nobody else ever lost 10,000 checker games in a row."[1]

Because of his inability to succeed, money and respectability were less important to Charlie Brown than the alleviation of his helplessness, loneliness and insignificance. In a society which Schultz portrayed as lacking care, Charlie Brown needed reassurance and solace. Charlie Brown felt unimportant not so much because he failed as because nobody was interested in his problems. His failings were made poignant because in his moments of suffering he was ignored by his dog, berated by his girl friend, laughed at by his peers and left alone and powerless to resolve his difficulties.

Although Schultz sensed that Americans lacked a sufficient spirit of care, he seemed determined to emphasize the belief that simple human kindness was a solution to man's stress. Consequently, he remained in the inspirational tradition that suggested suffering could best be resolved on a personal level without recourse to institutional or cultural reform. Describing himself as an Eisenhower Republican, he contended that "you've just got to let things to along . . . ride them out and see how they turn out in the end. There's no use swinging right and left and trying to solve all your problems in one day. It's a policy of moderation."[2]

Thus, Charlie Brown mainly served, as Morrow noted, as "a national symbol of the little man who defeats life's comic outrages simply by surviving them, who solves his insurmountable problems by determined inactivity." Rather than experiment with alternative life styles or political reforms, Charlie Brown simply continued to live a life of quiet desperation according to traditional but no longer functional guides to living. In essence, he seemed more concerned with being reassured that he was a good person because he retained his conventional faith in morality, kindness and effort than with attempting to find solutions to his stress.[3]

Schultz's position was taken by other popular philosophers who expressed a desperate hope for human kindness. Implying that existence was characterized by suffering, many writers made confrontations with sickness and death metaphors for the problem of living. *Reader's Digest* published many articles in which kindhearted doctors and beleaguered individuals struggled for faith and courage to cope with the sadness inflicted by the illness or demise of a loved one. In *The Saturday Evening Post*, Stanley Hyman asked his readers to remember that "the human spirit is stronger than death" even though men tragically failed. Similarly, Catherine Marshall's *To Live Again* was written to weary and fearful Americans hoping to find love and meaning in the face of loneliness and grief. At the conclusion of her book, Marshall insisted that only if her readers regarded other people as important could they overcome their sense of insignificance and aloneness. And using a different approach in *Dear Abby*, Abigail Van Buren published a collection of letters from her advice-to-the-lovelorn column which described the sufferings of lonely Americans who needed to turn to someone who cared.[4]

Image as Reality

While popular philosophers increasingly were recognizing the frustrations caused by the absence of care, many self help writers continued to insist that citizens remain competitive and self-interested so that the traditional American faith in self-reliance would be retained. To preserve such an exaggerated concept of individual power in a period marked

by desperation, success writers had to offer arguments as
vacuous as those presented in the early Fifties.

Self help writers maintained that the *dream* of success
was more important than the *attainment* of success. They
demanded that people rationalize emotional discontents as
inevitable burdens which had to be accepted or minor irrita-
tions which could be ignored. Having put out of mind the
sense of futility which suggested the meaninglessness of
striving, Americans then were asked to make the preservation
of the means to success the very end of life itself.

In taking this approach, success writers hoped to reinvigorate what Norman Vincent Peale called "the astonishing
number of tired and weary people . . . crawling through life"
who were "filled with gloom and apprehension." To counteract this stress, Eric Hoffer attempted to celebrate anxiety by
arguing in *Reader's Digest* that "it is questionable whether
tranquillity is the boon it is made out to be. . . . In human
affairs, the best stimulus for running ahead is to have something to run from." Similarly, Howard Upton contended
in *The Saturday Evening Post* that "life has never been, for
anyone anywhere, a serene uninterrupted flow of ecstasy.
Happiness comes, at best, in infrequent periods of contentment or bursts of triumph." Thus, Upton argued, it was best
to "conclude that being in the Old Rat Race, with all its
defects, is preferable to being out of it."[5]

By suggesting the inevitability of stress, Upton contradicted the success ethic's basic premise that an ambitious
person could find a satisfying life through the exertion of his
will. To sidestep the contradiction, Upton argued that the
individual had a free will if he chose to recognize that the
acutely limited number of options available to achievers was
sufficient to insure a wide degree of choice. The American
had either to "sacrifice his family life, his hobbies, his cultural
ties and even, perhaps, his health in the process" of striving
for large rewards or "cling to a forty-hour week, escape
extended business trips and avoid heavy responsibility, if he

wishes. The material rewards will not be nearly so great, of course, but the point is that *he* makes the decision."[6]

Similarly, Peale insisted that "in most cases . . . ineptness is inherent in the individual rather than the circumstances" and demanded that his readers become submissive to preserve their fiction of freedom of choice. To those who regarded their "work as dull and unromantic," he retorted that "actually it is made that way if the person who works at that job becomes dull." Thus, instead of suggesting that unhappy workers change either their occupations or devotion to the success ethic, Peale told his readers to accustom their minds "to block off worry and frustration" so that they could "absorb tension rather than rigidly battle it."[7]

Through such advice, Peale asserted that the frustrated achiever could learn again "How to Believe" in the possibility of success. But the definition of success Peale offered was nebulous. To be sure, Peale promised that his out-of-sight-out-of-mind philosophy induced joy, but he considered happiness to be more a means than an end. Maintaining that joy "would certainly not be a worthy motive for living," Peale suggested that joy be used to free the individual from stress so that he could be more efficient and productive. And while telling how businessmen could make profits by thinking positively, Peale contended: "By success, of course, I do not mean that you may become rich, famous or powerful for that does not, of necessity, represent achievement." Instead, Peale argued that the development of a "mature and constructive personality" which encouraged diligence and enthusiasm was the purpose to which the American should direct his life.[8]

Because success writers asked Americans to pursue lifestyles which had no tangible goals, they often considered the attainment of an image of success sufficient to make life meaningful. Although success writers prior to the Fifties had made status a worthwhile end, they always considered it distinctly secondary to monetary achievement. In contrast, they devoted much more attention to status in the late

Fifties. Between 1957 and 1959, status goals were advocated
only six fewer times than monetary goals in the articles
analyzed in *Reader's Digest* and only seven fewer times in *The
Saturday Evening Post.*

The emphasis placed on status was accentuated greatly
by the profusion of advertisements suggesting that popularity,
prestige, emotional gratification and a sense of advancement
could be attained through the consumption of material
products. Advertisements in *The Saturday Evening Post* and
Reader's Digest regularly implied that elegance, sex appeal,
affection and success resulted from the purchase of diamonds,
carpets, washing machines and even soft drinks.

The dreams of success promulgated by Peale, Upton and
advertisements were oriented more towards the interests of
employers than the needs of the average American. If citizens
would passively accept occupational frustrations and make
work an end in itself, management could be insured of an
obedient labor force. If Americans could be persuaded to
make their dreams of success more important than the attainment of success, corporations could maintain the unequal
distribution of wealth. And if industries could entice Americans to feel that they could attain the image of success
through consumption, they would be able to profit from the
public's desperate desires for companionship, contentment
and meaningfulness.

Most Americans, however, did not recognize the degree
to which their lifestyles and personal philosophies were being
directed towards their capacities to produce and consume
instead of their hopes for happiness and meaning. Accustomed
to make the struggle for success a substitute for the search
for the self, most continued their futile attempt to satisfy
emotional needs through compensatory and largely illusory
rewards.

Many attempted to alleviate their loneliness by substitut-
ing the competitive goal of popularity for the deeper satisfactions of actual friendships. Lured by advertisements
suggesting that sexual gratification and happiness could be

attained through consumption, Americans went shopping
when they felt lonely or distraught. Feeling unimportant, they
prized occupational titles such as "sales representative" and
"management engineer" which corporations used to uplift
the prestige and devotion of salesmen and office workers
without necessarily granting a promotion or raise. In searching
for reassurance through status striving, Americans accentuated their stress by forcing each other to conform, judge
people by meaningless symbols and consequently lose the
individuality which could have helped them attain a sense of
self.

To be sure, not all Americans completely succumbed to
the conformist success ethic of the late Fifties. In 1959,
Vance Packard's best-selling book, *The Status Seekers,* roundly
condemned the advocacy of conspicuous consumption as a
ploy to convince people that they were advancing during a
period when occupational mobility was lessening. Packard
recognized that the promotion of status striving severely distorted American values and blinded citizens to the existence
of poverty.[9]

Even so, his alternative to status striving remained
closely tied to the success ethic. Although he called for individuality and spontaneity to replace conformity, Packard
argued that status seeking could best be obliterated if Americans once again were given the opportunity actually to
succeed. Packard's solution indicated that although the success
ethic had become increasingly hollow by the late Fifties,
liberals as well as conservatives continued to demand that it
be retained.[10]

New Goals—Old Behavior

As Americans entered the 1960s, then, they were motivated by two distinct and conflicting desires. On the one
hand, they increasingly wanted significance, care and control.
On the other, they insisted upon preserving a success ethic

which stifled their individuality and accentuated their
loneliness and helplessness. Both *The Saturday Evening Post*,
which had a liberal orientation in the Sixties, and *Reader's
Digest*, which remained conservative throughout the decade,
reflected this ambivalence.

As indicated on Chart XVI, both magazines continued
to emphasize non-material ideals over material goals by a
margin of almost two to one. In *The Saturday Evening Post*,
non-material goals were praised in ninety-seven articles, while
material goals were only praised in fifty-three. Similarly, in
Reader's Digest non-material standards for a significant life
were praised one hundred eighty-nine times while monetary
goals were espoused in ninety-seven articles. The most popular
non-material goals for both magazines were the feelings of
usefulness derived from service to others, being loved, happiness and control of one's life.

The success figures praised in both magazines also
indicated an emphasis on emotional gratification. In *The
Saturday Evening Post,* the most popular heroes were entertainers who exuded youth and pursued pleasure, politicians
who exerted influence and served their nation, and professionals whose efforts assisted their fellow man and were rewarded
with status. In *Reader's Digest*, foreign political leaders who
possessed power were the most generally admired characters
while entertainers and professionals were the magazine's
favorite American heroes.

At the same time, strong vestiges of the success ethic
remained in both magazines. In *The Saturday Evening Post*
sample issues studied, the possession of wealth was admired
more often than any other single goal with the exception
of usefulness to mankind through service. Similarly, *Reader's
Digest* devoted more attention to the attainment of money
or profit than to leisure, peace of mind, or happiness in one's
work. In addition, both magazines' propensity to retain the
success ethic was very evident in the standards of behavior
they advocated. *Reader's Digest* especially encouraged a
fundamental Horatio Alger life style based on diligence, vir-

tue and will power while *The Saturday Evening Post* made hard work and virtue its most admired standards. Although both magazines recognized the influence which talent had on the attainment of success, they no longer emphasized luck as an important factor in shaping people's destinies. Thus, the concept of self-reliance continued to be admired at a time when the need for care was increasingly advocated.

Such ambivalent feelings inclined Americans towards three conflicting forms of behavior. Because of their admiration for service, Americans were predisposed to find meaningfulness and community through social reform. However, because they idealized achievement-oriented and humanistic values, many continued to ignore poverty and romanticize that people were sufficiently kind to the less fortunate. And because their wills had been paralyzed and insecurity intensified, they were ready to support an increasingly belligerent anti-Communist foreign policy.

Care, Individualism and the Liberal Dilemma

During the Presidential campaign of 1960, the ambivalences of middle class thought and their behavioral ramifications began to emerge. Both Nixon and Kennedy confronted the problems of helplessness, isolation and insignificance by maintaining that the individual still could control his destiny. Both agreed that the quality of American life could be evaluated by the dream of success, although Nixon opposed Medicare on the assumption that the success ethic applied equally to all citizens whereas Kennedy urged reform so that more could participate in the American dream. Both candidates stressed in their television debates that traditional values should be preserved and significance and community be attained through a unified nationalistic opposition to Communism.

Because of their ambivalent attitudes, most Americans listened to the candidates without much sense of direction.

Consequently, they recognized neither the warlike implications of both candidates' positions nor the differences in their
attitudes towards reform. Confused and image-oriented, they
gave the election to Kennedy largely on the basis of his
favorable appearance in the television debates with his dour
opponent.

Once in office, however, Kennedy displayed emotional
and ideological characteristics which made him an inter-
mediary between the fears of the Fifties and the dreams of
the Sixties. His inaugural address, as Stewart Alsop noted in
The Saturday Evening Post, was "a strange mixture of foreboding and of hope. . . . But the dominant note [was] the
note of hope. . . ." Lamenting the weariness and apathy of
the Fifties, he called for vigor and courage. Through his
sense of humor and intense enjoyment of recreation Kennedy
stirred the hearts of a bored constituency wanting happiness.
And while displaying a dignity, wealth and glamour admired
by status seekers, Kennedy advocated poverty programs
appealing to those hoping to reinvigorate the American dream
through the practice of care.[11]

To revitalize America, Kennedy offered a philosophy
which was both humanitarian and belligerent. Internationally,
the President promised to extend the dream of success
through foreign aid and fight any country which contested the
American way of life. Domestically, he attempted to merge
the growing desire for service with the middle class faith in
individualism, pleading with Americans to "ask not what your
country can do for you—ask what you can do for your
country."

Because of its ambivalences, Kennedy's philosophy contained the seeds of its own destruction. Promising peace and
yet threatening war, Kennedy's foreign policy presaged not
only a resurgent humanitarian idealism but also the drift
towards Vietnam. Recognizing the limits of American opportunity and yet wishing to retain the success ethic, calling
for cooperation while urging individualism, and displaying
sincerity although relishing status, Kennedy's compassionate

advocacy of care sometimes degenerated into symbolic attempts to preserve the fictions of self-reliance, American kindness and inevitable progress.

Unaware of these implications, Americans felt that Kennedy's eclectic dream offered the opportunity to retain traditional values while satisfying emotional needs and humanitarian impulses. Soon after his inauguration, as Alsop observed, "people sensed . . . [that there] was something new in the White House—youth, vigor, self-confidence, purpose. . . . [T] he underlying mood in the White House was one of hope, of confidence, even of gaiety. The mood quickly communicated itself outward, by an osmotic process, to the whole nation."[12]

Because Kennedy considered foreign policy his most important mission, he oriented the majority of his speeches and serious efforts towards diplomatic affairs. Apparently, the public was quite willing to find security through anti-Communism, approving Kennedy's Bay of Pigs invasion, intensification of the Cuban missile crisis, and encounter with the Soviets in Berlin.

While Kennedy's actions were mainly bellicose, his rhetoric of reform stirred the nation to some extent and was the part of the President's philosophy best remembered after his death. During his years in office, self help writers echoed Kennedy's contention that significance, vitality and community could be attained through the fusion of care and individualism. In *Reader's Digest*, Arthur Gordon quoted Socrates' maxim that " 'before a man can move the world, he must first move himself.' " "It does take courage to care, to fling open your heart and react with sympathy or compassion or indignation or enthusiasm when it is easier—and sometimes safer—not to get involved." But, Gordon promised, ". . . *the more intensely you care, the more alive you become.*"[13]

Similarly, Morton Hunt insisted that "in a world that is increasingly too big and too complicated, we desperately *need* to get involved if we are to live our lives fully." "Every little act of genuine involvement, in fact, encourages the growth of the identity beyond the Me to the We, intertwining us with other selves until the thread of each life is no longer a single strand but a part of the fabric of humankind."[14]

The assumption that care only could be inspired by the re-emergence of an individualistic temperament stemmed from a realization that the other-directedness of the Fifties encouraged apathy. Contending that the quest for reassurance through conformity had failed to develop Americans' self confidence, Vice Admiral H. G. Rickover argued in *The Saturday Evening Post* that citizens had to "reject the notion that man is no longer master of his own and of his society's destiny." Each person could thereby find the inner direction needed to exert himself and revitalize the nation as a whole. In an article which Sargent Shriver asked *Reader's Digest* to reprint, I. A. R. Wylie stressed that since happiness was not a birthright and security was an illusion, Americans had to confront problems by possessing confidence in their moral integrity so that they could have the courage to care about and serve others.[15]

While individual self-assurance was necessary for service, the advocacy of individualism also served as a rationale for those opposed to liberal reform. Arguing that the concept of self-reliance had to be preserved and that the dollar sign was preferable to the Christian cross, Ayn Rand denounced governmental efforts to assist the poor. She considered "altruism evil because it treats man as a sacrificial animal. Man should neither sacrifice himself to others, nor others to himself."[16]

Similarly, in *Reader's Digest*, Charles Stevenson condemned federal relief projects for destroying self-reliance while praising a California program in which the unemployed supposedly were given "rehabilitation" and "therapy" by learning to make baskets. Robert Stother's "Self-Help: An Answer to Urban Renewal" lauded a project in Texas where Chicano families, often with incomes under $3,000, took out loans to install sewer extensions and pave streets in their own neighborhoods.[17]

To protect their absolutist faith in the American dream, success advocates also recommend positive thinking to persuade people that poverty and discrimination were small problems easily remedied without liberal efforts. Senator Olin Johnson maintained in *Reader's Digest* that the South had made great progress without governmental assistance. "From abject poverty and devastation . . . the South has raised itself back into the national picture by its own bootstraps, until now it is . . . one of the foremost 'lands of opportunity' in our nation. The progress that has been made, in the absence of anything from the outside but criticism, has been one of the most glorious stories of perseverance, humanitarianism and sacrifice ever told." Johnson contended that "it was the white Southerner, who shrugged off his bitterness and humiliation . . . to help the Negro," and maintained that "looking at the South during the last 20 years, there is not much evidence of discrimination against voters." Apparently, the Senator did not find it inconsistent to couple his claims of Southern benevolence and harmony with his contention that "the Supreme Court had no business reversing its historic separate-but-equal doctrine . . . [since] the practice or non-practice of segregation is a matter for local people to determine for themselves."[18]

When compared to the actual extent of poverty in America, the positive thinkers' arguments were highly unrealistic. *The Saturday Evening Post* observed that if the annual income required for a minimum standard of living was $1,000 for an individual and $3,000 for a family, then 36 million Americans were poor. If the standards rose to $2,000 and $4,000 respectively, 54 million lived in poverty. Compared to the statistics gathered by academic and government experts, *The Saturday Evening Post*'s statistics were accurate and even lower than the government Conference on Economic Progress's estimate that 77 million Americans lived in poverty or deprivation in 1960.[19]

Nevertheless, conservative arguments stymied the New Frontier and the public seemed willing to be reassured by Kennedy's faith in care instead of insisting upon reform.

Kennedy's assassination, however, reversed the public's temperament. Having called for care and been martyred, Kennedy emerged after his death as a symbol of the inability of care to counteract social injustice. Consequently, inspired by Lyndon Johnson's assertion that "no memorial oration or eulogy could more eloquently honor President Kennedy's memory than the earliest possible passage of the civil-rights bill for which he fought," citizens demanded reform to reaffirm the power and existence of American kindness. Johnson's call for a War on Poverty led Americans to sublimate their belligerent tendencies into support of poverty programs in the hope of uniting the nation and preserving their faith in American opportunity.[20]

As a result, the institutionalization of Kennedy's and Johnson's programs served more to placate the middle class's need for reassurance than help the less fortunate. Public opinion polls taken after the passage of the Civil Rights Act indicated that the majority of Americans believed problems created by prejudice would be ended by that piece of legislation even though the law did little to ameliorate black economic difficulties. And while the War on Poverty alleviated impoverishment slightly, appropriations for the program were far too small to provide adequate assistance for the poor.[21]

As the reform spirit dissipated, many liberals became apathetic. In part, this disillusionment resulted from the public's lethargy. But to some extent, the diminished liberal spirit of care also resulted from the Kennedy philosophy itself. By maintaining that a person could find significance through service, self help writers and New Frontier advocates not only inspired a reform impulse but also redirected the essential focus of care back to the reformer's self interest. In treating reform as glamorous, Kennedyites brought into their movement status seekers concerned more with their image than with the welfare of others. As a result, reformers often lost interest when their paternalistic efforts satisfied personal desires for significance. This dissipation especially was evident in the civil rights movement where liberals could find it comfortable and exciting to urge black suffrage and equal public accommodation but often would not continue to care about the more serious black goals of open housing and economic power.[22]

The glamor and vitality surrounding Kennedyism, more than a genuine social concern, motivated many bored Americans. Symptomatic of their fascination with the excitement rather than the effects of political reform was the popularity of radio and television talk shows which encouraged argument over rather than analysis of social problems.

The short-lived infatuation with reform, however, was not enough to satisfy Americans' need for the reaffirmation of care. As a result, the stress which plagued the late Fifties began to return. The best seller charts in 1963 and 1964 reflected a tremendous growth in the popularity of Charles Schultz's "Peanuts." The titles of Schultz's books, *I Need All the Friends I Can Get, Christmas Is Together-Time, Security Is a Thumb and a Blanket* and *Happiness Is a Warm Puppy*, suggested the persistence of the problems of loneliness and the need for solace.[23]

Similar problems again became dominant subjects in *The Saturday Evening Post* and *Reader's Digest*. The former magazine consistently noted the isolation of their heroes. Melvin Durslag felt that actor Richard Chamberlain portrayed a "lonely, almost eerie picture" when he jogged. Football star Ernie Davis's life was described as a "lonely struggle" and writer Bill Davidson claimed that while Jack Benny was "beloved by millions . . . he often presents the image of a lonely, troubled man."[24]

Reader's Digest reverted to publishing inspirational articles which tried more to reassure Americans that care still did exist rather than motivate people to care. Interestingly, writers often chose acts of kindness in foreign countries rather than in the United States to prove that people still cared. Oscar Schisgall wrote about Swiss villagers who helped victims of an airplane crash because "in a world often accused of not caring, of not wanting to become involved in other people's troubles, the things that have happened in this stricken village deserve to be recorded." Leland Stowe likewise admired the successful efforts of social workers in Vicos, Peru because he "like[d] to think . . . [that] what has happened there, high in the Peruvian Andes, proves that men with faith in their fellow man can still work miracles."[25]

Feeling the absence of care, many found it easier to be self-interested than concerned. In Shirley Jackson's fictional social commentary, "The Possibility of Evil," one of the characters argued, "Doesn't seem to me anybody around here cares about us. . . . Why should we care about them?" As a result, Americans like the black quoted in *The Saturday Evening Post* lamented, "Nobody cares. Nobody. That's what you grow up with. The people on the outside, they have their own immediate problems, so they got no time for our problems."[26]

Pleasure, Passivity, and Death

Having sensed their emotional needs in the late Fifties and been led by Kennedy to expect the attainment of those needs while retaining traditional success-oriented and humanistic beliefs, Americans entered the mid-Sixties lacking the sense of aliveness, community, meaning and control essential to the development of the self. Consistent with their tendency to satisfy such needs through compensatory goals, they became engrossed with an exorbitant number of fads and a frantic search for pleasure.

In different ways, such actions indicated the continuing American attempt to retain an illusion of individualism while striving for emotional gratification. Abandoning the spirit of care for a more self-interested pursuit of pleasure meant forsaking sensitivity for sensationalism. In turn, this sensationalism suggested that Americans were even further abnegating their wills, wanting to be passively stimulated rather than actively involved.

The popularization of encounter groups and middle class aestheticism reflected these tendencies. Such modes of behavior did allow growth in expressing emotions and enjoying the present. Unfortunately, some Americans used simplified Gestalt techniques more to justify remaining fixated with themselves than develop social perspectives. The demand for "experiences" and "consciousness" often stemmed from boredom rather than a desire for knowledge. Sensitivity marathons became devices to vent rather than understand emotions. The plea for universal love towards oneself replaced the practice of care towards others, the cry for "meaningful relationships" supplanted the promise of a sense of usefulness through service, and the word "feeling" became more important than "commitment."

Similarly, self help writers in *Reader's Digest* eulogized nature appreciation. Although such writers often quoted William Blake, they generally seemed typically middle class in that the purpose of their version of aestheticism was mainly to relieve tension. In their rhetoric, writers often offered formulas for fusion and love which appealed to Americans plagued by a sense of helplessness and loneliness. Through quotations from his cousin's philosophy of life, Wayne Amos treated the quest for the self as the attainment of consciousness through "open[ing] your senses to anything—a sunset, a waterfall, a stone, a blade of grass. . . ." Asking his readers "to drop out of the future and the past and remain for a time . . . [in] the present," Amos promised that a person could be passive while "joy steps in, unasked." Amos assured his readers that through such practices "most men can have their glimpses of the eternal . . . almost any time they choose" and could learn to love so that they would experience their senses and love.[27]

Emotional tension and the need for escapism also led to a harried pursuit of pleasure. In *Reader's Digest*, William Zinsser lamented that Burma Shave signs were disappearing in the United States because the "*pursuit* of leisure is now the most frantic sport in America. Roads are no longer for browsing; they are for getting as fast as possible from one place to another." Articles on planning holiday excursions in *Reader's Digest* likewise emphasized that Americans had to slow down to keep their vacations free from exhaustion and family fights.[28]

Recreational tastes revealed an increased fascination with danger and violence, suggesting that Americans' senses had become so numbed by the boredom and frustration of everyday life that only intense excitement could move them. Authors in *Reader's Digest* presaged such tastes in the late Fifties by writing of feeling exhilarated by the "near-suicidal sport" of tobogganing and the "tinge of life-or-death" in skindiving. In the mid-Sixties, Phil Edwards justified surfing on the basis that "there is a need in all of us . . . for an activity that puts us—however briefly—on the *edge* of life. Civilization is breeding it out of us, or breeding it *down* in us, this go-to-hell trait. There are uncounted millions of people right now who are going through life without any sort of real, vibrant kick."[29]

The Saturday Evening Post worried about the growing number of boating enthusiasts engaged in "Water Torture" who treated "other crafts as though they were enemy destroyers." Sports writers noted that restless and frustrated Americans were making football rather than baseball their most popular sport. Even Schultz's Snoopy began fantasizing battles with the fierce Red Baron.[30]

The public's captivation with the James Bond movies revealed similar temperaments. The Bond fantasies displayed an admiration for the successful individual who did not need to exert his will, make moral commitments or feel. "To enter Bondsville," William Zinsser noted, "is to escape into the life of a man who always wins. In the elaborate mythology of a suave British spy, with his miraculous gadgets that rub out bad guys, and miraculous girls who sleep with good guys, modern man has found a perfect security blanket for the nervous 1960's." As a spy licensed to kill, Bond could act in any manner he wished without having to make a moral choice. Women were sexual objects with whom Bond never had to give of himself and enemies were always expendable. In essence, Bond was secure not only because of the power he possessed but also because his human relationships were based upon utilitarian standards rather than sensitivity.[31]

As spy fantasies became popular, they suggested that the public was reverting to a quest for security through belligerent anti-Communism. Indicative of this shift was the transformation which occurred in the television series "I Spy." In its first season, "I Spy" served as a model of the Kennedy dream of racial harmony, in which a black and a white secret agent worked together. By its third season, the television show focused on violent plots oriented towards the destruction of Communist agents.

Moderates and liberals began to drift towards the predispositions of their conservative counterparts who throughout the early Sixties wanted to preserve the American dream through anti-Communism instead of reform. Charles H. Brower was disturbed that the traditional success devotee was not "thriving too well in the current climate. He doesn't fit neatly into the current group of angle players, corner cutters, sharpshooters and goof-offs. He's burdened down with old-fashioned ideas of honesty, loyalty, courage and thrift. And he may already be on his way to extinction." Brower insisted that school books promulgate the belligerent nationalistic statements of Nathan Hale and Patrick Henry so that Americans could again "dare to be square." Similarly, although he recognized that his remarks might appear warlike, James Farley demanded that Americans prove through aggressive anti-Communism that they had not gone soft.[32]

In 1964, the Presidential campaign of Barry Goldwater vented conservative frustrations. Suggesting that the preservation of the success ethic was more vital than the practice of care through reform, Goldwater denounced Medicare, urged sale of the TVA, and argued against the continuance of the progressive income tax on the basis that a man with five million dollars should pay the same tax rate as a person with five thousand so that the poor would benefit from the rich's investments. Because of his faith in self-reliance, Goldwater opposed school desegregation, contending, "I don't think there's any legal way to solve this thing. It's a question of man himself, his own worst enemy." Regarding virtue more powerful than prejudice, the Republican candidate optimistically assured voters that discriminatory practices would change because ". . . decent people won't take that." Above all, Goldwater insisted that the defeat of world Communism and total victory in Vietnam be our paramount objectives to prove that the United States was not as weak as traditional success advocates feared.[33]

While Goldwater's positions forecast the escalation of our Vietnam involvement, his forthrightness was not well suited to an image-oriented culture which used rhetoric filled with pleas for brotherhood and care as a rubric for retaining traditional values. The country was more impressed by Lyndon Johnson's promise to be "the President of all the people" and keep our involvement in Vietnam from escalating than by Goldwater's hard-line image. As a result, Goldwater lost the votes of moderates who basically accepted his ideological beliefs but feared being labeled as extremists.

Johnson's actions after the election, however, indicated that liberals as well as conservatives were easily inclined to tolerate escalation. Because the causes of the war were complex, it would be erroneous to conclude that the war directly represented a symbolic defense of the success ethic. Nevertheless, the dream of success played an important role in instigating American support of the war. Following the liberal tradition of Kennedy, Johnson wished to extend American opportunity to Vietnam and considered Communism a force which prevented the attainment of success in underdeveloped countries. It was after the North Vietnamese rejection of Johnson's promise to extend the Great Society to Vietnam that the President began American escalation. Consistent with the concept of self-reliance, the President demanded that the South Vietnamese be given the right to determine their own

destiny. Inasmuch as the Vietnamese conflict already was a
civil war fought for that purpose, Johnson's justification
for American intervention implied that self-determination
could only be preserved under a success-oriented economic
system.

The varied responses to the war similarly revealed the
effect which the success ethic exerted over the public's
attitude towards Vietnam. Conservatives bellicosely demanded
allegiance to the government's attempt to extend American
values. They predicted total victory because of America's
virtue, strength and perseverance. Politicians held forth on
the domino theory under the assumption that American
abundance would be threatened unless Communism was destroyed at a distance of seven thousand miles. The press
recited body counts as if they were box scores. And a positive
thinking public expressed concern for the soldiers' morale
rather than the morality of the war.

With their senses numbed, many lacked a sufficient
respect for life to be appalled at the brutality of the war. Citizens shrugged off Vietnamese casualties as no more significant
than the thousands of deaths on American highways.

Ironically, Vietnam intensified rather than satisfied
ideological and emotional desires. Instead of extending
American values and fostering a sense of community and
importance as World War II had done, the war brought out our
political and cultural inadequacies and polarized our society.
Governmental disdain towards legitimate antiwar protests
raised questions about the extent of democracy and self-
determination in America. The "credibility gap" caused people
to wonder if moral values placed adequate restraints on the
exercise of power. The callous response of hawks and moderates towards antiwar pleas exposed the lack of care which
permeated our outwardly idealistic society. Most of all, the
American failure to win a war oriented in part towards justifying and extending the dream of success proved galling to
those already fearful of the inefficacy of their traditional
creed. And the inability of most government leaders and their

followers to find a feasible solution to the war increased
Americans' tendencies to doubt the power of their wills.

Love, Will and the Generation Gap

As Rollo May explained in his best selling psychology
book *Love and Will*, many Americans had become "obsessed
with the new form of the problem of identity, namely, Even-
if-I-know-who-I-am, I-have-no-significance. I am unable to
influence others." This sense of impotence made many people
feel out of touch with the world, avoid close relationships
and fear that nothing mattered. In such a situation, the concepts of love and will, which formerly might have served as
solutions to problems had become problems in themselves.[34]
Unsure of their capacity to love or be loved, May contended, Americans were looking for substitutes to fill their
lives. They found it difficult to give themselves and preferred
the release of tension to the development of creativity. They
searched for instant happiness through pleasure seeking
instead of constructively risking themselves in the attempt to
care for others. With their senses numbed and wills paralyzed,
Americans were perpetuating their tendency to divide reason
and emotion to the point excluding one or the other. Inclined to forego sensitivity for sentimentalism or thought for
sensationalism, rationalists and romantics were discarding
self-direction in favor of mind cure philosophies, sensory
expansion formulas or drugs. Americans undergoing such isolation vacillated between being apathetic since they felt
nothing mattered or violent because they strongly needed to
affect others.
May insisted that to counteract such behavior, Americans
had to realize that their faith in self-reliance was extremely
questionable. Moreover, it was necessary for people to recognize suppressed feelings and channel them in creative directions. In contrast, those who had decided to live by their
emotions had to recognize the need for reason to direct their

senses. In sum, May contended that the individual should accept his feelings, recognize that an improved life and society must be based upon a realistic evaluation of human potentiality and needs and work for that improvement by blending the emotional force of love with the powers of reason and will in a spirit of care.

Many Americans, however, did not want to give up their exaggerated concept of individualism or recognize their feelings. They continued using mental manipulations, rationalizations or self-righteous moralism to protect their beliefs and justify passivity. Still maintaining that the individual rather than society was the cause of stress, Maxwell Maltz argued that Americans had to ignore tension through the mechanistic formula of cybernetics. "In using a computer, the operator must clear the machine of the previous problem before undertaking a new one," Maltz explained. "In the same manner, we must clear our . . . emotions and moods."[35]

Others, like Billy Graham, used apocalyptic arguments to contend that the end of the world was insured unless Christian beliefs were retained. Considering protests, lawlessness, bigotry, Communism and nuclear weapons to be signs of world destruction, Graham insisted that the church not get involved in politics and people be satisfied with the condition in which God placed them. Arguing that humanistic crusades and liberal politics could not solve national problems, Graham predicted the second coming of Christ and asked Americans to let God direct their spirits to the coming of a new millennium.[36]

Politically, Americans became both violent and apathetic. Blacks rioted against a society which shunned them; students rebelled against universities which ignored reasonable demands; and middle America continued to support the violence of Vietnam while remaining unconcerned with our own societal deficiencies.

In essence, the two cultural processes that had emerged in the mid-Fifties had crystallized ten years later. Most people had taken sides in the conflict of either preserving traditional standards of behavior through rationalizations or satisfying basic emotional needs through political and cultural change. The "generation gap" which exploded in the mid-Sixties vividly exemplified this polarization. The immediate catalysts of youthful discontent were the spirit of Kennedy, the civil rights movement and the Vietnamese War; but the fundamental causes of dissension between adults and youths stemmed more from the general cultural dislocation and emotional milieu of the Fifties and early Sixties. With increased middle class affluence, children were freed from their parents' concerns for achievement and financial security to examine the quality of their lives. And exposure to the frustrations and meaninglessness of parental lives unfulfilled by the success ethic left many youths without an appealing philosophy of life to emulate.

Some adults recognized that the emptiness of traditional values and social policies had stimulated youthful quests for alternative life styles and beliefs. Joan Didion suggested in *The Saturday Evening Post* that youths might have discarded middle class values because parents themselves no longer possessed sufficient faith in their own beliefs. Buell Gallagher told readers to ask, "Does the older generation really have a compelling dream of the future to pass along?" when they wondered about the sources of youthful discontent.[37]

Most adults, however, finding it difficult to change personal values which debilitated their lives, urged children to follow in their footsteps and passively accept the limitations of their beliefs. Maintaining that "there is only one rule that applies in virtually every case: control yourself. That is the secret: control, control, control," Peale demanded that youths restrain and channel sexual impulses to insure civilized progress. Dr. John Miller counseled against the use of drugs because it weakened the discipline needed to work hard. Unable to comprehend drug experimentation, Miller argued that youths could get varied perceptions better than those induced by drugs "simply by moving from one part of town to another at an unusual time of day, or by coming on familiar places from a new angle."[38]

Distressed that youths looked for happiness rather than social advancement in marriage, Ernest Havemann similarly argued that dating be regarded as a "bargaining process . . . in the open market for the best possible mate. . . ." Baffled, he exclaimed, "Why dating should have replaced dolls and baseball gloves is one of the great mysteries of our time," and suggested that parents arrange marriages since "finding the right mate is too difficult and important a job to trust to the young."[39]

Other writers told youths to accept the limitations which "the real world" placed on religion, honesty and the preservation of life. April Ousler Armstrong, the daughter of the author of *The Greatest Story Ever Told*, criticized those deploring the materialism accompanying Christmas. "If Christmas becomes for some people primarily a subject for commercials," Ousler argued, "at least God is getting equal time with toothpaste." Angered by youths demanding honesty, D. W. Brogan contended that "Hypocrisy is no sin" and insisted that had Hitler been less forthright "he would have been more open to argument and prudence if not to humanity." Irritated by those more concerned with the threat Vietnam posed to their lives than with their level of affluence, Spencer Brown argued that while "the draft . . . does cramp youth somewhat," young people should be grateful to a nation which had given them so much abundance.[40]

Such remarks revealed not only how little adults understood or empathized with the youthful rebellion but also how much self help writers were willing to sacrifice to preserve the success ethic. The goals of countercultural youths were precisely those repressed or sublimated by success devotees. Disillusioned youths specifically considered loneliness, alienation, and societal inequities more important than self-interested monetary pursuits. Love, happiness, individuality, variety and life itself were infinitely preferable to existence in a conventional culture willing to fight to preserve the competition, conformity and blandness which accompanied its abundance.

Consequently, the counterculture focused on liberation

from the mores which inhibited middle class America; and
it was precisely this demand for liberation which angered those
compelled by the success ethic to restrain themselves. Because
rebellious youths in essence told adults that they had wasted
their lives and suppressed their emotions, such youths represented a threatening temptation to inhibited Americans who
needed reaffirmation of their doubted beliefs.

Aside from publishing some articles praising children
who had learned to work hard, be virtuous and emulate
parental behavior, *Reader's Digest* launched a substantial
attack on youth. According to Hervey Allen, *"Every new generation is a fresh invasion of savages."* Angered at the demand
for freedom and self-expression, John Logan exhorted adults
and youth alike to reject the concept of complete equality in
favor of obedience to the rules of society and to accept
self-restraint and devotion to hard work rather than pleasure
seeking. Otherwise, he warned, "we will transform ourselves
into a society of adolescents." In a reply to Logan's article,
Reader's Digest's editors agreed that youths had to restrain
themselves to develop achievement orientations. Readers'
letters to Logan expressed concern that students were in serious need of "authority and discipline [since] they need to
feel that someone is watching them. . . ."[41]

As the counterculture grew, the authoritarian temper-
ment of conventional America became more violent. During
the People's Park controversy, Berkeley resembled an occupied
town when Ronald Reagan allowed the police and national
guard to establish command posts on street corners, strafe
students with gas poured out of Army helicopters, shoot
numerous bystanders and kill one dissenter. Similarly, the
Chicago police brutally clubbed protestors during the 1968
Democratic convention and the Ohio national guard killed
four students during the tragedy of Kent State. Inasmuch as
public opinion polls indicated that a majority of conventional
citizens approved such repression, it seemed that many
Americans could more easily tolerate killing the young than
listening to their criticisms.

In the face of such resistance, the counterculture remained as helpless and isolated as much of conventional America. Some rebellious youths began to affect dysfunctional modes of apathetic and violent behavior resembling that of their middle class counterparts. Like parents who had hoped to get away from it all by going to mountain retreats and islands in the Fifties, many youths left the city for the countryside. Like adults who used the mechanical manipulations of cybernetics and positive thinking, many youths turned on with drugs to escape a society which made them helpless. They reacted to our culture's separation of reason and emotion by preferring sensation to thought rather than attempt the synthesis which was necessary for self-actualization.

In selecting certain religious experiences, some members of the counterculture created fantasied views of the world as dogmatic as those of conventional self help writers. Just as passive moralists sought reassurance in Billy Graham's apocalyptic predictions at religious revivals, many youths at rock festivals became entranced with musicians who preached love but condoned social withdrawal and drug abuse on the basis that the end of the world was inevitable. Messianic characteristics similar to those in success literature and stemming from equivalent sources of helplessness were evident in rock music. Through his songs, Jimi Hendrix boasted of his power to create and destroy land but lamented that a world bent on annihilation would not listen to his advocacy of love. Three Dog Night issued an album in which their lead singer was photographed stripped to his waist, with lash marks on his back and a crown of thorns on his head, singing to a frenzied audience which stretched out their hands to him. Fan magazines regularly described the Doors' Jim Morrison as Christ.[42]

Just as apathy, hedonism, reassurance and fantasy failed to alleviate middle class stress, so also did such behavior fail to placate disaffected youth. Thus, some youths turned to violence after sensing that social withdrawal only reflected and perpetuated their sense of impotence and did not alleviate their suffering. But since violence was met by society's greater force, such youths again retreated to non-involvement with a heightened sense of desperation.

The behavior advocated by the Jefferson Airplane, a popular rock group which consistently articulated rebellious discontent and heightened exasperation, reflected such vacillation. From 1965 to 1971, the Airplane changed from first reassuring youths that "Love Is" to advocating social withdrawal and mysticism, demanding confrontation and revolution, urging dropping out of the world and coming back from space to save society from its own destruction.

The Retreat to Illusion

In foreclosing alternatives to our culture, Americans were left again with the achievement ethic. Success books, which had disappeared from the best seller charts after 1959, re-emerged in 1967. Morton Shulman promised in the title of his book that *Anyone Can Make a Million*. Adam Smith similarly advised readers in *The Money Game* on how to increase their earnings. Robert Townshend's *Up the Organization* resembled Peale's demand for corporate obedience and the sublimation of emotional needs to the goals of efficiency and productivity. After boasting that his book allowed disgruntled workers to revolt against organizational society, Townshend encouraged employers to make the employee prefer his work to his wife, family and leisure.[43]

While the resurgent popularity of success books suggested a reversion to the temperament of the late Fifties, the tenor of these books indicated that Americans were not accepting a commitment to upward striving as wholeheartedly as they had in the previous decade. Shulman's book was filled with technical stock marketing advice rather than philosophical justifications for achievement life styles. Adam Smith considered striving a game capable of providing enjoyment but not identity. Moreover, Smith cheerfully and apocalyptically predicted the disappearance of success-oriented life styles after American productivity ushered in a new millennium of abundance which would provide happiness. And with all his insistence on efficiency, Townshend seemed to regard organizational life as essentially absurd.

The election of Richard Nixon as President symbolized politically the increased emptiness which turned Americans back towards the Fifties. Starved for significance and unwilling to accept failure after having been defeated in the elections of 1960 and 1962, Nixon appealed to frustrated Americans determined to strive. Praising his followers as "the silent majority," Nixon unconsciously used a classical metaphor for "the living dead" which recalled the apathy of the lethargic silent generation of the Fifties.

Ideologically, Nixon appealed to an image-oriented constituency wanting to retain the dream of success under the rubric of care. While voicing disapproval of poverty and discrimination, he followed a policy of benevolent neglect by advocating self-reliant black capitalism rather than broad economic assistance. Although disturbed by inflation and unemployment, Nixon emulated Herbert Hoover's policy of expressing confidence in our system while the economy faltered. In so doing, Nixon followed a let's pretend, out-of-sight-out-of-mind theory which resembled more a positive thinker's magic wish than an economist's sound judgment. Nixon's chief adviser, Paul McCracken, described the President's full employment budget as a "self-fulfilling prophecy: By operating as if we were at full employment, we will help to bring about that employment."[44]

While Nixon claimed empathy towards the young, he displayed a lack of sensitivity and understanding when he asked students who had travelled to Washington to protest the Cambodian invasion about their opinions on college football. And although calling for peace, Nixon seemed more intent on saving America's image rather than human lives. He chose de-escalation over immediate withdrawal to help Americans rationalize that their military retreat was a tactic for a South Vietnamese victory.

Although the discrepancy between his rhetoric and

actions further revealed the inadequacies of the success ethic, Nixon attempted to convince America of the soundness of his values. But typical of the proponents of positive thinking, Nixon himself occasionally revealed doubts. His continual references to the fact that he was President long after he was elected suggested that Nixon consistently had to reassure himself of his own significance even after attaining his dream of success. His sense of inferiority inclined him to engage in messianic self-descriptions to enhance his self esteem. During the Fifties and Sixties, Nixon offered himself as a leader capable of determining "the difference between life and death, slavery and freedom, plenty and poverty, and happiness and sorrow for millions of people on this earth." He hoped to protect "freedom for all mankind and the survival of civilization." As President, Nixon remained prone to hyperbole. Though playing an insignificant role in the moon landing, he hailed the event as "the greatest week in the history of the world since the creation." And while his dollar devaluation program had limited importance, he claimed that it was "the most significant monetary agreement in the history of the world."[45]

The dream of success which Nixon offered Americans was just as barren as it had been in the Fifties. Maintaining that "it's time to move on to a new freedom . . . [since] the old negative freedoms—freedom from hunger, freedom from want, freedom from fear—are no longer enough," Nixon argued that Americans suffered from a "crisis of spirit" which could be cured by an optimistic reaffirmation of the free enterprise system.[46]

Nixon offered a nationalistic dream of success to Americans plagued by loneliness, boredom and a sense of insignificance. Believing that anti-Communism could unite the nation, Nixon had said in 1960 that he offered Americans "not the grim sacrifice of desperation but the rewarding sacrifice of choice that lifts us out of the humdrum life in which we live and gives us the supreme satisfaction which comes from working together in a cause greater than ourselves, greater than our nation, as great as the whole world itself."

In his 1969 inaugural address, Nixon used almost identical words to make the abnegation of the will to the state and the pursuit of a life lacking happiness appealing. "I do not offer a life of uninspiring ease. I do not call for a life of grim sacrifice. I ask you to join in a high adventure—one as rich as humanity itself, and as exciting as the times we live in. The essence of freedom is that each of us shares in the shaping of his own destiny. Until he has become part of a cause larger than himself, no man is truly whole."[47]

Because he was aware of the weariness and polarization caused by Vietnam, Nixon considered the nation's cause for the late Sixties and Seventies to be a contradictory reaffirmation of middle and lower class self-reliance and corporate welfarism rather than an intense confrontation with Communism. Accepting his nomination in 1968, Nixon argued that "we are a great nation. And we must never forget how we became great. America is a great nation, not because of what government did for the people, but because of what people did for themselves. . . . Instead of Government jobs and Government housing and Government welfare, let Government use its tax and credit policies to enlist in this battle the greatest engine of progress ever developed in the history of man—American private enterprise."[48]

By the beginning of the Seventies, then, the New Frontier, Great Society and new Nixonianism had culminated in little more than a return to the preservation of the dream of success through the ultranationalism and corporatism which characterized the Fifties. Looking back at the Sixties, Americans had been led to believe that they were beginning to envision a new path in the search for the self. This belief was valid in that Americans were beginning to realize that care and emotionality were necessary for the social and individual dimensions of the self.

Still, the Sixties which most Americans fondly remembered actually existed for only a brief period of time. Americans did not really act upon the need for care, cooperation and self-expression until Kennedy's assassination in mid-1963, and the reform stemming from such actions generally ended after 1965. The rest of the decade was marked more by violence and apathy oriented towards the preservation of traditional assumptions than by progress towards societal reforms and cultural change.

The quest to preserve the American dream thus ended in an American tragedy. To preserve their faith in self-reliance, Americans shunned the cooperation which could have lessened their helplessness. Going into their shells to fantasize through positive thinking and drugs that they were not isolated, Americans accentuated their loneliness. Having struggled to make the gospel of success a substitute for religious conviction, Americans continued to find meaninglessness in a mundane world where conformity and apathy replaced commitment to social justice.

Since Americans had sacrificed autonomy for the fiction of individualism, they had to repress much of what they desired. While sensing that their lives needed emotionality and community, they used the rhetoric of care mainly as a cathartic device to vent frustrations instilled by our culture. Having closed off so many areas of their lives, they could not tolerate the emergence of a counterculture which itself suffered from fantasy and passivity. As individualism blunted our spirit of care, violence erupted. Many conventional citizens identified with the corporation and the state to the extent that in fearing the collectivism of Marxism they paid allegiance to their corporate state's warfare against nations struggling for their own definitions of freedom and self-determination. Similarly, countercultural adherents accepted the violence which drugs exerted on their minds to attain a false sense of messianic power and transcendent apathy.

Through such behavior, Americans expressed a need for a final answer to the meaning and practice of life so that they could alleviate their insecurity. Ironically, by searching for reassuring solutions to lessen their tensions rather than confront their stress by questioning the adequacy of their beliefs, Americans found anxiety instead of awareness and paralysis rather than power over their lives.

EPILOGUE

The unsatisfactory solutions advocated by self help philosophers and some contemporary social critics suggest the impossibility of giving simple answers to complex problems. Success advocates have preached self-reliance to the helpless, diligence to the unemployed and progress to the defeated. Humanists have spoken of the need for care to an apathetic nation and hippies have preached the power of love to a society which steadily has become more callous. Mystics recently have called for religious experiences in a bland culture and intellectuals have urged consciousness to a society blinded by its myths. All of these solutions have been the antitheses rather than the antidotes to our behavior and problems—they have represented wishes rather than cures.

Our loss of identity cannot be rectified simply by reassuring ourselves that humanistic and pleasure-oriented values are preferable to moralistic philosophies and the success ethic or vice versa. All of us share the contradictory values of our culture. Attempts to ignore the impact that our culture has upon us, as countercultural adherents unsuccessfully tried to do through innocence in the Sixties, only tends to make us more susceptible to the stifling effects of our outdated myths.

It is important for us to realize that we have lost ourselves not only because we have retained cultural values but also because we have developed behavioral responses which impede the questioning of dysfunctional beliefs. From the advent of industrialism to the present, Americans have displayed an increasing propensity to hope that the self can be found by an avoidance of the tension which by necessity accompanies thought, creativity and growth through the engagement of complex problems.

This reluctance was especially evident in Douglas Fairbanks' recommendation to laugh and live rather than reflect upon the contradictions of being both present- and future-minded, competitive and friendly, consumptive and thrifty, and inner- and other-directed. Similarly, Alger's and Schultz's reassurance philosophies revealed a desire to assume that the acceptance rather than the questioning of inadequate myths could quell doubt. The get away from it all dreams of pleasure seekers, the "mind blowing" drugs of the counterculture, and the out-of-sight-out-of-mind formulas of positive thinkers likewise reflect an aversion to the uneasiness attending consciousness.

In effect, the avoidance of consciousness results in apathy, or the belief that nothing matters. But while apathy largely accounts for our nation's inability to recognize and reform its inadequacies, Americans have not become so anesthetized that they completely lack concern for themselves and their fellow man. Our reform movements have indicated that Americans do possess a capacity to care; and as their growing stress indicates, citizens seem to have a vague awareness of the deficiencies in their lives. Unfortunately, Americans have been increasingly conditioned to remain passive even if they are emotionally dissatisfied.

Corporate apologists, moralists, humanists and even countercultural spokesmen have contributed to the assumption that it is unnecessary to act to alleviate stress. Success writers such as Link and Peale have told beleaguered workers to abnegate their wills to their employers' dictates. Similarly, moralists such as Billy Graham and Fulton Sheen have asked citizens to ignore necessary political reforms in favor of being directed and comforted by a paternal God. Advertisers have asked Americans to pacify themselves through the purchase of material goods. And while Charlie Brown passively takes

life's insults out of a hope that things will turn out in the
end, Charles Reich has reassured dissatisfied youth that
Consciousness III will overcome our culture without the need
for political effort.

The unwillingness to admit the emptiness of their achievement-oriented life styles has made citizens susceptible to
ideological rationalizations. As a result, many have closed off
the areas of their lives which seemed incompatible with
their achievement philosophies and increasingly resorted to
fantasy and the sublimation of their desires.

In remaining receptive to a process whereby they restrict
their abilities to think and to exert themselves to find a more
functional set of beliefs, Americans have failed to recognize
how our cultural standards lead us away from rather than
towards self development. It is difficult to make any sense of
the process by which the self in America is stifled unless we
recognize how terms connected with the concept of identity
have become inverted in our attempts to rationalize the
preservation of the American Dream.

Central to our loss of identity has been the confusion
surrounding our concept of individualism. Inasmuch as this
concept has been defined as self-reliance, it has been used to
reduce the points of conflict between the American and
his society. If destiny was completely within an individual's
hands, success advocates could rationalize that the American
had no reason to challenge his employer, question the economic structure of his society or consider his responsibilities
to the impoverished. For their part, in accepting the concept
of self-reliance, Americans have hoped to simplify their
difficulties. By assuming that the causes of their stress were
personal rather than societal, Americans could hope that
simple personality readjustments rather than substantial social
reforms were all that were necessary to correct problems.

In blunting the contact points between themselves and
their society, Americans have become isolated outsiders who
are bewildered when they seek to understand the workings
of their nation. Moreover, by retaining an exaggerated faith in

their powers, Americans have been led to feel guilty for not living up to their society's standards of success. Consequently, they have attempted to exonerate themselves through status illusions and occasional messianic and paranoid fantasies.

The deficiencies caused by our individualistic culture cannot be rectified by the simple advocacy of a spirit of community. While cooperation could alleviate the stress imposed by our faith in self-reliance and would encourage the care necessary for reform, we have been so conditioned to accept the need to control our lives to establish our identities that we cannot deny this basic urge. Utopian communities established in the course of our history have often shown authoritarian tendencies similar to those of exteme individualists, largely because our desire for power needs to be expressed in some way to give a sense of significance to life.

Economic self-sufficiency, however, is not the only means whereby we can search for a sense of control and significance. If Americans were to recognize that individualism can be defined as autonomy, or the self-determination of their own ideals, instead of as self-reliance, or the pursuit of culturally defined goals, they would be inclined to develop self-confidence rather than require reassurance, enjoy diversity rather than demand sameness and consequently find the freedom which accompanies self-expression rather than the dependence required by conformity.

Such an autonomous orientation places more emphasis on the possibilities for growth than on the need for security. The autonomous individual is inclined to encounter rather than escape reality, reflect upon rather than ignore his experiences, perceive and respect the uniqueness in people rather than manipulate them for his protection, and accept the ambiguities encountered in confronting the unfamiliar rather than reduce mystery through cultural rationalizations. Since such a person searches for his role in society and recognizes that suffering is a part of life to be confronted rather than an aberration to be ignored, he can develop the empathy, sense of tragedy and desire for cooperation necessary to sustain a spirit of care. And since the autonomous individual finds diversity and ambiguity as necessary as order, he can tolerate the necessity of conflict in bringing about substantial social change rather than yearn for an apathetic consensus which blunts the polarities of dispute necessary for social progress.[1]

To be sure, few Americans have been or are able to develop lives with such a degree of autonomy. All of us desire security as well as independence and are strongly subject to our culture even in our attempts to break from it. However, it is the grappling with these polarities which stimulates our thought and consequently allows us to find alternatives to broaden our perspectives and make our lives more controllable.

The recognition and creative use of ambivalence plays a significant role in encouraging maturity as the dominant characteristic in the creation of the self. Even in our youngest years, we are torn between our desires for security and self-expression or, as Ernest Schactel has termed them, the childish and childlike facets of the self. Through our childish urges, we fear separating from our parents, encountering the unfamiliar; we seek to avoid sensations which are new and bewildering and consequently remain passive rather than curious. Feeling insecure, the child gains affirmation by exchanging obedience for approval and productive behavior for love. As Schactel has noted, however, children are not simply childish. In their childlike moments, they wish to break away from their parents and reach out to explore their surroundings. Such behavior allows the child to be active and reflective, find enjoyment through curiosity, understand the objects he perceives and affirm himself by achieving a sense of distinctness and confidence in his ability to exert his own will. He thereby becomes increasingly autonomous and develops himself.[2]

Inasmuch as our culture encourages the quest for security, dependence and reassurance, it has failed to encourage the development of a mature concept of self. Americans, in periods of stress, have tended to identify with childish heroes. During the rise of industrialism, citizens identified with Horatio Alger's orphans. During the depression, Little Orphan Annie warmed many persons' hearts. In the Sixties and Seventies, many found much of themselves in the little characters in "Peanuts."

All of these characters seemed filled with innocence and courage. Yet Alger's upward striving heroes were markedly passive and obedient to their employers. As orphans, they found happiness in attaching themselves to parental employers who gave approval in return for jobs well done. Similarly, Annie's jaunty efforts were always rewarded with the admiration of a benevolent Daddy Warbucks. And through his passivity and retention of conventional beliefs, Charlie Brown reflected an acute preference for the approval of his peers over the possibility of growth which could have come from confronting his stress.

While partially alleviating their anxiety, this affectation of innocence has made Americans susceptible to the power exerted by corporate and political leaders. In a culture which ambivalently calls for self-control and yet demands dependence and passivity, the individual affecting childish behavior is prone to become so disoriented that, in seeking approval and direction, he accepts the guidance of father figures. And in our society, corporate and political leaders have been willing to affect paternalistic styles to retain their positions of privilege.

While Alger was encouraging Americans to remain children, Andrew Carnegie defined himself as a steward of wealth who supposedly knew what was best for America. As a result of the confluence between Americans' attempts to find reassurance for their success-oriented philosophies and Carnegie's use of the success ethic to justify corporate power, Americans took the first step in becoming dependent upon our industrial leaders for direction and sustenance. Through the innocence of Progressivism, they lost the opportunity to restrain corporate power and consequently circumscribed their freedom and control in the twentieth century.

Later defenders of corporate subservience similarly used the success ethic to call upon workers to trade their individuality for their employers' largesse. As Link bluntly put it, the American was to learn to behave himself rather than understand himself. And as paternalistic corporations in the Fifties encouraged conformity through adherence to the "one big happy family," their foremost spokesman, Norman Vincent Peale, reflected our cultural propensity to invert the meaning of words by reassuring Americans that maturity was displayed by efficient docility.

Because the encouragement of immaturity belies a desire for power, success-oriented paternalism has been marked by a lack of concern for the public. Most Americans have failed to recognize such intent because the success ethic has conditioned citizens to fear that their independence is threatened more by governmental "paternalism" than corporate power. By demanding limits on governmental services, Americans have been acculturated to support corporate interests rather than their own. Such dysfunctional political behavior was most apparent in the Twenties, when Americans applauded Harding's, Coolidge's and Hoover's denunciations of public assistance while permitting federal assistance to industry and the upper class.

More recently, Richard Nixon has obtained similar support for a program which justifies industrial aid at the expense of the average citizen on the stark basis of paternalistic rhetoric. While Nixon found it appropriate to help American business remain "the greatest engine of progress ever developed in the history of man," he insisted in less flattering terms that "the average American is just like the child in the family: You give him some responsibility, and he is going to amount to something; he is going to do something. If, on the other hand, you make him completely dependent and pamper him and cater to him too much, you are going to

make him soft, spoiled and eventually a very weak individual."
As a stern father, Nixon made it clear that he preferred social
control to social welfare. He demanded that Americans
acquire "a new feeling of self-discipline, rather than go back
to the thoughts of the '60s that it was Government's job every
time there was a problem . . . to give way to their [the public's] whims."[3]

Distrustful of democracy, Nixon thus offered Americans
this empty platitude: "We are going to promise to give you
the chance to help yourself." True to his word, Nixon has
reduced programs on health, education, welfare, housing and
environmental reform while consistently using his power to
aid corporations at the expense of the consumer, assist
corporate agriculture to the detriment of the family farm, and
inflate defense budget subsidies to American industry so as to
strain the American taxpayer.[4]

The dispute over welfare and taxation perhaps most
vividly indicates how the retention of the success ethic has
restricted Americans' spirit of care and caused them to act
against their self interests. Although middle class Americans
assume that relief expenditures are too high, only 22 percent
of the poor receive governmental assistance at all. Monthly
relief checks in eighteen states in 1965 were $40 or less for
families of four. And contrary to the myth that the poor are
lazy, 42 percent of the impoverished are children under 18
and 8 million are citizens over 65. Of the few who receive welfare, Gabriel Kolko has noted that in the sample year 1958,
41 percent were blind, disabled or over 65, 36.5 percent were
dependent children, and the remaining 22.5 percent were
composed mainly of citizens temporarily unemployed as a result of an economic recession. Moreover, while the middle
class has resented relief out of the assumption that their taxes
go to the indolent, in actuality the millions of Americans
who constitute the impoverished class in America pay an
amount in sales, gasoline and other taxes which is slightly
larger than the amount given to the few on relief.[5]

Such statistics indicate strongly that the government has

done too little rather than too much in coping with poverty. Most of the effective attempts to reduce poverty came during the New and Fair Deals. Under FDR, poverty was reduced by 24 percent from the 1929 level. Under Truman, poverty was cut at twice that rate. In contrast, under the Eisenhower-Nixon administration, the level of poverty remained the same and the plight of black Americans actually became worse. The fact that the rate of poverty reduction from 1929 to 1960 was only .7 percent annually indicates how meager both conservative and liberal efforts have been.[6]

Although affluent Americans have considered the poor a burden for dubious reasons, poverty does affect the middle class detrimentally. Because our economy is based on the consumption rather than the production of material goods, the insufficient purchasing power of the 77 million Americans who live in poverty or deprivation causes prices to remain high. It would be to the advantage of the middle class to encourage more assistance to the poor. With larger incomes, the poor could purchase more goods and, theoretically, prices would drop to the benefit of the middle class consumer as well. And as more goods were purchased, industry could increase production, provide more jobs and consequently reduce the ranks of the unemployed needing assistance.

Such a policy is incomprehensible to the middle class, who fear that increased relief expenditures necessitate higher middle income taxes. This fear reflects the extent to which affluent Americans have had their imaginations blunted by a success ethic promulgated for corporate interests. Though middle class taxes have risen sharply since 1939, they have done so because of increasing defense expenditures which subsidize much of American industry. While corporate welfare has increased, corporate taxes have remained exceptionally low. Increased relief could be financed by closing tax loopholes, but again the middle class would lament that such taxes would be passed on to the consumer through higher prices. While this inflation could be halted by price controls, most Americans would be disturbed by such a governmental

restraint on their supposedly free economy. And by dis-
trusting governmental "paternalism" and restraint, the middle
class remains subject to the prices our corporations impose,
and vote out of a false sense of economic self interest which
perpetuates a system providing assistance for the rich at
the expense of the poor and middle class alike.

The retention of the success ethic has not only stifled
our spirit of care but also has inclined us to become violent as
a nation. If violence is defined as the infliction of physical
suffering, our tolerance of the persistent suffering experienced
by the impoverished is far more disturbing than the sporadic
riots which conventional Americans abhorred in the Sixties.
Lacking a sense of aliveness, the majority of Americans were
so offended by the temptations of a vital counterculture
that they condoned the oppression and occasional killing of
antiwar dissenters.

In foreign policy, the magnitude of the violent effects of
the retention of the success ethic has been far more severe.
While the acceptance of passivity may have led to an aversion
to war in the late Fifties, it also enhanced a sense of helplessness which inclined Americans to desire security through
power and overaggressiveness a decade later. In protecting
the success ethic to the point of preferring the image of success over the recognition of the emptiness of their lives,
Americans became oriented to desiring the illusion of victory
in a war which has cost over two million American and
Vietnamese lives. Out of our unwarranted compulsion for
optimism, we lost the recognition of tragedy which would
have made clear the brutality and meaninglessness of our
military involvement. We have achieved our illusions of success and security at the cost of severely diminishing our
commitment to life itself.

To become disentangled from our present malaise,
Americans would have to accept their capabilities to exert
their wills. Such a statement may seem paradoxical in a
culture which claims its citizens possess complete power over
their destinies and has inspired messianic self-descriptions

and paranoid tendencies through an exaggerated emphasis on self-reliance. However, the paradox disappears if we remember that our society has inverted the concept of will to mean dependency and resignation. The tension between the success ethic's demands for self-power and submission compounded by the sense of inferiority generated by passivity, creates the feeling of helplessness which fosters paranoid tendencies. While it would be detrimental to reiterate the traditional success ethic's demand for self-reliance, since the alleviation of our economic problems necessitates collective political efforts, Americans could begin to reduce their cultural confusion by recognizing their ability to work towards the definition of their own goals rather than continue to be misguided by our ideological myths.

Such a recognition would take into account the legitimate role of resistance in the development of the self. While our culture generally has deplored resistance as disruptive, it is important to recognize that success advocates themselves have demanded resistance, although of a dysfunctional sort, by insisting that Americans avoid the temptation to perceive and reflect upon their societal inadequacies. Resisting this culturally ascribed avoidance of reality is at least the first step that can lead to the development of the self.

Most Americans, however, are not willing to risk such an exercise of their wills because resistance isolates the individual from his culture and peers. This aloneness is precisely what security-minded Americans fear most. However, until citizens confront their problems and test their ability to cope with their stress both through individual and cooperative forms of behavior, they will remain unsure of themselves and consequently fail to escape the isolation they already experience.

The concept of resistance, however, is not a total answer to our stress. Many Americans, but especially the young, recognized the need for resistance in the Sixties only to become entangled in the confusing definition our society gives to freedom. Freedom, to most Americans, implies liberation

from requirements. Such an orientation, while a part of
the overall concept of freedom, is incomplete and often becomes a vehicle for escapism. The success advocates' demand
for free enterprise not only calls for a lack of governmental
restraint but also serves to justify the abnegation of social
responsibility. Similarly, some countercultural proponents
have used the concept of liberation not only for resisting
their culture but also for the self-interested purpose of dropping out.

Liberation from stress by itself is ultimately self-defeating because the resultant apathy serves as a symbol of helplessness and fails to protect the individual from a society
which demands conformity. A more effective concept of will
must couple the need for liberation *from* cultural restraints
with the desire for freedom *to* search actively for alternative
beliefs and forms of effective behavior.

Such freedom is difficult for Americans to accept
because it engenders the tension which accompanies the
possibility of guilt. Most Americans find it almost sinful to
resist their culture because its mores are filled with religious
connotations. In a different fashion, a subtle fear of guilt
has affected some countercultural adherents as well. In
deviating from one's culture and developing self ideals, one
must accept responsibility for the effects of his actions and
consequently remain open to the possibility of guilt. Such
guilt differs from that experienced by most Americans in that
it stems from not living up to one's own expectations rather
than from disobeying the dictates of one's culture. Countercultural advocates who have denied the possibility of guilt
and call for innocent apathy or useless violence without
accepting responsibility for their actions in effect tolerate or
enhance social suffering and limit their autonomy by short-
circuiting the process whereby the individual seeks a creative
role in society.

If Americans wish to consider a spirit of care the nexus
between the self and society, they would have to recognize
that our culture's aversion to tension has also blinded citizens
to the realization that care necessitates conflict as well as

cooperation. In their quest for reassurance, Americans have wished more to be cared about than to care for others. And when Kennedy liberals attempted to broaden our concept of care to encompass social service, their efforts were stifled by their mistaken assumption that a success-oriented society would easily abandon its self-interested inclinations. The liberal propensity to use consensus politics to attain reform left them ill-prepared, when their movement faltered, to accept the social tension necessary to support the demands of black Americans who more clearly recognized the need for conflict in effecting change.

The concept of care requires with it a recognition of the need for power. Just as power without care leads to irresponsible dominance, the lack of ability to alleviate suffering makes the advocacy of care mainly sentiment. Americans are disturbed by the demand for power because of our cultural distortions. While our success-oriented values have construed power to be a means by which to attain superiority over others, the term also can mean the ability to affect one's own condition. In this latter sense, the demand for power is a legitimate response to our helplessness.[7]

Still, most citizens consider power a negative force, in much the same way that they are conditioned to consider resistance evil. Such connotations are understandable inasmuch as power has been misused so often in our society. However, the identification of power with evil has been engrained in us by irresponsible institutional leaders. It is difficult to imagine a politician who would express his delight in achieving power, not only because such an admission would seem inegalitarian, but also because it would make such a politician accountable for his actions. Consequently, we often are given the rationalization that the President is forced to act against the public's interest because of Congressional obstinacy or vice versa. Similarly, corporate presidents never justify price increases on the fact that they have the power to do so; instead, such actions are always rationalized on the grounds that labor unions or consumer demand forces inflationary rates. And in our foreign policy, Americans have heard the most paradoxical rationalization when Presidents have likened America to a "helpless giant" forced to continue a supposedly undesired war because of the resistance of the North Vietnamese in letting us depart.

It is understandable, then, in a society which encourages public passivity and laments the exertion of will on the part of our leaders, that Americans have been unable and largely uninterested in attempting to define alternatives. In living under the illusion that the twentieth century has been an age of reform, we forget that aside from the New Deal, Americans have failed to alter measurably values already dysfunctional in the 1870s. In the half century since World War I, we have had less than ten years of major attempts at national reform.

Through our continual use of cultural clichés which assume progress and change, we have ignored the disturbing drift of modern America towards a decrease in commitment to the quality of our lives and a diminished respect for the needs and rights of the suffering both in America and the world at large. Our forgetfulness of history, which makes it difficult to mature as a nation, is similar to the difficulty we experience in trying to recall the possibilities lost in our early childhoods. We forget our childlike capacities for freedom and exploration because cultural demands and the difficulties of our lives make us wish to simplify our existence. Similarly, our ignorance of history allows us to deny the complexities of our problems and the uncomfortableness attending responsibility. As long as we remain amenable to our culturally ascribed amnesia we will continue to experience our loss of the self.[8] And as long as Americans fail to realize that security is not a place of ideological stability but a direction inspired by curiosity and that the complexity of existence negates simple and absolute answers, the quest for reassurance will continue to keep Americans from the engagement of mystery which allows us to learn and find alternatives amidst our paralysis.

APPENDIX

The following are content analysis charts categorizing the goals, success formulas and biographical heroes contained in *The Saturday Evening Post* and *Reader's Digest*. Five sample issues of *The Saturday Evening Post* published in every other year from 1917 through 1967 were analyzed. Four issues of *Reader's Digest* randomly selected for 1926 and every other year from 1927 through 1969 also were studied. In all, 707 stories and articles in *The Saturday Evening Post* and 1140 articles in *Reader's Digest* were analyzed.

Note: Minus numbers on charts below indicate the number of times a certain item was characterized as not beneficial or unworthy by either *The Saturday Evening Post* or *Reader's Digest*.

CHART I

The following are definitions of success contained in *The Saturday Evening Post* sample issues, 1917–1929 and *Reader's Digest* sample issues, 1926–1929. Statistics are based upon one hundred fifty-two articles and stories in *The Saturday Evening Post* and ninety-six articles studied in *Reader's Digest*.

MATERIAL SUCCESS:	TIMES MENTIONED	
	SEP	RD
Money or Profit	24	12–2
Wealth	22	10
Prosperity	14	7
Promotion	7	0
$5,000–$20,000	3	2
Security	2	2
Job	2	1
Total	74	34–2

STATUS:

Fame or Recognition	18–1	6
Respectability	5	1
Popularity	3	1
Total	26–1	8

POWER:

Power	18	7

NON-MATERIAL SUCCESS:

Love or Marriage	11	4
Happy Job	9	3
Leisure and Enjoyment	7–1	5–2
Happiness	4	7
Friendship	4	3
Usefulness to Mankind (aside from involvement in business)	6	7
Peace of Mind	0	4
Total	41–1	33–2

CHART II

The following are methods stressed in the formulas for success contained in *The Saturday Evening Post* sample issues, 1917–1929 and *Reader's Digest* sample issues, 1926–1929. Statistics are based on one hundred fifty-two articles and stories in *The Saturday Evening Post* and ninety-six articles studied in *Reader's Digest*.

REQUIREMENTS FOR SUCCESS:	TIMES MENTIONED	
	SEP	RD
Diligence	31–2	14–2
Virtuous Character	30–7	10–1
Salesmanship	26–1	9–4
Frugality	24–3	1–1
Ambition and Will Power	17	14
Imagination	12	1
Luck	12	3
Efficiency	11	4
Positive Thinking	10	6
Talent	10	4
Courage	8	4
Prudence or Common Sense	7	2
Connections	3	–1

CHART III

The following is a list of success heroes praised in *The Saturday Evening Post* sample issues, 1917–1929 and *Reader's Digest* sample issues, 1926–1929. Statistics are based upon one hundred fifty-two articles and stories in *The Saturday Evening Post* and ninety-six articles studied in *Reader's Digest*.

SUCCESS FIGURES:	*TIMES MENTIONED*	
	SEP	*RD*
Big Businessmen	20	12
Entertainers	15	3
Small Businessmen	9	2
Politicians and Diplomats	6	3
White Collar Employees	5	2
Writers	6	0
Farmers	4	2
Blue Collar Employees	4	2
Military Leaders	4	0
Professionals	3	2

CHART IV

The following are definitions of success contained in *The Saturday Evening Post* and *Reader's Digest* sample issues, 1930–1939. Statistics are based on one hundred eleven articles and stories in *The Saturday Evening Post* and one hundred sixty-seven articles studied in *Reader's Digest*.

MATERIAL SUCCESS:	*TIMES MENTIONED*	
	SEP	*RD*
Wealth	27	21–1
Money or Profit	15	11
Prosperity	9	10
Job	9	5
Promotion	7	3
Security	4	4
$5,000–$20,000	6	0
Total	77	54–1

STATUS:		
Fame or Recognition	9	11
Respectability	6	1
Popularity	1	3
Total	16	15

POWER:		
Power	8	11

NON-MATERIAL SUCCESS:

Usefulness to Mankind (aside from involvement in business)	11	10
Happiness	3	5
Leisure and Enjoyment	2	6
Love or Marriage	5	2
Friendship	0	3
Happy Job	1	2
Peace of Mind	1	1
Total	23	29

CHART V

The following are methods stressed in the formulas for success contained in *The Saturday Evening Post* and *Reader's Digest* sample issues from 1930–1939. Statistics are based on one hundred eleven articles and stories in *The Saturday Evening Post* and one hundred sixty-seven articles studied in *Reader's Digest*.

REQUIREMENTS FOR SUCCESS:	*TIMES MENTIONED*	
	SEP	*RD*
Diligence	15–1	17–3
Salesmanship	17–1	13
Luck	13	8
Ambition and Will Power	11	11–1
Talent	11–1	8
Virtuous Character	10–1	9
Imagination	8	11
Courage	8	6
Confidence	8	4
Common Sense	7	2
Frugality	8–2	3–5
Efficiency	0	5
Education	3	1
Connections	1	1

CHART VI

The following is a list of success heroes praised in *The Saturday Evening Post* and *Reader's Digest* sample issues, 1930–1939. Statistics are based upon one hundred eleven articles and stories in *The Saturday Evening Post* and one hundred sixty-seven articles studied in *Reader's Digest*.

SUCCESS FIGURES:	*TIMES MENTIONED*	
	SEP	*RD*
Entertainers	23	12
Big Businessmen	10	10
Politicians and Diplomats	3	11

Small Businessmen	7	5
White Collar Employees	5	2
Professionals	4	1
Military Leaders	1	2
Blue Collar Workers	2	0

CHART VII

The following are definitions of success contained in *The Saturday Evening Post* and *Reader's Digest* sample issues, 1941–1945. Statistics are based on seventy-five articles and stories analyzed in *The Saturday Evening Post* and one hundred twenty articles studied in *Reader's Digest*.

MATERIAL SUCCESS:	TIMES MENTIONED	
	SEP	RD
Money	13	12
Wealth	8	11
$5,000–$20,000	3	4
Prosperity	0	7
Job	1	4
Promotion	0	5
Total	25	43
STATUS:		
Fame or Recognition	7	9
Respectability	4	2
Popularity	4	3
Total	15	14
POWER:		
Power	14	5
NON-MATERIAL:		
Usefulness to Mankind (aside from involvement in business)	4	9
Happy Job	10	0
Desire for Worthwhile Existence	5	4
Leisure and Enjoyment	1	4
Happiness	1	3
Friendship	0	2
Love or Marriage	0	2
Peace of Mind	0	1
Total	21	25

CHART VIII

The following are methods stressed in the formulas for success contained in *The Saturday Evening Post* and *Reader's Digest* sample issues, 1941–1945, and are based on seventy-five articles and stories analyzed in *The Saturday Evening Post* and one hundred twenty articles studied in *Reader's Digest*.

REQUIREMENTS FOR SUCCESS:	TIMES MENTIONED	
	SEP	RD
Diligence	13	21
Salesmanship	7	19
Will Power and Ambition	11	14
Courage	10	10
Virtuous Character	7–3	15
Luck	8	9
Imagination	10	7
Talent	6	9
Positive Thinking	5	11–1
Education	7	3
Frugality	3	4
Connections	3	1
Prudence	3	1

CHART IX

The following is a list of success heroes praised in *The Saturday Evening Post* and *Reader's Digest* sample issues, 1941 to 1945. Statistics are based on seventy-five articles and stories analyzed in *The Saturday Evening Post* and one hundred twenty articles studied in *Reader's Digest*.

SUCCESS FIGURES:	TIMES MENTIONED	
	SEP	RD
Entertainers	14	11
Politicians and Diplomats	6	9
Blue Collar Workers	5	8
Military	8	7
Big Businessmen	5	3
Professionals	4	0
White Collar Workers	3	1
Small Businessmen	1	1

CHART X

The following are definitions of success contained in *The Saturday Evening Post* and *Reader's Digest* sample issues, 1947–1955. Statistics are based on two hundred thirty-three articles studied in *Reader's Digest* and one hundred thirteen articles and stories analyzed in *The Saturday Evening Post*.

MATERIAL SUCCESS:	*TIMES MENTIONED*	
	SEP	RD
Wealth	17	37
Money or Profit	14	23
Prosperity	5	9
Security	4	7
Job	6	3
$5,000–$20,000	5	4
Promotion	4	2
Total	55	85
STATUS:		
Fame or Recognition	7	13
Popularity	7	8
Respectability	3	10
Total	17	31
POWER:		
Power	15	13
NON-MATERIAL SUCCESS:		
Happy Job	11	14
Usefulness to Mankind (aside from involvement in business)	3	15
Peace of Mind	1	13
Love or Marriage	7	5
Leisure and Enjoyment	4	8
Friendship	2	8
Desire for Worthwhile Existence	2	6
Happiness	1	7
Total	31	76

CHART XI

The following are methods stressed in the formulas for success contained in *The Saturday Evening Post* and *Reader's Digest* sample issues, 1947–1955. Statistics are based on two hundred thirty-three articles studied in *Reader's Digest* and one hundred thirteen articles and stories analyzed in *The Saturday Evening Post*.

REQUIREMENTS FOR SUCCESS:	TIMES MENTIONED	
	SEP	RD
Diligence	20	40
Positive Thinking	10	25
Salesmanship	12	21
Will Power or Ambition	9	20
Courage	7	21
Virtuous Character	12	16
Talent	11	16
Imagination	12	15
Luck	7	17
Education	6	7
Efficiency	3	7
Frugality	4–7	7–7

CHART XII

The following is a list of success heroes praised in *The Saturday Evening Post* and *Reader's Digest* sample issues, 1947–1955. Statistics are based upon one hundred thirteen articles and stories in *The Saturday Evening Post* and two hundred thirty-three articles studied in *Reader's Digest*.

SUCCESS FIGURES:	TIMES MENTIONED	
	SEP	RD
Entertainers	19	19
Big Businessmen	9	21
Politicians and Diplomats	12	13
Small Businessmen	7	12
Professionals	4	14
White Collar Employees	10	2
Military	5	4
Blue Collar Workers	3	5

CHART XIII

The following are definitions of success contained in *The Saturday Evening Post* and *Reader's Digest* sample issues, 1957–1959. Statistics are based on one hundred eighty-one articles studied in *Reader's Digest* and seventy-eight articles and stories analyzed in *The Saturday Evening Post*.

MATERIAL SUCCESS:	*TIMES MENTIONED*	
	SEP	*RD*
Wealth	7	14
Money or Profit	7	5–3
Job	1	8
Prosperity	0	4
Security	1	1
$5,000–$20,000	2	0
Promotion	1	1
Total	19	33–3
STATUS:		
Respectability	8	9
Fame or Recognition	3	12
Popularity	1	5–1
Total	12	26–1
POWER:		
Power	8	7
NON-MATERIAL SUCCESS:		
Usefulness to Mankind (aside from involvement in business)	3	34
Happy Job	14	7
Love or Marriage	12	8
Leisure and Enjoyment	10	8
Happiness	6	10
Friendship	5	4
Peace of Mind	4	4
Desire for Worthwhile Existence	4	2
Total	58	77

CHART XIV

The following are methods stressed in the formulas for success contained in *The Saturday Evening Post* and *Reader's Digest* sample issues, 1957–1959. Statistics are based on one hundred eighty-one articles studied in *Reader's Digest* and seventy-eight articles and stories analyzed in *The Saturday Evening Post*.

REQUIREMENTS FOR SUCCESS:	TIMES MENTIONED SEP	RD
Virtuous Character	15	26
Courage	11	26
Diligence	15	22–1
Will Power or Ambition	7	29
Positive Thinking	3	27
Talent	5	21
Salesmanship	6	14
Imagination	2	10
Education	1	11
Luck	5	6
Efficiency	2	6
Thrift	0	4–1

CHART XV

The following is a list of success heroes praised in *The Saturday Evening Post* and *Reader's Digest* sample issues, 1957–1959. Statistics are based upon seventy-eight articles and stories in *The Saturday Evening Post* and one hundred eighty-one articles studied in *Reader's Digest*.

SUCCESS FIGURES:	TIMES MENTIONED SEP	RD
Professionals	6	19
Big Businessmen	4	17
Entertainers	10	8
Politicians	6	10–2
Small Businessmen	5	8
Military	4	9
Blue Collar Workers	4	6
White Collar Workers	4	1

CHART XVI

The following are definitions of success contained in *The Saturday Evening Post* and *Reader's Digest* sample issues, 1961–1969. Statistics are based on three hundred forty-three articles studied in *Reader's Digest* and one hundred seventy-eight articles and stories analyzed in *The Saturday Evening Post*.

MATERIAL SUCCESS:	TIMES MENTIONED	
	SEP	RD
Wealth	25-1	18
Money or Profit	15	29-8
Job	6	18
Prosperity	1	21
Promotion	1	5
$5,000–$20,000	1	2
Security	4-3	4-1
Total	53-4	97-9

STATUS:		
Respectability	15-2	38
Fame or Recognition	11	18-2
Popularity	5-1	7
Total	31-3	63-2

POWER:		
Power	12-1	34-1

NON-MATERIAL SUCCESS:		
Usefulness to Mankind (aside from involvement in business)	25	62
Love or Marriage	20-4	30
Desire for Worthwhile Existence	9	26
Leisure and Enjoyment	15	18-1
Happy Job	12-1	13
Peace of Mind	5	19
Happiness	7	16
Friendship	4	5
Total	97-5	189-1

CHART XVII

The following are methods stressed in the formulas for success contained in *The Saturday Evening Post* and *Reader's Digest* sample issues, 1961-1969. Statistics are based on three hundred forty-three articles studied in *Reader's Digest* and one hundred seventy-eight articles and stories analyzed in *The Saturday Evening Post*.

REQUIREMENTS FOR SUCCESS:	TIMES MENTIONED SEP	RD
Diligence	31-2	61
Virtuous Character	27-1	45
Will Power or Ambition	19-2	54-2
Talent	20	41
Positive Thinking	16-2	36
Courage	10	31
Education	11	27
Salesmanship	19-1	18
Imagination	3	22-1
Efficiency	0	18
Luck	6	11
Prudence	1	7
Thrift	7-4	7-4

CHART XVIII

The following is a list of success heroes praised in *The Saturday Evening Post* and *Reader's Digest* sample issues, 1961-1969. Statistics are based upon three hundred forty-three articles in *Reader's Digest* and one hundred seventy-eight articles and stories studied in *The Saturday Evening Post*.

SUCCESS FIGURES:	TIMES MENTIONED SEP	RD
Entertainers	26	16
Politicians and Diplomats	12-1	21
Professionals	8	15
Big Businessmen	11	11
Military	2	11
Blue Collar Workers	4	7
White Collar Employees	7	7
Small Businessmen	3	4

CHART XIX

The following is a comparison of the success formulas advocated in combined sample issues of *The Saturday Evening Post* and *Reader's Digest* published between 1917 and 1929 and 1947 through 1955. Statistics are based on two hundred forty-eight stories and articles published from 1917 through 1929 and three hundred forty-six articles and stories published from 1947 through 1955. Statistics indicating the emphasis which each magazine separately gave to the following success factors can be found in Appendix Charts II and XI.

REQUIREMENTS FOR SUCCESS:	TIMES ADVOCATED 1917-1929	REQUIREMENTS FOR SUCCESS:	TIMES ADVOCATED 1947-1955
Diligence	45	Diligence	60
Virtuous Character	40	Positive Thinking	35
Salesmanship	35	Salesmanship	30
Will or Ambition	31	Will or Ambition	29
Frugality	25	Courage	28
Positive Thinking	16	Virtuous Character	28
Efficiency	15	Talent	27
Luck	15	Imagination	27
Talent	14	Luck	24
Imagination	13	Education	13
Courage	12	Efficiency	10

CHART XX

The following is a comparison of the emphasis given material and non-material standards of success in sample issues of *Reader's Digest* and *The Saturday Evening Post* from 1917 through 1969. Statistics are based upon one thousand one hundred forty articles studied in *Reader's Digest* and seven hundred seven articles and stories analyzed in *The Saturday Evening Post*.

DEFINITION OF SUCCESS:	1917-29 SEP	RD*	1930-39 SEP	RD	1941-45 SEP	RD	1947-55 SEP	RD
Material	74	34-2	77	54-1	25	43	55	85
Non-material	35-1	33-2	13	29	21	25	31	76

	1957-59 SEP	RD	1961-69 SEP**	RD
	19	32-3	53-4	97-9
	58	77	97-5	189-1

*Statistics for *Reader's Digest* are for issues studied from 1926 to 1929 only.
**Statistics for *The Saturday Evening Post* are for issues studied from 1961 to 1967 only.

NOTES

Preface

1. Long after I had begun my research and writing on popular American philosophies of life, I came across Richard Weiss's use of the term "guides to living" to describe success tracts in the late nineteenth and early twentieth centuries. Since this term has been useful in writing the final version of this book, I would like to give credit to Weiss in publicizing it in *The American Myth of Success* (New York: Basic Books, Inc., Publishers, 1969).

2. In using psychology, I do not wish to suggest that I am analyzing the *minds* of the writers I discuss. I am interested only in the psychological characteristics of their *rhetoric*, which often reflect the advocacy of types of adaptive behavior to the growth of political, cultural and personal stress.

3. For discussions of the relationship of public opinion to the mass media, see Bernard Berelson, "Communications and Public Opinion," in Wilbur Schramm, ed., *Mass Communications*, 2nd ed., (Urbana: University of Illinois Press, 1960), pp. 527–543, and Charles Steinberg, *The Mass Communicators* (New York: Harper and Brothers, 1958), p. 116.

4. In selecting sample issues of *Reader's Digest* and *The Saturday Evening Post*, I used the following method: Four issues of *Reader's Digest* published in 1926 and thereafter for every other year from 1927 through 1969 were studied. Similarly, five issues of *The Saturday Evening Post* published in every other year from 1917 through 1967 were examined. The 1847 articles and stories read were those which promulgated and reflected cultural and political beliefs related to the American dream of success, consumption tastes, moralistic and humanistic approaches to living and the attainment of pleasure and friendship.

   I am indebted to Alice Hackett's *70 Years of Best Sellers:*

1895-1965 (New York: R. R. Bowker Company, 1967) for listing the most popular books of the twentieth century.
5. James Playsted Wood, ed., *Magazines in the United States*, 2nd ed. (New York: The Ronald Press Company, 1956), pp. 156, 221; *Life, Continuing Study of Magazine Audiences*, Report No. 9, November 15, 1947 (no city given: Time Incorporated, 1947), p. 14; John Bainbridge, *The Little Wonder: Or, The Reader's Digest and How It Grew* (New York: Reynal and Hitchcock, 1946), p. 114; Daniel Starch and Staff, Inc., "1972 Starch Demographic Report," (supplied by *Reader's Digest*), no pages given. According to *N. W. Ayer and Son's Directory of Newspapers and Periodicals*, the circulation of *The Saturday Evening Post* rose from 1,889,487 in 1917 to 2,924,363 in 1930; 3,231,496 in 1940; 4,069,220 in 1950 and 4,638,189 in 1955. In 1963, just before *The Saturday Evening Post* became a bi-weekly, the magazine's circulation rose to 6,589,050. By 1967, the magazine reached 6,747,424 Americans. While *Life* overtook *The Saturday Evening Post* as the top-selling weekly in the Fifties, over the entire course of the twentieth century *The Saturday Evening Post* was the most popular weekly.

John Bainbridge, the historian of *Reader's Digest*, has estimated that that magazine's circulation rose from 290,000 in 1929 to 1,800,000 in 1936. During World War II, *Reader's Digest*'s circulation leaped from under four million to over nine million. In 1955, the magazine had a circulation of 10,239,057 and by 1969 *Reader's Digest* reached 17,585,611 Americans.

Because *The Saturday Evening Post* had a higher circulation than *Reader's Digest* from 1917 to the middle of the depression, whereas *Reader's Digest* was more popular from 1940 to 1969, I have given greater attention to *The Saturday Evening Post*'s attitudes in the post-World War I–depression era and have emphasized *Reader's Digest*'s opinions in the World War II and modern periods.

Since *The Saturday Evening Post* went into bankruptcy in 1968, some might question why I should use the magazine at all in my discussion of the 1960s. I have chosen to use *The Saturday Evening Post* until its demise because, as the circulation figures indicate, the magazine continually remained popular with the public. During the Sixties, it continued to remain the second most popular magazine of its type in America. Internal editorial conflicts and unfortunate financial policies far more than a decelerated yet still increasing subscription rate accounted for the demise of *The Saturday Evening Post*. Modern magazines make their profit on advertising revenues rather than subscription rates. The bank-

ruptcy of *The Saturday Evening Post* largely was precipitated by
the loss of important advertising accounts just at the time when
they lost a $460,000 libel suit. In fact, *The Saturday Evening Post*
desperately but unsuccessfully tried to decrease the number of
their subscribers while attempting to change from a middle class
magazine to an upper class publication to remain solvent.

6. Phillips Wyman, *Magazine Circulation* (New York, 1936), pp. 34–36;
Roland Wolseley, "Social Effects of Magazines," and James Playsted Wood, "Magazine Publishing Today" in Charles Steinberg,
ed., *Mass Media and Communication* (New York: Hastings House,
1966), pp. 188, 174–175.

7. Unfortunately, a more specific economic breakdown of *The Saturday Evening Post* readership was not given by *Life* Magazine,
Continuing Study of Magazine Audiences, Report No. 9 November 15, 1947, pp. 21, 15. While demographic variations in *The
Saturday Evening Post* were not striking, the magazine reached
slightly more urban than rural groups, and slightly more mid-
western and eastern than western and southern audiences. Almost
49 percent of their readers were from 20–44 years of age.

The class and educational backgrounds of *Reader's Digest*
followers comes from Daniel Starch and Staff, "1972 Starch
Demographic Report," no pages given. A slight majority of the
Reader's Digest audience was over fifty years of age. While almost
two-thirds of *Reader's Digest* subscribers resided in metropolitan
centers, the magazine did reach 31 percent of rural America in
1972. No information on sectional characteristics of the *Reader's
Digest* audience was provided by the Starch Report.

No statistics regarding race, religion or ethnic background
were given for either magazine. *The Saturday Evening Post* was
read by slightly more men than women. The ratio in *Reader's
Digest* was just the reverse. Throughout the period I researched,
the success ethic was essentially a male philosophy. Alger wrote
of Ragged Dick but not Ragged Jane. Yet the dream of success
had enormous consequences for women. Wherever possible, I
have noted this dimension of the success ethic. However, to examine these consequences and the relationship of the new feminism
to the dream of success in any detail would require another book.

Moreover, since pluralistic variations exist in our society,
I do not wish to suggest that this book describes the American
character. Nevertheless, I believe the philosophies of life I discuss
do affect to varying extents young and old, Catholics, Protestants
and Jews different ethnic groups and geographical sections. I have
not attempted a specific statistical breakdown of which Americans held which values. Different social types possessed different

cultural concepts in differing degrees of intensity and complexity. I do feel comfortable in using the term "middle class" in reference to the people and concepts I discuss because of the obvious general middle class character of the readerships of the magazines I have researched.

8. "Tranquilizers in Print," *Time* LXIX (March 25, 1957), 114.

Chapter 1.

1. For discussions of the concept of identity, see Alfred Adler, *The Practice and Theory of Individual Psychology*, rev. ed. (London: Routledge and Kegan Paul, Ltd., 1955), pp. 8–9, 102–103; Helen Lynd, *On Shame and the Search for Identity* (New York: Harcourt, Brace and Company, 1958), pp. 15, 204, 210; Erik H. Erikson, "The Problem of Ego Identity," and Maurice R. Stein and Arthur J. Vidich, "Identity and History: An Overview," in Maurice R. Stein, Arthur J. Vidich, and David Manning White, eds., *Identity and Anxiety* (Glencoe: The Free Press of Glencoe, 1960), pp. 37–87, 17–33, 45–46, but esp. 25, 69; Allen Wheelis, *The Quest for Identity* (New York: W. W. Norton and Company, Inc., 1958), p. 19; Alfred Adler, *The Science of Living* (Garden City: Garden City Publishing Company, 1929), pp. 16–17; Sigmund Freud, *Civilization and Its Discontents* (London: The Hogarth Press, Ltd., 1957), Ch. I, II, but esp. p. 26; Robin Williams, Jr., *American Society: A Sociological Interpretation*, second ed., rev. (New York: Alfred A. Knopf, 1960), pp. 391, 395, 396; and Rollo May, *Man's Search for Himself* (New York: W. W. Norton and Company, Inc., 1953), p. 210.

2. *Cf.* Williams, *American Society*, pp. 24–30.

3. *Cf.*, Reinhold Bendix, *Work and Authority in Industry* (New York: John Wiley and Sons, Inc., 1956), p. 199; Francis X. Sutton et al. *The American Business Creed* (Cambridge: Harvard University Press, 1956), pp. 2, 275.

4. *Cf.* Williams, *American Society*, p. 31; Sutton, *The American Business Creed*, pp. 276–279.

5. Anne Morgan, as told to Mary Margaret McBride, "Sidelights on the Woman Question," *The Saturday Evening Post* (hereafter referred to as *SEP*) CXCIX (March 26, 1927), 186; Judge Henry Neil, "Ford Discusses Human Flivvers," *Reader's Digest* V (October, 1926), 348 (condensed from *Everybody's Magazine*); Christa Winsloe, "Mad Marks," *SEP* CCVI (January 6, 1934), 23; Albert Wiggam, "Do Brains and Character Go Together?" *Reader's Digest* XXXIX (November, 1941), 110 (condensed from *School and*

Society); Dale Carnegie, *How to Win Friends and Influence People* (New York: Simon and Schuster, 1937), p. 133; Henry Link, *The Return to Religion* (New York: The Macmillan Company, 1936).

6. Arthur Wiltse, "The Abundant Life," *Reader's Digest* XXXI (December, 1937), 81; Vash Young, *A Fortune to Share* (Indianapolis: The Bobbs-Merrill Company, 1931), p. 155; for examples of men unable to enjoy retirement, see Earl Biggers, "Idle Hands," *SEP* CXCIII (June 11, 1921), 5-7, 41-42, 45-46, 48; and Arthur Stringer, "Power," *SEP* CXCVII (February 21, 1925), 3.

7. Link, *The Return to Religion*, pp. 99, 33.

8. Carnegie, *How to Win Friends and Influence People*, p. 98.

9. Dean Jennings, "Girl on the Glamour-Go-Round," *SEP* CCXXXIV (September 23, 1961), 38.

10. Ibid., 44; Elvis Presley, quoted in C. Robert Jennings, "There'll Always Be an Elvis," *SEP* CCXXXVIII (September 11, 1965), 78, 79.

11. Stanley Frank, "How the Giants Found a Pitcher in the Doghouse," *SEP* CCXXIII (May 5, 1951), 29; Arthur Mann, "How to Buy a Ball Club for Peanuts," *SEP* CCXXVII (April 9, 1955), 25.

12. Robert L. Murray, "$10,000—and One Year to Live," *Reader's Digest* VII (February, 1929), 622 (condensed from Hearst's *International Cosmopolitan*).

13. Isaac F. Marcosson, "Adventures in Interviewing Pershing and Some Other War Notables," *SEP* CXCII (July 5, 1919), 85, 88; Isaac F. Marcosson, "Marvels of Army Organization," *SEP* CXCI (January 4, 1919), 15.

14. Edward G. Lowry, "We, U. S., and Company," *SEP* CXCIII (February 5, 1921), 8; Isaac F. Marcosson, "The President Gets Down to Business," *SEP* CCII (December 21, 1929), 78; Richard Washburn Child, "Hoover—or Some Other?" *SEP* CCI (March 16, 1929), 25, 149.

15. "Norman Vincent Peale, Minister to Millions," *Look* XVII (September 22, 1953), 86; Meg Greenfield, "The Great American Morality Play," *The Reporter* XXIV (June 8, 1961), 16.

16. John A. Logan, Jr., "The Crisis on Our Campuses," *Reader's Digest* LXXXVI (February, 1965), 126 (condensed from *Town & Country*).

17. Hanson W. Baldwin, "Our Fighting Men Have Gone Soft," *Reader's Digest* LXXV (November, 1959), 97-98 (condensed from *SEP*).

18. Conference on Economic Progress, *Poverty and Deprivation in the United States* (Washington, 1962), pp. 30, 31; Seymour Lipset and Reinhard Bendix, *Social Mobility in Industrial Society* (Berkeley: University of California Press, 1966), p. 85.

19. Lipset and Bendix, *Social Mobility in Industrial America*, p. 102; Conference on Economic Progress, *Poverty and Deprivation in the United States*, pp. 2, 4, 3.
20. Joseph A. Kahl, *The American Class Structure* (New York: Rinehart, 1957), p. 263; Lipset and Bendix, *Social Mobility in Industrial Society*, p. 88; Robert Presthus, *The Organizational Society* (New York: Random House, Inc., Vintage Books, 1962), p. 207.
21. Mabel Newcomer, *The Big Business Executive* (New York: Columbia University Press, 1957), pp. 53–54; Warner and Abegglin, qt. in Kahl, *The American Class Structure*, p. 269.
22. For lengthy discussions by psychologists, sociologists, and organizational studies experts on the types of defense mechanisms which I describe in relation to success devotees who feel various degrees of helplessness, see Heinz and Rowena Ansbacher, eds., *The Individual Psychology of Alfred Adler* (New York: Harper and Row, Publishers, 1967), pp. 77–125, 239–325; Helen Lynd, *On Shame and the Search for Identity*, pp. 22–26, 44; Karen Horney, *The Neurotic Personality of Our Time* (New York: W. W. Norton and Company, Inc., 1937), pp. 171–172, 166, 179–180, 239; Robert Presthus, *The Organizational Society* (New York: Vintage Books, 1962), pp. 172–174; Sutton, *American Business Creed*, pp. 301–383, but esp. 334, 341–342, 371.
23. Carnegie, *How to Win Friends and Influence People*, p. 101; Bruce Bliven, "The Adventure of Being Human," *Reader's Digest* LXXV (August, 1959), 43. Italics Bliven's. Part of original in boldface type.
24. Dorothea Brande, *Wake Up and Live!* (New York: Simon and Schuster, 1936), pp. 8, 19, 22, 80, 71, 68–69, 84–85; Ansbacher and Ansbacher, *The Individual Psychology of Alfred Adler*, pp. 76–100, 233, 244–247.
25. Maxwell Maltz, M.D., "How to Stand Up Under Stress," *Reader's Digest* LXXVIII (June, 1961), 43, 44, 45; Norman Vincent Peale, *The Power of Positive Thinking* (Englewood Cliffs, N. J.: Prentice-Hall, Inc., 1953), pp. 72, 145, 124.
26. Norman Vincent Peale, "Trouble: Whetstone of Life," *Reader's Digest* LXXXII (January, 1963), 146.
27. Alexis de Tocqueville, *Democracy in America*, Vol. II (New York: Vintage Books, 1961), p. 4; Bruce Barton, *The Man Nobody Knows*, pp. 9, introduction (no pages given); Link, *The Return to Religion*, p. 79.
28. Frank Bettger, *How I Raised Myself from Failure to Success in Selling*, (Englewood Cliffs, N. J.: Prentice-Hall, Inc., 1950), p. 8; A. H. Z. Carr, "How to Attract Good Luck," *Reader's Digest* LXII (February, 1953), 16.

29. Gilbert Seldes, "Uneasy Chameleons," *SEP* CXCIX (January 1, 1927), 82; Editorial, "Civilization Shock," *SEP* CXCII (June 11, 1921), 20. Cf. Adler, *The Practice and Theory of Individual Psychology*, p. 9.

30. Link, *The Return to Religion*, pp. 169-170; Baldwin, "Our Fighting Men Have Gone Soft," pp. 97-98.

31. Adler, *The Practice and Theory of Individual Psychology*, pp. 255-260; Ansbacher and Ansbacher, *The Individual Psychology of Alfred Adler*, pp. 317-318; Richard Hofstadter, *The Paranoid Style in American Politics* (New York: Alfred A. Knopf, 1967), Ch. I, II.

32. Success writers such as Carnegie and Peale increasingly have emphasized the need for friendship and enjoyment and thus have contributed to the growing popularity of the pleasure-oriented consumption ethic. However, Peale and Carnegie differed from most consumption advocates insofar as the advocacy of pleasure did not damage their preference for the success ethic. Peale maintained that recreation could help the individual rejuvenate himself to continue to strive. And while Carnegie called for companionship, he phrased his advice in the achievement terminology of "winning friends" through salesmanship.

33. Walter Pitkin, *Life Begins at Forty* (New York: Whittlesey House, McGraw-Hill Book Company, Inc., 1932), pp. 70, 107; Marjorie Hillis, *Orchids on Your Budget* (Indianapolis: The Bobbs-Merrill Company, 1937), p. 64.

34. Hillis, *Orchids on Your Budget*, p. 65.

35. Katharine Anthony, "Love–Luxury or Necessity?" *Reader's Digest* L (February, 1947), 188 (condensed from *Delineator*); Pitkin, *Life Begins at Forty*, p. 16; Hillis, *Live Alone and Like It*, (Indianapolis: The Bobbs-Merrill Company, 1936), pp. 38-39.

36. George Dorsey, "How Much of Your Brain Do You Use?" *Reader's Digest* V (October, 1926), 323, 353 (condensed from *The American Magazine*).

37. Alan Devoe, "Profits from Idleness," *Reader's Digest* XXXV (October, 1939), 97 (condensed from *Coronet*).

38. Cf. Phillip Slater, *The Pursuit of Loneliness: American Culture at the Breaking Point* (Boston: Beacon Press, 1970), pp. 83-86.

39. Marion L. Boling, "The Best Hours of My Life," *Reader's Digest* LXXIV (February, 1959), 42-46.

40. Bill Koman, quoted in James Atwater, "Tormented Life of a Pro Linebacker," *SEP* CCXXXVIII (December 18, 1965), 28.

41. "Editorials," *Reader's Digest* V (October, 1926), 349; Ernest Dimnet, *What We Live By* (New York: Simon and Schuster, Inc., 1932), p. 247; Billy Graham, *The Secret of Happiness* (Garden City: Doubleday and Company, Inc., 1955), pp. 19, 111.

42. Graham, *The Secret of Happiness*, p. 16; Fulton J. Sheen, *Peace of Soul* (New York: Whittlesey House, McGraw-Hill Book Company, Inc., 1949), p. 20; Joshua Loth Liebman, *Peace of Mind* (New York: Simon and Schuster, Inc.), pp. 96–97.

43. Liebman, *Peace of Mind*, p. xi. Italics Liebman's. Sheen, *Peace of Soul*, p. 1.

44. Sheen, *Peace of Soul*, pp. 89–90, 26, 56–57. Italics Liebman's.

45. Liebman, *Peace of Mind*, pp. 24, 38, 53, 54.

46. Ibid., p. 53.

47. Sheen, *Peace of Soul*, p. 59; Graham, *The Secret of Happiness*, p. 44.

48. Cf. Rollo May, "Love and Will," *Psychology Today* III (August, 1969), 17–18, 59.

Chapter 2.

1. Crawford's and the Commissioner of Indian Affairs' quotations are taken from Michael Paul Rogin, "Liberal Society and the Indian Question," *Politics and Society* I (May, 1971), 280, 281.

2. Ralph Waldo Emerson, "Wealth," in Moses Rischin, ed., *The American Gospel of Success* (Chicago: Quadrangle Books, 1965), pp. 41, 40.

3. Ralph Waldo Emerson, qt. in John Ward, *Red, White and Blue* (New York: Oxford University Press, 1969), p. 235. Some of the positions taken in the first half of this chapter were inspired by Ward's excellent discussion of the changing concepts of individualism in the above-mentioned book.

4. Herbert Spencer, qt. in Sidney Fine, ed., *Laissez-Faire and the General-Welfare State* (Ann Arbor: Ann Arbor Paperbacks, The University of Michigan Press, 1964), p. 34; Spencer and Sumner, quoted in Richard Hofstadter, *Social Darwinism in American Thought*, rev. ed. (Boston: Beacon Press, 1955), pp. 37, 51.

5. Horatio Alger, *Ragged Dick and Mark, the Match Boy* (New York: Collier Books, 1962), p. 319.

6. Cf. Richard Weiss, *The American Myth of Success* (New York: Basic Books, Inc., Publishers, 1969), pp. 55, 60; Horatio Alger, "Struggling Upward, or Luke Larkin's Luck," in Rischin, *The American Gospel of Success*, p. 89.

7. Cf., John Cawelti, *Apostles of the Self-Made Man* (Chicago: The University of Chicago Press, 1968), pp. 101–123 for a discussion of the limited extent of mobility advocated in Alger's stories; Alger, *Ragged Dick and Mark, the Match Boy*, p. 308.

8. Andrew Carnegie, quoted in Ward, *Red, White and Blue*, p. 245.

9. John D. Rockefeller, quoted ibid., p. 250.

10. For a thorough content analysis of the treatment of the success

ethic in American popular magazines from 1890 to 1917, see
Theodore Greene, *America's Heroes* (New York: Oxford University Press, 1970), pp. 110–337.

11. Frank Haddock, quoted in Weiss, *The American Myth of Success*, p. 215.

12. Cf. Heinz and Rowena Ansbacher, eds., *The Individual Psychology of Alfred Adler* (New York: Harper and Row, Publishers, 1967), pp. 77–108, 239, 300, 282, 290–293, 281, 289, 296–297, 314.

13. Douglas Fairbanks, *Laugh and Live* (New York: Britton Publishing Company, 1917), pp. 17, 31. In the non-fiction class, Fairbanks's book was the sixth best seller in 1917 and the fifth best seller in 1918.

14. Ibid., pp. 50, 87, 18.

15. Ibid., pp. 47, 21, 109–124, 119, 75, 83. Italics Fairbanks's.

16. Cf. Rollo May, *Power and Innocence* (New York: W. W. Norton and Company, Inc., 1972), pp. 257–260.

17. Fairbanks, *Laugh and Live*, pp. 16, 23, 10. Italics Fairbanks's.

18. Emile Coué, *Self-Mastery Through Conscious Autosuggestion* (New York: American Library Service, 1922), pp. 110, 14, 26–27, 35, 31. Ford's statement appears on the end cover of Coué's book. Coué's book was the seventh best seller in the non-fiction class in 1923, and chapters of the Coué League of America dotted the nation in the early Twenties. Henry Ford, quoted in Richard M. Huber, *The American Idea of Success* (New York: McGraw-Hill Book Company, 1971), p. 117.

19. For the period from 1917 to 1929, wealth and status were more popular goals than power. Moreover, power and wealth were often praised together in articles. From 1917 to 1925, however, power often was mentioned in articles which did not discuss a success hero's material attainments.

20. Corine Lowe, "Alice through the Working Class," *The Saturday Evening Post* (hereafter referred to as *SEP*), CXCI (May 3, 1919), p. 18; Booth Tarkington, "Saving the Country," *SEP* CXCII (July 5, 1919), pp. 11, 76, 81; Judge Gary, quoted in Floyd W. Parsons, "Everybody's Business," *SEP* CXCI (July 5, 1919), p. 27.

21. Harry Leon Wilson, "Naughty Boys!" *SEP* CXCI (May 3, 1919), 3, 42; "Who's Who—and Why," *SEP* CXC (Dec. 1, 1917), 25; Editorial, "Civilization Shock," *SEP* CXCIII (June 11, 1921), 20.

22. Edward Filene, "Immigration, Progress, and Prosperity," *SEP* CXCVI (July 28, 1923), 8; Forrest Crissey, "New Feet Under the Table," *SEP* CXCII (Oct. 4, 1919), 82.

23. Anne Morgan, as told to Mary Margaret McBride, "Sidelights on the Woman Question," *SEP* CXCIV (March 26, 1927), 186; *Nation's Business*, quoted in William Leuchtenburg, *The Perils of Pros-*

perity, 1914–32 (Chicago: University of Chicago Press, 1963), p. 198.

24. Bruce Barton, *The Man Nobody Knows* (Indianapolis: The Bobbs-Merrill Company, 1925), Foreword (no pages given), pp. 179, 180, 8, 9. In the nonfiction class, Barton's book was the fourth best seller in 1925 and the top best seller in 1926. Italics Barton's.

25. Ibid., Foreword (no pages given), p. 167.

26. Ibid., pp. 73–75, Foreword (no pages given), 19, 104.

27. Bruce Barton, *The Book Nobody Knows* (Indianapolis: The Bobbs-Merrill Company, 1926), pp. 14, 51–52. This book was the seventh best seller in the nonfiction class in 1926.

28. Giovanni Papini, *The Life of Christ* (New York: Harcourt, Brace and Company, 1923), pp. 286–287, 251, 196. In the nonfiction class, Papini's book was the second best seller in 1923 and 1924, and the fifth best seller in 1925.

29. Barton, *The Man Nobody Knows*, Foreword (no pages given).

30. Ibid., p. 77.

31. Thomas Read, "The American Secret," *Reader's Digest* V (April, 1927), 721–722 (condensed from *The Atlantic Monthly*); Bishop Fiske, quoted in Richard M. Huber, *The American Idea of Success*, p. 203; Leuchtenburg, *The Perils of Prosperity*, p. 189.

32. Editorial, "The Golden Rule in Business," *SEP* CCI (March 16, 1929), 24.

33. Calvin Coolidge, quoted in Leuchtenburg, *The Perils of Prosperity*, p. 188; Judge Henry Neil, "Ford Discusses Human Flivvers," *Reader's Digest* V (Oct., 1926), 347–348 (condensed from *Everybody's Magazine*).

34. Judge Gary, quoted in Floyd Parsons, "Everybody's Business," *SEP* CXCI (July 5, 1919), 27; Samuel Insull, quoted in Forrest Crissey, "Getting On in the World," *SEP* CXCVIII (August 1, 1925), 34.

35. Editorial, "For President," *SEP* CXCII (Oct. 4, 1919), 28–29.

36. Leuchtenburg, *The Perils of Prosperity*, p. 90; President Harding, quoted in James D. Hart, *The Popular Book* (New York: Oxford University Press, 1950), p. 236.

37. Samuel G. Blythe, "A Calm Review of a Calm Man," *SEP* CXCVI (July 28, 1923), 73–74. Harding was so pleased with Blythe's article that the President asked his wife to read the article to him on his death bed.

38. Leuchtenburg, *The Perils of Prosperity*, p. 188.

39. President Hoover, quoted in Richard Hofstadter, *The American Political Tradition* (New York: Alfred A. Knopf, 1948), pp. 293–294. Original quote in italics.

40. President Hoover, quoted in Walter Johnson, *1600 Pennsylvania Avenue* (Boston: Little, Brown and Company, 1960), p. 6;

Robert S. and Helen Lynd, *Middletown in Transition* (New York: Harcourt, Brace and Company, 1937), p. 3; Bernard Baruch, quoted in John Kenneth Galbraith, *The Great Crash—1929* (Boston: Houghton Mifflin Company, 1955), p. 75.

41. Statistics on poverty and income distribution from Conference on Economic Progress, *Poverty and Deprivation in the United States* (Washington, 1962), p. 20 and Leuchtenburg, *The Perils of Prosperity*, pp. 194, 193.

42. Galbraith, *The Great Crash*, pp. 178, 182–183; John D. Hicks, *Republican Ascendancy* (New York: Harper and Row, Publishers, 1960), pp. 230–233.

43. Alonzo Englebert Taylor, "To Reduce the Cost of Eating," *SEP* CXCIII (March 5, 1921), 8.

44. President's Research Committee on Social Trends, quoted in Leuchtenburg, *The Perils of Prosperity*, p. 174.

45. Cornelia James Cannon, "The New Leisure," *Reader's Digest* V (October, 1926), 329–330 (condensed from *The North American Review*); Raymond Essen, "Less Money and More Life," *Reader's Digest* VII (February, 1929), 590 (condensed from *Harper's Magazine*).

46. James Truslow Adams, "Happiness and the Art of Living," *Reader's Digest* V (January, 1927), 523–524 (condensed from *McNaught's Monthly*); James Truslow Adams, "A Business Man's Civilization," *Reader's Digest* VIII (August, 1929), 364 (condensed from *Harper's Magazine*); Albert J. Nock, "The Decline of Conversation," *Reader's Digest* V (July, 1926), 158 (condensed from *Harper's Magazine*).

47. George Dorsey, *Why We Behave Like Human Beings* (New York: Harper and Brothers, 1925), pp. 469, 452, 449, 471. In the nonfiction class, Dorsey's book was the second best seller in 1926 and the ninth best seller in 1927.

48. Ernest Dimnet, *The Art of Thinking* (New York: Simon and Schuster, 1932), pp. 16, 27, 195–208, 29. In the nonfiction class, Dimnet's book was the top best seller in 1929 and the ninth best seller in 1930.

49. Forrest Crissey, "New Feet Under the Table," *SEP* CXCII (October 4, 1919), p. 10; James Collins, "Sobering Up the Business Conscience," *SEP* CXCIV (March 5, 1921), p. 20.

50. Barton, *The Man Nobody Knows*, p. 143.

51. Garet Garrett, "The Seven Sound Years," *SEP* CCI (April 13, 1929), 8, 9.

52. Ibid., 9, 117.

Chapter 3.

1. Dixon Wecter, *The Age of the Great Depression, 1929–1941* (New York: The Macmillan Company, 1969), p. 32.

2. On the characteristics of shame and guilt which I discuss in this section, see Helen Lynd, *On Shame and the Search for Identity* (New York: Harcourt, Brace and Company, 1958), pp. 22, 27, 35, 43, 58.

3. Robert and Helen Lynd, *Middletown in Transition* (New York: Harcourt, Brace and Company, 1937), p. 24; Wilbur Cash, *The Mind of the South* (New York: Alfred A. Knopf, 1950), p. 362; E. Wight Bakke, *Citizens Without Work* (New Haven: Yale University Press, 1940), pp. 22–23.

4. Vash Young, *A Fortune to Share* (Indianapolis: The Bobbs-Merrill Company, 1932), p. 10; Marjorie Hillis, *Orchids on Your Budget* (Indianapolis: The Bobbs-Merrill Company, 1937), p. 161. Young's book was the third best seller in the nonfiction class in 1932; Hillis's book was the fifth best seller in the nonfiction class in 1937. In fact, her books were the only self help works published for women which reached the best seller charts from 1917 to 1970. While it is interesting to note that her books emphasized a consumption-oriented lifestyle for women, Hillis was not popular merely for reinforcing this sexist aspect of American culture. During the depression, advice on making ends meet was useful for men, but especially important for women since marriage rates fell and desertion increased as a result of widespread financial difficulties.

5. Ernest Dimnet, *What We Live By* (New York: Simon and Schuster, Inc., 1932), p. 246; Henry Link, *The Return to Religion* (New York: The Macmillan Co., 1936), pp. 154–155. Dimnet's book was the sixth best seller in the nonfiction class in 1932; Link's book was the third best seller in the nonfiction class in 1937.

6. Link, *The Return to Religion*, pp. 180–181; Dale Carnegie, *How to Win Friends and Influence People* (New York: Simon and Schuster, Inc., 1937), p. 131. In the nonfiction class, Carnegie's book was the top best seller in 1937 and the sixth best seller in 1938.

7. William Leuchtenburg, *The Perils of Prosperity 1914–32* (Chicago: The University of Chicago Press, 1963), p. 250; Frederick Lewis Allen, *Since Yesterday 1929–1939* (New York: Bantam Books, Inc., 1965), p. 50.

8. Henry Ford, quoted in Keith Sward, *The Legend of Henry Ford* (New York: Atheneum, 1968), p. 224.

9. Garet Garrett, "America Can't Come Back," *The Saturday Evening Post* (hereafter referred to as *SEP*), CCIV (Jan. 23, 1932), 3–5, 92–95; Hillis, *Orchids on Your Budget*, pp. 162–163; Young, *A Fortune to Share*, p. 89; Frank Vanderlip, "From Farm Boy to Financier," *SEP* CCVII (Nov. 10, 1934), 68.

10. Wecter, *The Age of the Great Depression*, p. 17; Leuchtenburg, *The Perils of Prosperity*, pp. 250–251.

11. Myron Taylor, quoted in Arthur Schlesinger, Jr., *The Crises of the Old Order 1919–1933* (Boston: Houghton Mifflin Company, Sentry Edition, 1964), p. 180; Will Rogers, in Donald Day, ed., *Sanity Is Where You Find It* (Boston: Houghton Mifflin Company, 1955), p. 120.

12. Richard Hofstadter, *The American Political Tradition* (New York: Alfred A. Knopf, 1948), p. 305.

13. President Hoover, quoted ibid., p. 303 and Allen, *Since Yesterday*, p. 41.

14. President Hoover, quoted in Schlesinger, *Crisis of the Old Order*, p. 188; Leuchtenburg, *The Perils of Prosperity*, pp. 252, 253.

15. President Hoover, quoted in Schlesinger, *Crisis of the Old Order*, p. 242; Allen, *Since Yesterday*, p. 50.

16. Leuchtenburg, *The Perils of Prosperity*, p. 264; John Steinbeck, *The Grapes of Wrath* (New York: The Viking Press, 1964), p. 72; Wecter, *The Age of the Great Depression*, p. 35.

17. Charles Schwab, quoted in Allen, *Since Yesterday*, p. 58.

18. Will Rogers, in Day, ed., *Sanity Is Where You Find It*, pp. 129–130.

19. *New York Sun*, quoted in "Patter," *Reader's Digest* XXII (Jan., 1933), 90. Italics *Reader's Digest*.

20. Walter Pitkin, *Life Begins at Forty* (New York: Whittlesey House, McGraw-Hill Book Company, Inc., 1932), pp. 100, 7–8. Pitkin's book was the top best seller in the nonfiction class in 1933 and the second best seller in that class in 1934. Edmund Jacobson's *You Must Relax* (New York: Whittlesey House, McGraw-Hill Book Company, Inc., 1934) similarly criticized the exhausting effects of the American devotion to diligence and competition. Jacobson's book was the ninth best seller in the nonfiction class in 1934.

21. Emil Ludwig, "Briand," *SEP* CCIV (Feb. 27, 1932), 14; Pitkin, *Life Begins at Forty*, pp. 37, 143.

22. For an example of Octavus Roy Cohen's stories about blacks, see "5000 Feet Make One Smile," *SEP* CCII (Jan. 4, 1930), 16–17, 84, 87, 91; Paul Gallico, "Mean Man," *Reader's Digest* XXVII (Nov., 1935), 70 (condensed from *Vanity Fair*).

23. Carnegie, *How to Win Friends and Influence People*, p. 25; Helena

Huntington Smith, "Paderewski's Double Life," *Reader's Digest* XVIII (March, 1931), 995 (condensed from *The New Yorker*); Saul Hurok, "Ballet Business," *SEP* CCVI (July 21, 1934), 70, 21; David Lawrence, "There Is a Tide," *SEP* CCII (Jan. 11, 1930), 35, 162, 166.

24. Paul Hutchinson, "The Decline of Puritan Virtues," *Reader's Digest* XXIII (July, 1933), 99 (condensed from *The Forum*).

25. Ibid., 100.

26. Franklin Roosevelt, quoted in Leuchtenburg, *Franklin D. Roosevelt and the New Deal* (New York: Harper and Row, Publishers, 1963), p. 124.

27. A. A. Berle, Jr., "A High Road for Business," *Reader's Digest* XXIII (July, 1933), 22, 23 (condensed from *Scribner's Magazine*).

28. Henry Goddard Leach, "Religion and Recovery," *Reader's Digest* XXIII (Oct., 1933), 4 (excerpt from Editorial Forward, *The Forum*); Donald Richberg, "The Challenge of NRA," *Reader's Digest* XXIII (Oct., 1933), 90, 92.

29. Newton Baker, "The Decay of Self-Reliance," *Reader's Digest* XXVI (Feb., 1935), 21, 22 (condensed from *The Atlantic Monthly*); Marc Rose, "The Mormons March Off Relief," *Reader's Digest* XXX (June, 1937), 43 (condensed from *The Commentator*).

30. J. P. Morgan, quoted in Arthur Schlesinger, Jr., *The Coming of the New Deal* (Boston: Houghton Mifflin Company, Sentry Edition, 1965), p. 477.

31. Harold Gray, *Arf! The Life and Hard Times of Little Orphan Annie 1935-1945* (New Rochelle, New York: Arlington House, 1970), no pages given; quotations from comic strips appearing on Tuesday, April 21, 1936, Thursday, May 7, 1936, Friday, November 8, 1935, and Thursday, June 25, 1936.

32. Ibid., quotation from comic strip appearing on Wednesday, September 4, 1935.

33. Stanley High, "Jobs Preferred!" *Reader's Digest* XXXI (Sept., 1937), 20 (condensed from *The Saturday Evening Post*); Priscilla Pennypacker, "How to Raise a Family on $1800 a Year," *Reader's Digest* XVIII (March, 1931), 977 (condensed from *The Forum*). Frances Miller, "Not by Bread Alone," *Reader's Digest* XXX (June, 1937), 29.

34. Dorothea Brande, *Wake Up and Live!* (New York: Simon and Schuster, Inc., 1936), pp. 8, 10, 80, 54. Italics Brande's. Brande's book was the second best seller in the nonfiction class in 1936.

35. Carnegie, *How to Win Friends and Influence People*, pp. 4–6.

36. Carnegie, *How to Win Friends and Influence People*, p. 133.

37. Brande, *Wake Up and Live!*, p. 84, 8.

38. Ibid., 84–85; Link, *The Return to Religion,* p. 170.
39. Carnegie, *How to Win Friends and Influence People*, pp. 98, 19, 100.
40. Brande, *Wake Up and Live!*, p. 68.
41. Ibid., p. 80; Link, *The Return to Religion*, p. 73.
42. Henry Link, "Do the Thing You Fear—," *Reader's Digest* XXXI (Dec., 1937), 22; Link, *The Return to Religion*, pp. 169–170.
43. For a discussion of the House Un-American Activities Committee actions and Ickes' remark, see Leuchtenburg, *Franklin D. Roosevelt and the New Deal*, pp. 280–281.

Chapter 4.

1. John Kenneth Galbraith, *American Capitalism: The Concept of Countervailing Power* (Boston: Houghton Mifflin Company, Sentry Edition, 1956), p. 65.
2. Harry T. Paxton, "Firemen of the High Seas," *The Saturday Evening Post* (hereafter referred to as *SEP*) XXCVI (Oct. 9, 1943), 26, 27, 48; David O. Woodbury, "They Get Damaged Warships Back to Sea," *Reader's Digest* XLII (March, 1943), 107 (condensed from *Scientific American*).
3. Ernest W. Burgess, "The Family," and W. Lloyd Warner, "The American Town," in William Fielding Ogburn, ed., *American Society in Wartime* (Chicago: University of Chicago Press, 1944), pp. 36, 43, 46.
4. Raymond Rubicam, "Advertising," in Jack Goodman, ed., *While You Were Gone* (New York: Simon and Schuster, Inc., 1946), p. 435.
5. T. E. Murphy, "White Collars Go on the Production Line," *Reader's Digest* XLII (March, 1943), 13, 15 (condensed from *Forbes*); Peggy McEvoy, "Gun Molls of the U. S. A.," *Reader's Digest* XLII (March, 1943), 49 (condensed from *This Week, New York Herald Tribune*).
6. Editors, "Keeping Posted," *SEP* CCXII (April 19, 1941), 4. For examples of Thruelsen's articles, see "Men at Work," *SEP* CCXIII (April 19, 1941), 20, 21; and "Men at Work," *SEP* CCXIII (June 14, 1941), 18, 19.
7. Gretta Palmer, "Screen Appeal: Our Highest-Priced Commodity," *Reader's Digest* XLVII (Oct., 1945), 93 (condensed from *Woman's Life*).
8. Rubicam, "Advertising," in Goodman, ed., *While You Were Gone*, p. 435; Otis Graham, Jr., "Years of Crisis: America in Depression and War, 1933–1945," in William E. Leuchtenburg, ed., *The Un-*

finished Century: America Since 1900 (Boston: Little, Brown and Company, [Inc.], 1973), p. 448.

9. *Superman From the Thirties to the Seventies* (New York: Crown Publishers, Inc., 1971), p. 207.

10. Ibid., p. 19.

11. Bill Mauldin, *Up Front* (New York: Henry Holt and Company, 1945), pp. 7–8.

12. Ibid., p. 15.

13. Frederick Sodern, Jr., "There Are No Atheists in the Skies," *Reader's Digest* XLIII (Dec., 1943), 26 (condensed from *Air Facts*); The Reverend Dr. Peter Marshall, "Quicken the Spirit Within You," *Reader's Digest* XLVI (Jan., 1945), 1. Italics Marshall's.

14. Ibid., 1; A. F. Cronin, "Diogenes in Maine," *Reader's Digest* XXIX (Aug., 1941), 13 (condensed from *Harper's Bazaar*).

15. Jack Alexander, "Do-Gooder," *SEP* CCXIV (Dec. 6, 1941), 15.

16. Harry Emerson Fosdick, *On Being a Real Person*. (New York: Harper and Brothers, 1943), pp. 5, 16. Fosdick's book was the fourth best seller in the nonfiction class in 1943.

17. Ibid., p. 108.

18. Ibid., pp. 28, 44, 178, 181, 79, 47.

19. Ibid., p. 24.

20. Joshua Loth Liebman, *Peace of Mind*. (New York: Simon and Schuster, Inc., 1946), pp. 12, 13.

21. Ibid., p. 4.

22. Ibid., pp. 53, 38. Italics Liebman's.

23. Ibid., p. 53.

24. S/Sgt. Jameson G. Campaigne, "What's the Matter with the U. S. A.?" *SEP* CCXVIII (Nov. 3, 1945), 34.

25. Harland Manchester, "Simon Lake, Submarine Genius," *Reader's Digest* XLII (March, 1943), 94 (condensed from *Scientific American*); Ernest O. Hauser, "The World's Most Famous Optimists," *SEP* CCXVII (March 3, 1945), 9.

26. Editors, "The Meaning of Total," *SEP* CCXIV (Dec. 6, 1941), 28; "1022 Government-Owned War Plants," *Reader's Digest* XLII (June, 1943), 27–28 (condensed from *The United States News*).

27. J. P. McEvoy, "Our 110,000 New Boarders," *Reader's Digest* XLII (March, 1943), 65–68 (condensed from The Baltimore Sunday *Sun*); Joseph A. Livingston, "Let's Produce Jobs, Not Unemployment," *SEP* CCXVIII (Nov. 3, 1945), 132.

28. Friedrich Hayek, "The Road to Serfdom," *Reader's Digest* XLVI (April, 1945), 2, 3, 20, 17.

29. W. M. Kiplinger, "What the *Practical* Men See Ahead," *Reader's Digest* XLIII (Sept., 1943), 36, 37 (condensed from *Cosmopolitan*).

30. Marc Rose, "Cripple Creek Wins a Bet," *Reader's Digest* XXXIX
    (Nov., 1941), 119–122 (condensed from *Forbes*); Paul de Kruif,
    "Cooperative Health Harvest," *Reader's Digest* XLIII (Sept.,
    1943), 97; David Lilienthal, "An Alternative to Big Government,"
    Reader's Digest L (May, 1947), 75.
31. Bill Mauldin, *Back Home* (New York: William Sloane Associates,
    Publisher, 1947), pp. 110, 101. Italics Mauldin's.
32. Ibid., p. 154.

Chapter 5.

1. Henry Morgan, quoted in Eric Goldman, *The Crucial Decade—and
   After: America, 1945-1960* (New York: Vintage Books, 1960),
   p. 41; Norman Vincent Peale, quoted in "Pastor's Problem,"
   Reader's Digest LVIII (Jan., 1951), 47.
2. Bruce Barton, *The Man Nobody Knows* (Indianapolis: The Bobbs-
   Merrill Company, 1925), frontplate; Dr. John Schindler, *How to
   Live 365 Days a Year* (Englewood Cliffs, N. J.: Prentice-Hall, Inc.,
   1963), p. v. Italics and caps, Barton's and Schindler's. Schindler's
   book was the fifth best seller in the nonfiction class in 1955.
3. Catherine Marshall, *Mr. Jones, Meet the Master* (Los Angeles: Fleming H. Revell Co., 1949), p. 22; Fulton J. Sheen, *Peace of Soul*
   (New York: Whittlesey House, McGraw-Hill Book Co., Inc.,
   1949), p. 22; Dale Evans Rogers, *Angel Unaware* (Los Angeles:
   Fleming H. Revell Co., 1953), p. 22, 20; Italics Rogers's. Billy
   Graham, *The Secret of Happiness* (Garden City: Doubleday and
   Co., Inc., 1955), p. 1. In the nonfiction class, Marshall's book
   was the sixth best seller in 1950, Sheen's book the ninth best
   seller in 1949, Rogers's book the fourth best seller in 1953, and
   Graham's book the seventh best seller in 1955.
4. Eckert Goodman, "Richard Rodgers: Still Stage-Struck," *Reader's
   Digest* LXIII (Nov., 1953), 91 (condensed from *Harper's Magazine*); Eleanor Ruggles, "Destiny's Child," *Reader's Digest* LXIII
   (Nov., 1953), 137.
5. Jacob Hay, "Port of Little Ships," *The Saturday Evening Post* (hereafter referred to as *SEP*) CCXXII (Oct. 1, 1949), 112; Robert D.
   Wilcox, "Goldfish Made Him a Millionaire," *SEP* CCXXIII (May 5,
   1951), 17; George Sessions Perry, "Can This Man Clean Up New
   York?" *SEP* CCXXVIII (Nov. 12, 1955), 32.
6. Robert K. Merton, "Social Structure and Anomie," in *Social Theory
   and Social Structure*, revised and enlarged edition. (Glencoe,
   Illinois: The Free Press of Glencoe, 1963), pp. 131-160, esp. 134;
   Heinz and Rowena Ansbacher, eds., *The Individual Psychology of*

Alfred Adler (New York: Harper and Row, Publishers, 1967), pp. 317–318.

7. Cf. Hendrik M. Ruitenbeck, *The Individual and the Crowd: A Study of Identity in America* (New York: Thomas Nelson and Sons, 1964), pp. 104–123, 131–132 for a discussion of the relationship between identity, anomie and ultraconservative and paranoid activities.

8. James Gardner, quoted in Goldman, *The Crucial Decade*, p. 50.

9. James Hilton, quoted from his *New York Herald Tribune* review of *Nineteen Eighty-Four*, preceding George Orwell, "Nineteen Eighty-Four," *Reader's Digest* LV (Sept., 1949), 129 (condensed from the book by George Orwell); William Hard, "The Fight at Niagara," *Reader's Digest* LXIII (Aug., 1953), 31; Editors, "The Fair Deal is Part of Truman's Propaganda," *SEP* CCXXII (June 30, 1949), 10.

10. E. T. Leech, "The 'Gimmees' Sap the Nation's Strength," *Reader's Digest* LIV (March, 1949), 87 (condensed from *The Pittsburgh Press*).

11. Goldman, *The Crucial Decade—and After*, p. 213.

12. Abraham Lincoln Kilby, "A Missouri Mailman Looks at Britain," *SEP* CCXXIII (June 2, 1951), 26, 134.

13. Richard Hirsh, "The Soviet Spies," *Reader's Digest* L (May, 1947), 127–152; John T. Flynn, "Who Owns Your Child's Mind?" *Reader's Digest* LIX (Oct., 1951), 23, 24; Mrs. Thomas White, quoted in Goldman, *The Crucial Decade—and After*, p. 258.

14. Goldman, *The Crucial Decade—and After*, pp. 137–139.

15. H. I. Phillips, "Some Sneer, Some Don't," *Reader's Digest* LXIII (Aug., 1953), 26 (condensed from *New York World-Telegram* and *The Sun*).

16. Theodore Adorno, *The Authoritarian Personality* (New York: Harper and Brothers, Publishers, 1950), p. 676; see also Richard Hofstadter, *The Paranoid Style in American Politics* (New York: Alfred A. Knopf, 1966), pp. 43–44.

17. Jack Alexander, "The Great Gabbo," *SEP* CCIX (March 15, 1947), 47, 15, 16.

18. Ibid., 52.

19. Ibid., 15, 16, 56.

20. Ibid., 47.

21. Ibid., 17.

22. Gabriel Heatter in "Letters to the Editors," *SEP* CCIX (April 26, 1947), 4.

23. Cf. Ernest Schachtel, *Metamorphosis* (New York: Basic Books, Inc., Publishers, 1959), pp. 37–44.

24. William Campbell Gault, "Murder Car," *SEP* CCXXIII (June 2,

1951), 58; Bernice Fitz-Gibbon, "Wanted: More Bounce to the Ounce," *Reader's Digest* LIX (Oct., 1951), 3 (from *Harper's Bazaar*). Italics Fitz-Gibbon's.

25. Donald Meyer, *The Positive Thinkers* (Garden City: Doubleday and Company, Inc., 1965), pp. 282, 287.

26. Norman Vincent Peale, *The Power of Positive Thinking* (Englewood Cliffs, New Jersey: Prentice-Hall, Inc., 1953), pp. 1, 142. Peale's book was the sixth best seller in the nonfiction class in 1952 and the second best seller from 1953 through 1955. Norman Vincent Peale, *A Guide to Confident Living* (Englewood Cliffs, New Jersey: Prentice-Hall, Inc., 1948), pp. 46, 64, 115. *A Guide to Confident Living* was the ninth best seller in the nonfiction class in 1948 and the tenth best seller in 1949.

27. Peale, *The Power of Positive Thinking*, p. 22.

28. Ibid., pp. 120, 116, 106.

29. Norman Vincent Peale, *Stay Alive All Your Life* (Englewood Cliffs, New Jersey: Prentice-Hall, Inc., 1957), p. 114; Peale, *The Power of Positive Thinking*, pp. 205–209, esp. 208; Norman Vincent Peale, "Man, Morals and Maturity," *Reader's Digest* LXXXVII (Oct., 1965), 287.

30. Peale, *The Power of Positive Thinking*, pp. 16, 64, 66. Peale gave credit for the term "flash prayers" to Frank Laubach, *Prayer, the Mightiest Power in the World*.

31. Peale, *The Power of Positive Thinking*, p. ix.

32. Dale Carnegie, *How to Stop Worrying and Start Living* (New York: Simon and Schuster, Inc., 1948), pp. 52, 53, 54. Carnegie's book was the second best seller in the nonfiction class in 1948.

33. Ibid., p. 153.

34. Martin Marty, *The New Shape of American Religion* (New York: Harper and Row, Publishers, 1959), p. 10. Italics Marty's.

35. Ibid., pp. 15, 39.

36. Peter Marshall, in Catherine Marshall, ed., *Mr. Jones, Meet the Master*, p. 44; Billy Graham, *The Secret of Happiness*, p. 108.

37. Arthur W. Baum, "Everybody Wants to Be a Sailor," *SEP* CCXXVI (Oct. 10, 1953), 24–25, 126, 129, 131; Robert Froman, "Even You Can Own an Island," *SEP* CCXXII (July 30, 1949), 17–19, 45.

38. Margaret Blair Johnstone, "Sanctuary Is Where You Find It," *Reader's Digest* LXII (May, 1953), 123 (condensed from *Guideposts*).

39. Arthur Link and William Catton, *American Epoch* (New York: Alfred A. Knopf, 1965), p. 661; Marty, *The New Shape of American Religion*, p. 15.

40. Humphrey, Weeks and Wilson, quoted in Goldman, *The Crucial Decade—and After*, pp. 240, 239, 242.

Chapter 6.

1. Hugh Morrow, "The Success of an Utter Failure," *The Saturday Evening Post* (hereafter referred to as *SEP*) CCXXIX (Jan. 12, 1957), 34.
2. Charles Schultz, quoted ibid., 73.
3. Ibid., 34.
4. Stanley Hyman, "The Tragic Vision," *SEP* CCXXXI (June 13, 1959), 52; Catherine Marshall, *To Live Again* (New York: McGraw-Hill Book Co., Inc., 1957); Abigail Van Buren, *Dear Abby* (Englewood Cliffs, N. J.: Prentice-Hall, Inc., 1958). In the nonfiction class, Marshall's book was the fourth best seller in 1957 and Van Buren's book was the ninth best seller in 1958.
5. Norman Vincent Peale, *Stay Alive All Your Life* (Englewood Cliffs, N. J.: Prentice-Hall, Inc., 1957), pp. 121, 105. Peale's book was the third best seller in the nonfiction class in 1957. Eric Hoffer, in "Points to Ponder," *Reader's Digest* LXXI (July, 1957), 183 (quoted from *Harper's Magazine*); Howard Upton, "Had Enough of the Old Rat Race?" *SEP* CCXXX (Dec. 7, 1957), 117, 118.
6. Upton, "Had Enough of the Old Rat Race?" *SEP*, 118. Italics Upton's.
7. Peale, *Stay Alive All Your Life*, pp. 9, 94, 136, 158.
8. Ibid., pp. 22, 173, 4.
9. Vance Packard, *The Status Seekers* (New York: D. McKay Company, 1959), pp. 8, 317–318. Packard's book, which was a critique of American mobility rather than a self help book, was the fourth best seller in the nonfiction class in 1959.
10. Ibid., pp. 358, 329, 359, 290, 317.
11. Stewart Alsop, "How's Kennedy Doing?" *SEP* CCXXXIV (Sept. 16, 1961), 44.
12. Ibid., 44.
13. Arthur Gordon, "The Rewards of Caring," *Reader's Digest* LXXXIII (Oct., 1963), 84, 81 (condensed from *Guideposts*). Italics Gordon's.
14. Morton Hunt, "Get Involved!" *Reader's Digest* LXXVIII (March, 1961), 258, 259 (condensed from *Today's Living*).
15. Vice Admiral H. G. Rickover, "The Decline of the Individual," *SEP* CCXXXVI (March 30, 1963), 12; I. A. R. Wylie, "The Quest of Our Lives," *Reader's Digest* LXXIX (Sept., 1961), 129–132.
16. Ayn Rand, quoted in John Kobler, "The Curious Cult of Ayn Rand," *SEP* CCXXXIV (Nov. 11, 1961), 98, 99.
17. Charles Stevenson, "Must We Have Relief Programs That Make Chronic Dependents?" *Reader's Digest* LXXIX (Dec., 1961), 59; Robert S. Strother, "Self-Help: An Answer to Urban Renewal," *Reader's Digest* LXXXVI (Feb., 1965), 223–226 (condensed from *National Civic Review*).

18. Olin D. Johnson, U. S. Senator from South Carolina, "The Good Side of the South," *Reader's Digest* LXXIX (Dec., 1961), 117–118, 118, 120, 119 (condensed from *The New York Times Magazine*).

19. "Who Are the Poor," *SEP* CCXXXVI (Dec. 21–28, 1963), 37.

20. Lyndon Johnson, quoted in Paul Y. Hammond, *The Cold War Years: American Foreign Policy Since 1945* (New York: Harcourt, Brace and World, Inc., 1969), p. 214.

21. For an analysis of the limited effects which Kennedy's and Johnson's programs had on American poverty, see Herman Miller, *Rich Man, Poor Man* (New York: Crowell, 1970).

22. For an interesting discussion of the style and spirit of Kennedy and their effects on adults and youths, see John Ward, *Red, White and Blue* (New York: Oxford University Press, 1969), pp. 142–151. Also, regarding the detrimental effect that image-seeking exerted on Kennedyism, see Christopher Lasch, *The New Radicalism in America: 1889–1963* (New York: Vintage Books, 1967), pp. 313–318.

23. Charles Schultz, *Happiness Is a Warm Puppy* (New York: Determined Productions, 1963); Charles Schultz, *Security Is a Thumb and a Blanket* (New York: Determined Productions, 1963); Charles Schultz, *I Need All the Friends I Can Get* (New York: Determined Productions, 1964); Charles Schultz, *Christmas Is Together-Time* (New York: Determined Productions, 1964). *Happiness* and *Security* were the first and second best sellers in 1963; *Friends* and *Christmas* were the second and fifth best sellers in 1964.

24. Melvin Durslag, "Dr. Kildare Is a Doll," *SEP* CCXXXVI (March 30, 1963), 15; Ernie Davis with Bob August, "'I'm Not Unlucky,'" *SEP* CCXXXVI (March 30, 1963), 60; Bill Davidson, "Buck$ Benny Rides Again," *SEP* CCXXXVI (March 2, 1963), 27.

25. Oscar Schisgall, "The Village Where People Cared," *Reader's Digest* LXXXVI (Feb., 1965), 55; Leland Stowe, "Miracle at Vicos," *Reader's Digest* LXXXII (April, 1963), 222.

26. Shirley Jackson, "The Possibility of Evil," *SEP* CCXXXVIII (Dec. 18, 1965), 69; black American quoted in Ben H. Bagdikian, "The Black Immigrants," *SEP* CCXL (July 15, 1967), 68.

27. Wayne Amos, "Riley's Route to the Eternal Now," *Reader's Digest* LXXXVI (Feb., 1965), 228, 230.

28. William K. Zinsser, "Good-By, Burma Shave," *Reader's Digest* LXXXVI (Feb., 1965), 104 (condensed from *The Saturday Evening Post*). Italics Zinsser's.

29. Paul Gallico, "Wildest Ride in the World," *Reader's Digest* LXX (Jan., 1957), 69 (condensed from *True*); John Knowles, "Half

Man—Half Fish," *Reader's Digest* LXXV (Aug., 1959), 97 (condensed from *Holiday*); Phil Edwards, "You Should Have Been Here An Hour Ago," *SEP* CCXL (July 1, 1967), 33.

30. "Water Torture," *SEP* CCXXXVI (Aug. 24–31, 1963), 32.

31. William K. Zinsser, "The Big Bond Bonanza," *SEP* CCXXXVIII (July 17, 1965), 77.

32. Charles H. Brower, "Let's Dare to Be Square," *Reader's Digest* LXXXII (April, 1963), 50, 51; James A. Farley, "A Creed for a Time of Danger," *Reader's Digest* LXXXIII (July, 1963), 49–52.

33. Barry Goldwater, quoted in Stewart Alsop, "Can Barry Goldwater Win?" *SEP* CCXXXVI (Aug. 24–31, 1963), 21, 24.

34. Rollo May, *Love and Will* (New York: W. W. Norton and Co., Inc., 1969), pp. 14, 16, 13.

35. Maxwell Maltz, "How to Stand Up Under Stress," *Reader's Digest* LXXVIII (June, 1961), 45.

36. Billy Graham, *World Aflame* (Garden City, N. Y.: Doubleday and Co., Inc., 1965), pp. xiii–xiv, 2, 42, 45, 138–139, 170, 181–182, 185–186, 203. Graham's book was the fourth best selling book in the nonfiction class in 1965.

37. Joan Didion, "The Hippie Generation: Slouching Towards Bethlehem," *SEP* CCXL (Sept. 23, 1967), 94; Buell G. Gallagher, "Our Students Have No Utopia," *SEP* CCXL (May 6, 1967), 10.

38. Norman Vincent Peale, "Man, Morals and Maturity," *Reader's Digest* LXXXVII (Oct., 1965), 277, 269, 268, 267, 265, 256, 280, 281–283, 285; Jonathan Miller, "I Won't Pay for the Trip," *Reader's Digest* XCI (Dec., 1967), 131, 134 (condensed from *Vogue*).

39. Ernest Havemann, "Modern Courtship: The Great Illusion?" *Reader's Digest* LXXIX (Dec., 1961), 82, 81, 80 (condensed from *Life*). Havemann gave credit to Drs. James H. H. Bossard and Clifford Kirkpatrick for some of his ideas.

40. April Ousler Armstrong, "Let's Keep Christmas Commercial," *SEP* CCXXXVIII (Dec. 18, 1965), 10; D. W. Brogan, "Hypocrisy Is No Sin," *SEP* CCXXXVIII (Aug. 14, 1965), 10, 14; Spencer Brown, "What's the Matter with the Younger Generation?" *Reader's Digest* XC (March, 1967), 58, 59–60 (condensed from *New York Times Magazine*).

41. Hervey Allen, no title, *Reader's Digest* XC (June, 1967), 164. Italics Allen's. John A. Logan, "The Crisis on Our Campuses," *Reader's Digest* LXXXVI (Feb., 1965), 126 (condensed from *Town and Country*); "What Parents Think About Campus Morals," *Reader's Digest* LXXXVI (May, 1965), 141, 142 (condensed from *Town and Country*).

42. For an extended discussion of the growth of awareness and confu-

sion of the counterculture upon which I am basing my remarks concerning the dysfunctional behavior rhetoric which unfortunately short-circuited part of the youthful rebellion, see Lawrence Chenoweth, "The Rhetoric of Hope and Despair: A Study of the Jimi Hendrix Experience and the Jefferson Airplane," *American Quarterly* XXIII (Spring, 1971), 25–45.

43. Morton Shulman, *Anyone Can Make a Million* (New York: Bantam Books, 1967); Adam Smith, *The Money Game* (New York: Dell Publishing Co., Inc., 1969); Robert Townsend, *Up the Organization* (New York: Alfred A. Knopf, 1970), esp. p. 142.

44. Paul McCracken, quoted in J. A. Livingston, "McCracken: A Babe Ruth or Fred Merkle," *Milwaukee Journal* (Feb. 11, 1971), 22.

45. *The New York Times*, August 24, 1956, p. 10; *The New York Times*, July 29, 1960, p. 9. I am indebted to a former student of mine, James Lapsley, for finding the statements which are included in this section. These quotations formed part of the basis for an excellent but unfortunately unpublished paper done by this student which was entitled "Richard Nixon: See How He Runs."

46. Richard Nixon, quoted in Robert B. Semple, Jr., "A Crisis of Spirit in U. S., Nixon Says," *The New York Times*, Feb. 4, 1968, p. 31.

47. *The New York Times*, July 29, 1960, p. 9; *The New York Times*, Jan. 21, 1969, p. 21.

48. *The New York Times*, August 9, 1968, p. 20.

Epilogue

1. My definition of autonomy and most of the psychological assumptions I make in this epilogue are based on: Otto Rank, *Will Therapy Truth and Reality* (New York: Alfred A. Knopf, 1968); Ernest Schachtel, *Metamorphosis* (New York: Basic Books, Inc., Publishers, 1959); and Rollo May, *Power and Innocence* (New York: W. W. Norton and Company, Inc., 1972).

2. Schachtel, *Metamorphosis*, pp. 5, 6, 9, 15, 25, 54, 132, 150.

3. Richard Nixon, "A New Feeling of Self-Discipline," *U. S. News and World Report* (Nov. 20, 1972), 73. Excerpts from interview with Garnett D. Horner, published originally in *The Washington* (D. C.) *Star-News*.

4. Ibid., 73.

5. Michael Harrington, *Toward a Democratic Left* (Baltimore: Penguin Books Inc., 1969), pp. 57, 62; Gabriel Kolko, *Wealth and Power in America* (New York: Frederick A. Praeger, Publishers, 1966), pp. 94–95, 39.

6. Conference on Economic Progress, *Poverty and Deprivation in the United States* (Washington, 1962), pp. 20, 22, 29.

7. Cf., May, *Power and Innocence*, esp. p. 250.

8. Cf., Schachtel, *Metamorphosis*, pp. 279–322.

BIBLIOGRAPHY

Primary Sources

Self Help and Inspirational Books

Alger, Horatio, *Ragged Dick and Mark, the Match Boy*. New York: Collier Books, 1962.

Barton, Bruce, *The Book Nobody Knows*. Indianapolis: The Bobbs-Merrill Company, 1926.

_____, *The Man Nobody Knows*. Indianapolis: The Bobbs-Merrill Company, 1925.

Bettger, Frank, *How I Raised Myself from Failure to Success in Selling*. Englewood Cliffs, New Jersey: Prentice-Hall, Inc., 1958.

Boone, Pat, *'Twixt Twelve and Twenty*. Englewood Cliffs, New Jersey: Prentice-Hall, Inc., 1958.

Brande, Dorothea (Thompson), *Wake Up and Live!* New York: Simon and Schuster, Inc., 1936.

Carnegie, Dale, *How to Stop Worrying and Start Living*. New York: Simon and Schuster, Inc., 1948.

_____, *How to Win Friends and Influence People*. New York: Simon and Schuster, Inc., 1937.

Coué, Emile, *Self-Mastery Through Conscious Autosuggestion*. New York: American Library Service, 1922.

Dimnet, Ernest, *The Art of Thinking*. New York: Simon and Schuster, Inc., 1932.

_____, *What We Live By*. New York: Simon and Schuster, Inc., 1932.

Dorsey, George, *Why We Behave Like Human Beings*. New York: Harper and Brothers, 1925.

Du Nuoy, Lecomte, *Human Destiny*. New York: Longman's, Green, 1947.

Fairbanks, Douglas, *Laugh and Live*. New York: Britton Publishing Company, 1917.

Fosdick, Harry Emerson, *On Being a Real Person*. New York: Harper and Brothers, 1943.

Graham, Billy (William Franklin), *The Secret of Happiness*. Garden City, New York: Doubleday and Company, Inc., 1955.

_____, *World Aflame*. Garden City, New York: Doubleday and Company, Inc., 1965.

Hauser, Gaylord, *Look Younger, Live Longer*. New York: Farrar, Strauss, 1950.

Hayes, Helen, *A Gift of Joy*. Greenwich, Connecticut: Fawcett Publications, Inc., 1965.

Hillis, Marjorie (Roulston), *Live Alone and Like It*. Indianapolis: The Bobbs-Merrill Company, 1936.

_____, *Orchids on Your Budget*. Indianapolis: The Bobbs-Merrill Company, 1937.

Jacobson, Edmund, *You Must Relax*. New York: Whittlesey House, McGraw-Hill Book Company, Inc., 1934.

Liebman, Joshua Loth, *Peace of Mind*. New York: Simon and Schuster, Inc., 1946.

Link, Henry Charles, *The Return to Religion*. New York: The Macmillan Company, 1936.

Marshall, Catherine, *Mr. Jones, Meet the Master*. Los Angeles: Fleming H. Revell Company, 1949.

_____, *To Live Again*. New York: McGraw-Hill Book Company, Inc., 1957.

Merton, Thomas, *The Seven Story Mountain*. New York: Harcourt, Brace and Company, 1948.

Overstreet, H. A., *The Mature Mind*. New York: W. W. Norton and Company, Inc., 1949.

Papini, Giovanni, *Life of Christ*. New York: Harcourt, Brace and Company, 1923.

Peale, Norman Vincent, *A Guide to Confident Living*. Englewood Cliffs, New Jersey: Prentice-Hall, Inc., 1948.

_____, *The Power of Positive Thinking*. Englewood Cliffs, New Jersey: Prentice-Hall, Inc., 1956.

_____, *Stay Alive All Your Life*. Englewood Cliffs, New Jersey: Prentice-Hall, Inc., 1957.

Pitkin, Walter Boughton, *Life Begins at Forty*. New York: Whittlesey House, McGraw-Hill Book Company, Inc., 1932.

Rogers, Dale Evans, *Angel Unaware*. Los Angeles: Fleming H. Revell Company, 1953.

Roth, Lillian, *I'll Cry Tomorrow*. New York: Frederick Fell, Inc., Publishers, 1954.

Schindler, John A., *How to Live 365 Days a Year*. Englewood Cliffs, New Jersey: Prentice-Hall, Inc., 1954.

Sheen, Fulton, *Life Is Worth Living*. New York: McGraw-Hill Book
    Company, Inc., 1953.
_____, *Peace of Soul*. New York: Whittlesey House, McGraw-Hill Book
    Company, Inc., 1949.
Shulman, Morton, *Anyone Can Make a Million*. New York: McGraw-Hill
    Book Company, Inc., 1966.
Smith, Adam, *The Money Game*. New York: Dell Publishing Company,
    Inc., 1969.
Swing, Raymond, ed., *This I Believe*, Vol. II. New York: Simon and
    Schuster, Inc., 1954.
Townsend, Robert, *Up the Organization*. New York: Alfred A. Knopf,
    1970.
Van Buren, Abigail, *Dear Abby*. Englewood Cliffs, New Jersey: Prentice-
    Hall, Inc., 1958.
Young, Vash, *A Fortune to Share*. Indianapolis: The Bobbs-Merrill
    Company, 1932.

Cartoon and Comic Strip Sources

Galewitz, Herb, ed., *The Celebrated Cases of Dick Tracy, 1931–1951*.
    New York: Chelsea House, 1970.
Gray, Harold, *Arf! The Life and Hard Times of Little Orphan Annie*,
    1935–1945. New Rochelle, New York: Arlington House, 1970.
Mauldin, Bill, *Back Home*. New York: William Sloan Associates, Pub-
    lishers, 1947.
_____, *Up Front*. New York: Henry Holt and Company, 1945.
Schultz, Charles, *Christmas Is Together-Time*. New York: Determined
    Productions, 1964.
_____, *Happiness Is a Warm Puppy*. New York: Determined Produc-
    tions, 1963.
_____, *I Need All the Friends I Can Get*. New York: Determined Pro-
    ductions, 1964.
_____, *Security Is a Thumb and a Blanket*. New York: Determined
    Productions, 1963.
Superman from the Thirties to the Seventies. New York: Crown Pub-
    lishers, Inc., 1971.

Miscellaneous

Day, Donald, ed., *Sanity Is Where You Find It*. Boston: Houghton
    Mifflin Company, 1955.

Lait, Jack, ed., *Will Rogers Wit and Wisdom.* New York: Frederick A. Stokes Company, 1936.

Love, Paula McSpadden, ed., *The Will Rogers Book.* Indianapolis: The Bobbs-Merrill Company, 1961.

Periodicals

Reader's Digest
The Saturday Evening Post

Secondary Sources

Books on the Dream of Success

Cawelti, John G., *Apostles of the Self-Made Man.* Chicago: University of Chicago Press, 1968.

Huber, Richard M., *The American Idea of Success.* New York: McGraw-Hill Book Company, 1971.

Kennedy, Gail, ed., *Democracy and the Gospel of Wealth.* Boston: D. C. Heath and Co., 1949.

Meyer, Donald B., *The Positive Thinkers.* Garden City, New York: Doubleday and Company, Inc., 1965.

Rischin, Moses, ed., *The American Gospel of Success.* Chicago: Quadrangle Books, 1965.

Weiss, Richard, *The American Myth of Success.* New York: Basic Books, Inc., Publishers, 1969.

Wyllie, Irvin Gordon, *The Self-Made Man in America.* New Brunswick, New Jersey: Rutgers University Press, 1954.

Articles on the Dream of Success

Griswold, A. Whitney, "New Thought: A Cult of Success," *American Journal of Sociology,* XL (Nov., 1934), 309–318.

Books on American Character

de Tocqueville, Alexis, *Democracy in America,* Vols. I, II. New York: Vintage Books, 1961.

Hartz, Louis, *The Liberal Tradition in America*. New York: Harcourt, Brace and Company, 1955.

Petersen, William, ed., *American Social Patterns*. Garden City, New York: Doubleday and Company, Inc., 1956.

Potter, David Morris, *People of Plenty*. Chicago: University of Chicago Press, 1963.

Riesman, David, Nathan Glazer and Reuel Denney, *The Lonely Crowd*. Garden City, New York: Doubleday and Company, Inc., 1953.

Slater, Philip E., *The Pursuit of Loneliness: American Culture at the Breaking Point*. Boston: Beacon Press, 1970.

Ward, John William, *Red, White, and Blue*. New York: Oxford University Press, 1969.

Williams, Robin Murphy, *American Society: A Sociological Interpretation*. Second ed., rev., New York: Alfred A. Knopf, 1960.

Books on Content Analysis, Mass Media and Best Selling Publications

Bainbridge, John, *The Little Wonder: Or, The Reader's Digest and How It Grew*. New York: Reynal and Hitchcock, 1946.

Berelson, Bernard, *Content Analysis in Communication Research*. Glencoe, Illinois: Free Press of Glencoe, 1952.

_____, and Morris Janowitz, eds., *Reader in Public Opinion and Communication*. Glencoe, Illinois: Free Press of Glencoe, 1953.

Couperie, Pierre, and Maurice C. Horn, *A History of the Comic Strip*. New York: Crown Publishers, Inc., 1968.

Hackett, Alice Payne, *Seventy Years of Best Sellers, 1895–1965*. New York: R. R. Bowker Company, 1967.

Hart, James D., *The Popular Book*. New York: Oxford University Press, 1950.

Huebel, Harry Russell, ed., *Things in the Driver's Seat: Readings in Popular Culture*. Chicago: Rand McNally and Company, 1972.

Mott, Frank Luther, *Golden Multitudes*. New York: R. R. Bowker Company, 1956.

Peterson, Theodore, *Magazines in the Twentieth Century*, 2nd ed. Urbana: University of Illinois Press, 1964.

Rosenberg, Bernard, and David Manning White, eds., *Mass Culture*. Glencoe, Illinois: Free Press of Glencoe, 1963.

Schramm, Wilbur Land, ed., *Mass Communications*. Urbana: University of Illinois Press, 1960.

Steinberg, Charles Side, *The Mass Communicators*. New York: Harper and Brothers, 1958.

_____, ed., *Mass Media and Communication*. New York: Hastings House, 1966.

Waugh, Coulton, *The Comics*. New York: The Macmillan Company, 1947.

Wilson, Louis Round, ed., *The Practice of Book Selection*. Chicago: University of Chicago Press, 1940.

Wood, James Playsted, *Magazines in the United States*. New York: Ronald Press Company, 1956.

_____, *Of Lasting Interest: The Story of The Reader's Digest*. Garden City, New York: Doubleday and Company, Inc., 1958.

Articles on Magazine Analysis

Halsey, Van. R., "Fiction and the Businessman: Society Through All Its Literature," *American Quarterly*, XI, No. 3, (Fall, 1959), 391–402.

Klapp, Orrin, "The Creation of Popular Heroes," *American Journal of Sociology*, LIV (Sept., 1948), 135–141.

_____, "Hero Worship in America," *American Sociological Review*, XIV (Feb., 1949), 53–62.

Lazarfeld, Paul, "Magazines in Ninety Cities: Who Reads What?" *Public Opinion Quarterly*, I (Oct., 1937), 29–41.

Psychology

Adler, Alfred, *The Practice and Theory of Individual Psychology*, rev. ed. London: Routledge and Kegan Paul, Ltd., 1955.

_____, *The Science of Living*. Garden City, New York: Garden City Publishing Company, 1929.

Adorno, Theodore W., *The Authoritarian Personality*. New York: Harper and Brothers, 1950.

Ansbacher, Heinz Ludwig and Rowena R., eds., *The Individual Psychology of Alfred Adler*. New York: Harper and Row, Publishers, 1967.

Brown, Norman Oliver, *Life Against Death*. Middletown, Connecticut: Wesleyan University Press, 1959.

Freud, Sigmund, *Civilization and Its Discontents*. London: The Hogarth Press, Ltd., 1957.

Hook, Sidney, *The Quest for Being*. New York: St. Martin's Press, 1961.

Horney, Karen, *The Neurotic Personality of Our Time*. New York: W. W. Norton and Company, 1937.

Laing, R. D., *The Divided Self*. Baltimore: Penguin Books, 1960.

Lynd, Helen, *On Shame and the Search for Identity*. New York: Harcourt, Brace and Company, 1958.

May, Rollo, *Love and Will*. New York: W. W. Norton and Company, Inc., 1969.

_____, *Man's Search for Himself*. New York: W. W. Norton and Company, Inc., 1953.

_____, *Power and Innocence*. New York: W. W. Norton and Company, Inc., 1972.

McClelland, David Clarence, *The Achieving Society*. Princeton, New Jersey: Van Nostrand, 1961.

Rank, Otto, *Will Therapy and Truth and Reality*. New York: Alfred A. Knopf, 1968.

Reik, Theodor, *Myth and Guilt*. New York: G. Braziller, 1957.

Ruitenbeek, Hendrik Marinus, *The Individual and the Crowd: A Study of Identity in America*. New York: Nelson, 1965.

Schachtel, Ernest G., *Metamorphosis*. New York: Basic Books, Inc., Publishers, 1959.

Stein, Maurice Robert, David Manning White and Arthur J. Vidich, eds., *Identity and Anxiety*. Glencoe, Illinois: Free Press of Glencoe, 1960.

Wheelis, Allen, *The Quest for Identity*. New York: W. W. Norton and Company, Inc., 1958.

Articles

Hollingshed, A. B., R. Ellis, and E. Kirby, "Social Mobility and Mental Illness," *American Sociological Review*, XIX (1954), 577–584.

History

Abrams, Richard M., and Lawrence W. Levine, eds., *The Shaping of Twentieth Century America*. Boston: Little, Brown and Company, 1965.

Allen, Frederick Lewis, *Since Yesterday, 1929–1939*. New York: Bantam Books, 1965.

Bakke, Edward Wight, *Citizens Without Work*. New Haven: Yale University Press, 1940.

Cash, Wilbur Joseph, *The Mind of the South*. New York: Alfred A. Knopf, 1950.

Diamond, Sigmund, *The Reputation of the American Businessman*. New York: Harper and Row, Publishers, 1966.

Faulkner, Harold, *Politics, Reform, and Expansion: 1890–1900.* New York: Harper and Row, Publishers, 1963.

Fine, Sidney, *Laissez-Faire and the General-Welfare State.* Ann Arbor, Michigan: University of Michigan Press, 1964.

Friedel, Frank, *The New Deal and the American People.* Englewood Cliffs, New Jersey: Prentice-Hall, Inc., 1964.

Goldman, Eric Frederick, *The Crucial Decade—And After.* New York: Alfred A. Knopf, 1960.

Goldman, Jack, ed., *While You Were Gone.* New York: Simon and Schuster, Inc., 1946.

Hammond, Paul Y., *The Cold War Years: American Foreign Policy Since 1945.* New York: Harcourt, Brace and World, Inc., 1969.

Hicks, John Donald, *Republican Ascendancy.* New York: Harper and Row, Publishers, 1960.

Hofstadter, Richard, *The Age of Reform.* New York: Alfred A. Knopf, 1965.

_____, *The American Political Tradition.* New York: Alfred A. Knopf, 1948.

_____, *The Paranoid Style in American Politics.* New York: Alfred A. Knopf, 1967.

_____, *Social Darwinism in American Thought.* Boston: Beacon Press, 1955.

Hurst, James Willard, *Law and the Conditions of Freedom in the Nineteenth Century United States.* Madison: University of Wisconsin Press, 1964.

Johnson, Walter, *1600 Pennsylvania Avenue.* Boston: Little, Brown and Company, 1960.

Lasch, Christopher, *The New Radicalism in America: 1889–1963.* New York: Random House, Inc., Vintage Books, 1965.

Leuchtenburg, William Edward, *Franklin D. Roosevelt and the New Deal.* New York: Harper and Row, Publishers, 1963.

_____, *The Perils of Prosperity, 1914–32.* Chicago: University of Chicago Press, 1963.

Lynd, Robert Staughton and Helen Merrell, *Middletown in Transition.* New York: Harcourt, Brace and Company, 1937.

Marty, Martin E., *The New Shape of American Religion.* New York: Harper and Row, Publishers, 1959.

May, Henry Farnham, *Protestant Churches and Industrial America.* New York: Harper and Row, Publishers, 1949.

McConnell, Grant, *Private Power and American Democracy.* New York: Alfred A. Knopf, 1966.

Ogburn, William Fielding, ed., *American Society in Wartime.* Chicago: The University of Chicago Press, 1944.

Prothro, James, *The Dollar Decade: Business Ideas in the 1920s.* Baton
Rouge, Louisiana: Louisiana State University Press, 1954.

Schlesinger, Jr., Arthur M., *The Crisis of the Old Order, 1919-1933.*
Boston: Houghton Mifflin Company, Sentry edition, 1964.

_____, *The Coming of the New Deal.* Boston: Houghton Mifflin
Company, Sentry edition, 1965.

Selznic, Phillip, *TVA and the Grass-Roots.* Berkeley: University of
California Press, 1953.

Soule, George, *Prosperity Decade.* New York: Holt, Rinehart and
Winston, 1962.

Sward, Keith, *The Legend of Henry Ford.* New York: Atheneum, 1968.

Wecter, Dixon, *The Age of the Great Depression, 1929-1941.* New York:
The Macmillan Company, 1969.

White, Morton, *Social Thought in America.* Boston: Beacon Hill, 1964.

Wiebe, Robert H., *The Search for Order: 1877-1920.* New York: Hill
and Wang, 1968.

Articles

Rogin, Michael Paul, "Liberal Society and the Indian Question," *Politics
and Society,* I (May, 1971), 269-312.

Economics and Social Mobility

Caudill, Harry, *Night Comes to the Cumberlands.* Boston: Little, Brown
and Company, 1963.

Conference on Economic Progress, *Poverty and Deprivation in the
United States.* Washington, 1962.

Durkheim, Emile, *The Division of Labor in Society.* Glencoe, Illinois:
Free Press of Glencoe, 1949.

Galbraith, John Kenneth, *American Capitalism: The Concept of Countervailing Power.* Boston: Houghton Mifflin Company, 1952.

_____, *The Great Crash—1929.* Boston: Houghton Mifflin Company,
1955.

Harrington, Michael, *The Other America.* New York: The Macmillan
Company, 1964.

Kahl, Joseph Alan, *The American Class Structure.* New York: Rinehart,
1957.

Keynes, John Maynard, *Essays in Persuasion.* New York: Harcourt,
Brace and Company, 1932.

_____, *A Treatise on Money,* Vol. II. New York: Harcourt, Brace and
Company, 1930.

Kolko, Gabriel, *Wealth and Power in America*. New York: Frederick A. Praeger, Publishers, 1962.

Lipset, Seymour Martin, and Reinhard Bendix, *Social Mobility in Industrial Society*. Berkeley: University of California Press, 1966.

Mayer, Kurt, *Class and Society*, rev. ed. New York: Random House, 1964.

Miller, Herman Phillip, *Rich Man, Poor Man*. New York: Crowell, 1964.

Newcomer, Mable, *The Big Business Executive: The Factors That Made Him, 1900-1950*. New York: Columbia University Press, 1957.

Sorokin, Pitirim Aleksandrovich, *Social and Cultural Mobility*. Glencoe, Illinois: Free Press of Glencoe, 1959.

Thernstrom, Stephan, *Poverty and Progress: Social Mobility in a Nineteenth Century City*. New York: Atheneum, 1964.

Social Structure and Thought

Lipset, Seymour Martin, and Reinhard Bendix, *Class, Status, and Power*. Glencoe, Illinois: Free Press of Glencoe, 1953.

Merton, Robert K., *Social Theory and Social Structure*, revised and enlarged. Glencoe, Illinois: Free Press of Glencoe, 1963.

Packard, Vance Oakley, *The Status Seekers*. New York: D. McKay Company, 1961.

Weber, Max, *The Protestant Ethic and the Spirit of Capitalism*. New York: Scribner, 1958.

Articles

Chinoy, Ely, "The Tradition of Opportunity and the Aspirations of Automobile Workers," *American Journal of Sociology*, LVII (1952), 453.

Lenski, Gerhard E., "Social Correlates of Religious Interest," *American Sociological Review*, 18 (1953), 533-544.

Organizational Studies

Bendix, Reinhold, *Work and Authority in Industry*. New York: John Wiley and Sons, Inc., 1956.

Ghiselli, Edwin Ernest, and Clarence W. Brown, *Personnel and Industrial Psychology*. New York: McGraw-Hill Book Company, Inc., 1955.

Marrow, Alfred Jay, *Making Management Human*. New York: McGraw-Hill Book Company, 1957.

Presthus, Robert, *The Organizational Society*. New York: Random House, Inc., Vintage Books, 1962.

Sutton, Francis X., et. al, *The American Business Creed*. Cambridge: Harvard University Press, 1956.

Whyte, William Hollingsworth, Jr., *The Organization Man*. Garden City, New York: Doubleday and Company, Inc., 1956.

INDEX

Adams, James Truslow: on conformity, 58
Adorno, Theodore: on pseudo-conservativism, 118
Alexander, Jack: on Marshall Field, 98
Alger, Horatio: compared with Barton, 49; compared with "Little Orphan Annie," 80–81; compared with "Superman," 95; and employee obedience, 35; on free will, 35; indications of middle class childishness in works of, 170; and limits on opportunity, 35; philososphy of, 34–35; and reassurance, 34–35, 166; re-invigoration of his values in the 1960s, 140–141
Allen, Hervey: on savagery of all generations, 158
Alsop, Stewart: on Kennedy, 142, 143
Ambivalence: creative use of, 168–169; and guilt, 5
Ambivalent principles in guides to living: 1, 3–5, 31; during—
    the rise of industrialism, 32–33, 33–35
    Progressive era, 38
    1917–1929, 42–45, 58–59
    the depression, 71–78, 82–89
    World War II, 94–97, 99–100
    1947–1955, 110–113
    1957–1959, 131–139
    1960s, 139–141.
    See also Tension
American dream of success: changing goals of (1957–1970), 131–135, 139–141; citizen treated as function in, 9, 12; confused defense of

in 1930s, 82–89; contradictory defense in post-World War II era, 118–122; as a corporate ideology, 10–12, 16, 31, 35–37, 42, 47–48, 50, 51–55, 67–69, 138–139, 173–174; and the counterculture, 155–157, 159–160; defended during World War II, 103–106; definition, 3; effects of World War II on, 90–96; emotional gratification as emphasized goal of, 139–141; and emotional repression, 5, 7, 15–16, 40–41, 136–138, 156–157; and future-orientation, 7; guilt induced by, 6–8, 49, 64–67, 167–168; inspirational books contrasted to, 111–112; Kennedy's views on, 141–143; money more important than life, 8; moralistic character of, 6, 48–51; moralistic critiques of, 24, 49, 98, 99, 101–102, 112, 125, 129; moralistic guides to living similar to, 126; Nixon's views on, 141, 161–163; politics as a business enterprise, 9–10, 53–55, 128; and power, 10, 18; rationalizations of, 135–139; and self-development, 5–6; social function of, 3–4, 31; and status, 137–138; supremacy as motivation of, 10; and Vietnam, 9, 152–154, 174; violent effects of, 8–9, 152–154, 158, 174; weakened defense of in 1930s, 82–87; weakened defense of in 1950s, 118–120, 122, 135–141; World War I effects on, 39–40, 8–9; World War II effects on, 90–97.
See also Content Analysis; Individ-

227

ualism; Self-Reliance; Will Power
Amos, Wayne: and middle class aestheticism, 149
Anomie: definition, 113–114; relationship to paranoia, 114
Anthony, Katharine: on friendship, 20
Anti-communism: and care, 141; and "I Spy," 151; Kennedy's sentiments on, 141–143; McCarthyism, 115–118; 1920s success advocates on, 46–47; 1960s success advocates on, 151–152; Nixon's views on 141, 162–163; The Red Scare, 46–47. *See also* Paranoia
Armstrong, April Ousler: on materialism and Christmas, 157
Autonomy: care, community and, 101–103, 108, 169; conflicts between security and independence, 169; definition, 168; Liebman's views on, 101–103, 108; self-reliance versus, 164

Bakke, E. Wight: on workers' guilt during depression, 66
Barton, Bruce: and abnegation of will power, 129; on advertising, 60; and Bernard Baruch, 55; biographical background, 47–48; on Christ, 17, 48–49; compared to Alger, 49; and confluence of success, moralistic and humanistic principles, 47–50; on power, 49, 123; on service, 49, 50
Benny, Jack: as a depression hero, 73; as a lonely image, 147; on World War II, 94–95
Berle, A.A., Jr.: on New Deal and individualism, 79
Bettger, Frank: *How I Raised Myself from Failure to Success in Selling*, 112
Black Americans: and the decline of care, 148; discussed during depression, 73–74; Nixon's policy toward, 161; and poverty, 12–13; Southern attitude toward, 145
Boling, Marion: pleasure seeking and occupational stress, 23
Bond, James: 150–151
Brande, Dorothea: and abnegation of will power, 129; "as if" philosophy

of, 15–16, 83, 84, 85; biographical information, 83; confusion over goals, 86; misuse of Adler's and Vaihinger's theories, 15–16; on power, 86
Brogan, D.W.: on Hitler and hypocrisy, 157
Brower, Charles H.: on nationalism and declining achievement motivation, 151
Brown, Charlie: indication of middle class childishness in, 170; and passivity, 166–167. *See also* "Peanuts"
Brown, Spencer: on youth and the draft, 157

Calkings, Earnest Elmo: on individual responsibility during the depression, 67
Campaigne, S/Sgt. Jameson G.: defends success ethic, 103
Cannon, Cornelia James: on compulsive diligence, 57
Care: ambivalence in "Peanuts" regarding, 29, 132–135; and anti-communism, 141; and autonomy, 168–169; and Barton, 49–50; as business service, 50–51; cathartic rhetoric of, 164; conservative attitudes toward, 144–145; conservative and liberal views of, 125–126; contrasted to sentimentalism, 27–29, 125, 147–148, 177–178; definition, 28; as dominant goal from 1957 to 1970, 131–135, 139–141; Fairbanks's ambivalence on, 43; humanistic limitations on, 27–29; and individualism, 131, 139–141; individualism and the liberal dilemma, 141–148; and Kennedy's death, 146; love, will and, 154–155; Rollo May's attitudes toward, 154–155; moralistic limitations on, 26–27, 126; 1960s ambivalence toward, 139–148; and pleasure, 148–149; and power, 177–178; and self-reliance, 144–145; success ethic's effects on, 50, 139–148, 174; and tragedy, 168–169; universality of, 126; and violence, 174
Carnegie, Andrew: on the gospel of

wealth, 36; on individualism, 36; and middle class interests, 37; paternalism of, 170

Carnegie, Dale: and abnegation of will power, 129; confusion over goals, 85–86; and emotional repression, 7; and optimism, 123; popularity of, xii, 83, 84; and power, 86; on religion, 124; on salesmanship as Golden Rule, 6; on salesmanship techniques, 7, 15, 84; on talent, 74; on virtue and failure, 67; on work, 123–124

Cash, Wilbur: on Southern guilt for the depression, 66

Child, Richard: on Calvin Coolidge, 9

Childhood: conflicting emotions of, 169; and success ethic, 6, 169–172

Civil Rights Act: as symbolic legislation, 146

Cloud, John: on 1950s island retreats, 127

Community: and autonomy, 100, 101–103, 108, 168–169; and conformity, 82, 100, 109–110; Fosdick on, 99–101; inadequacies in concept of, 108, 168; and individualism, 168; and individualism during the depression, 78–82; and individualism during World War II, 90, 91, 98–103, 108; influences of World War II on, 91, 94, 95; Liebman on, 25–26, 101–103, 108; relationship to empathy and idealism, 97; and shame, 64; during World War II, 91–92, 94–95

Confluence of beliefs: corporate ideologies and success philosophies in late 1800s, 36–37; moralism and success in 1920s, 47–51; pleasure, consumption and corporate interests in 1920s, 57–58; power, community, morality and care in "Superman" comics of 1940s, 95–96; success behavior and humanistic ideals in late 1950s and 1960s, 131–133, 139–143; success, moralistic, and pleasure-oriented advocacies of early 1950s, 126–127; success, status, consumption and corporate interests in late 1950s, 138

Conformity: as a defense mechanism, 17–18; demands for, 134–135,

109–110, 108; and immigrants, 47; Liebman's criticisms of, 101–103; psychological cost of, 40; and the Red Scare, 45–47

See also Anti-communism; Other-directedness; McCarthyism; Salesmanship

Consciousness: passivity, will power and, 166–167; and tension, 165–166

Consumption: and changing popular heroes, 56–57, 73; and emotional stress, 4, 20, 21, 23–24, 57–58, 138–139; and guilt, 59–61, 67; Hillis on, 20, 72, 74; as a necessity for economic stability and growth, 56, 70, 173; Pitkin on, 20, 72; and status, 138–139; during World War II, 92, 107

Content analysis of: changing emphasis given to material and non-material goals from 1917–1955, 112–113; changing in success formulas between 1917–1929 and 1947–1955, 110–111; success formulas in Reader's Digest and The Saturday Evening Post for—

    1917–1929, 53, 57
    1930–1939, 67, 72, 73, 88–89
    1940–1945, 104
    1947–1955, 110–111
    1957–1959, 133
    1961–1969, 140–141

success goals in Reader's Digest and The Saturday Evening Post for—

    1917–1929, 45, 52
    1930–1939, 88
    1940–1945, 93
    1947–1955, 112–113
    1957–1959, 132
    1961–1969, 140

success heroes in Reader's Digest and The Saturday Evening Post for—

    1917–1929, 51
    1930–1939, 73
    1940–1945, 93–94
    1947–1955, 113
    1957–1959, 132
    1961–1969, 140

Coolidge, Calvin: 9, 51, 54, 55, 171

Corporate interests: and the advocacy of passivity, 166; and Barton, 47,

50; Andrew Carnegie's statements for, 35–37; encouragement of childish behavior, 170–171; middle class identification with, 11–12, 37, 172–174; response to the depression, 67–69, 80–82; and paternalism, 170–172, 174; use of consumptive pleasure ethic, 22–23, 57–58, 138–139; John D. Rockefeller on, 36–37; use of Social Darwinism, 35–37; use of the success ethic, 10–12, 16, 35–37, 67–69, 173–174

Couéism: 44–45, 129

Counterculture: 155–160; and innocence, 165; relationship to consumptive pleasure ethic, 21–22

Crawford, Secretary of War; on property, 32

Cronin, A.F.: on changing values during World War II, 98

Davidson, Bill: on Jack Benny, 147

Davis, Ernie: as a lonely figure, 147

Death: as a metaphor for life in success literature, 135; and pleasure, 148–150; public tolerance of, 153, 158, 174; and the Silent Majority, 161; success ethic's effects on the meaning of, 8, 153, 158, 174

Defense mechanisms: and conformity, 18; and escapist pleasure seeking, 23–24, 126–127; pseudo-realism, 18; the uses of magic, 17. *See also* Guilt; Messianic self-descriptions; Paranoia; Positive thinking; Salesmanship

de Kruif, Paul: on community self-help, 106

Democracy: success ethic's conflicts with, 10–12, 37, 50

Depression, the: causes of, 55–56; changing attitudes toward success principles, 71–75; guilt, shame and, 64–67

Didion, Joan: on generation gap, 156

Dimnet, Ernest: on humanism and success, 24; on pleasure, success and individuality, 59

Dissenters: success advocates on, 17–18, 46–47, 87, 156–158

Dorsey, George: on diligence, pleasure and idealism, 58–59; on success and leisure, 22

Durslag, Melvin: on Richard Chamberlain, 147

Economic Opportunity. *see* Social mobility

Edwards, Phil: on boredom and surfing, 150

Eisenhower, Dwight D.: 127, 128

Emerson, Ralph Waldo: on American Dream of Success, 32–33; compared to Carnegie and Rockefeller, 37; and New Thought, 40

Emotional repression: and ambivalence, 5; and success ethic, 5, 7, 15–16, 40–41, 136–138, 156–157

Equality: ambivalent concepts of, 11; conflict with desire for supremacy, 10–11; Fairbanks's attitudes toward, 43; John Logan on, 10–11. *See also* Social mobility

Essen, Raymond: on leisure, 57

Fairbanks, Douglas: ambivalences of, 42–43; and avoidance of tension, 166; on optimism, 44

Farley, James: on anti-communism, 151

Field, Marshall: 98

Fitz-Gibbon, Bernice: on retaining success ethic, 120

Flynn, John T.: on teaching socialism, 116

Ford, Henry: Christ-like virtues attributed to, 51; of Coué, 44–45; response to the depression, 68

Fosdick, Harry Emerson: on power, community and individualism, 98–100

Francis, Connie: compulsive diligence, loneliness and, 7–8

Friendship: and Carnegie, 86, 198; compared to popularity, 138; Fairbanks's ambivalent attitudes toward, 43; Hillis on, 20; and Pitkin, 20

Froman, Robert: on purchase of islands in 1950s, 127

Galbraith, John Kenneth: on World War II experience, 91

Gallagher, Buell: on generation gap, 156

Gardner, James: on post-World War

II desires for significance, 114–115
Garrett, Garet: on causes of the depression, 68; forebodings in late 1920s, 60–61
Gary, Elbert H.: on opportunity, 52
Gault, William Campbell: on retaining success ethic, 120
Generation gap. *See* Counterculture
Goldman, Eric: on communist candy wrapper controversy, 116
Goldwater, Barry: 151–152
Gordon, Arthur: on care, 143
Graham, Billy: apocalyptic views of, 155; and guilt, 27, 126; Liebman contrasted to, 24–27, 125–126; on materialism, 24, 112, 129; and passivity, 126, 166; politics of, 27, 125–126, 155; on self-reliance, 24
Gray, Harold: "Little Orphan Annie," 80–82
Guilt: and compulsive diligence, 6–8; conformist and autonomous versions of, 176; and consumption in 1920s, 59–61; corporate scape-goating and, 67–69; cultural foundations of, 5; as a defense mechanism, 65; and the depression, 64–67; and freedom, 176; Fosdick's views on, 100; Graham's and Sheen's views on, 25–27, 126; and human-istic guides to living, 26; Liebman's views on, 102; over materialism in 1920s, 49; and moralistic guides to living, 25–26; and paranoia, 18; and pleasure, 22; and politics, 26–27; self-reliance as cause of, 14, 65, 167–168; and shame, 64–67

Hackett, Alice: and best selling books, 192–193
Hard, William: on threat of govern-ment power, 115
Harding, Warren G.: 53–54, 171
Havemann, Ernest: on marriage, 157
Hayek, Friedrich: *The Road to Serf-dom*, 105–106
Heatter, Gabriel: on success, failure and optimism, 16, 118–120
Hendrix, Jimi: apocalyptic message of, 159
Hillis, Marjorie: on budgeting, 74; on consumption, 20; on the depression and thrift, 72; on failure, 67–68;

on pleasure, 20
Hilton, James: on Orwell's *Nineteen Eighty-Four*, 115
Hoffer, Eric: on stress, 136
Hoover, Herbert: corporate-minded-ness of, 171; Marcosson on, 9; politics in the 1920s, 54–55; public reaction to, 71; response to the depression, 69–71;
Hope: characteristics of, 120
House Committee on Un-American Activities: on Shirley Temple, 87
Humanistic guides to living: attacks on pleasure and success ethics in the 1920s, 58–59; characteristics of, 24–26; definition of, 4; and guilt, 26; as inspirational literature in 1950s and 1960s, 28, 112, 125–126, 133–135, 147–148; lack of popularity in 1930s, 66; and peace, 25; relation-ship to moralistic guides during World War II, 90, 91, 98–103; and self-reliance, 24–25; social function of, 4
Humphrey, Treasury Secretary: on Hemingway, 128
Hunt, Morton: on care, 143–144
Hyman, Stanley: on tragedy, 135

Individualism: and autonomy, 168; Newton Baker on, 79–80; A.A. Berle on, 79; Earnest Elmo Calkings on, 67; and care, 131, 139–141, 154–155, 168; Andrew Carnegie on, 36; and community, 168; and community during the depression, 78–82; and community during World War II, 90, 91, 98–103, 108; Emerson's definition of, 33; Hoover on, 55; Paul Hutchinson on, 75; Kennedy liberals' views on, 141–144, 146; Liebman's criticisms of, 25, 101–102; Donald Richberg on, 79; Vice Admiral Rickover on, 144; Rockefeller on, 36; World War I effects on, 39–40; World War II effects on, 90–98. *See also* Autonomy; Self-reliance; Will power
Inspirational literature: characteristics of, 28, 112; popularity of in 1950s, 112, 124–125, 133–135; resurgence in 1960s, 147–148

Insull, Samuel: on government regulation, 52

Jackson, Shirley: on absence of care, 148
Jefferson Airplane: as indicator of countercultural trends, 160
Johnson, Lyndon: on Kennedy, 146; presidency of, 152–153
Johnson, Olin: on Southern progress and opportunity, 145
Johnstone, Margaret Blair: on positive thinking, 127

Kennedy, John F.: ambivalent philosophy of, 141–143; consequences of his assassination, 145–147; Lyndon Johnson's eulogy for, 146
Kennedyism: and conflict, 177; and image-seeking, 146–147
Kilby, Abraham: on English socialism, 116
Kiplinger, W.M.: predictions of post-World War II conservatism, 106
Kolko, Gabriel: on welfare deficiencies, 172
Koman, Bill: on football, 23–24

Leech, E.T.: on America's decline because of welfare programs, 116
Liebman, Joshua: on guilt, repression and politics, 26, 102–103; on peace of mind, 25, 101–102; on religion and psychology, 101; on self-reliance, 25, 101–103
Lilienthal, David: criticizing TVA, 106
Link, Arthur: on "bargain-counter" religions, 127
Link, Henry: and abnegation of will power, 129; authoritarian overtones in, 86–87; on businessmen as messiahs, 17; and future-orientation, 7; on liberalism, communists and self-discipline, 86–87; on obedience, 85, 171; and passivity, 166; and power, 86; on the Protestant ethic, 67; on salesmanship and conformity, 84; on salesmanship as a religion, 6
"Little Orphan Annie": 80–82; indication of middle class childishness in, 170
Livingston, Joseph: concerns about governmental power, 105
Logan, John: on equality, 10–11; on self-restraint and the generation gap, 158
Loneliness: caused by the success ethic, 5, 7–8, 167; of Connie Francis, 7–8; indications of in 1950s, 134, 135; indications of in 1960s, 147; and sensitivity groups, 149; and success, 7–8; treatment of during the depression, 81–82, 85–86; during World War II, 94–95
Luck: and Alger, 34–35; changes of emphasis on—
   in 1920s, 53
   in 1930s, 73–75
   in 1940s, 94
   in early 1950s, 110–111
   in 1960s, 141

McCarthyism: 115–118
McEvoy, J.P.: on Japanese relocation, 105
McEvoy, Peggy: on boredom and war effort, 92
Maglie, Sal: 8
Maltz, Maxwell: on psycho-cybernetics, 16, 155
Marcosson, Isaac: on business and war, 8–9; on Herbert Hoover, 9
Marshall, Catherine: on love and loneliness, 135; *The Prayers of Peter Marshall*, 112
Marshall, Rev. Peter: contrasted to Liebman, 125; on morality, materialism and the self, 98; on success and happiness, 112
Marty, Martin: on revival of religious interest, 124
Mass media: as corporate ideologists, 10
Mauldin, Bill: 96–97, 107
May, Rollo: *Love and Will*, 154–155
Messianic self-descriptions: and the generation gap, 159; individualism as a cause of, 17, 167–168; Liebman's views on, 102, 103; and New Thought, 40–41; and Nixon, 162; and paranoia, 18–19, 114
Middletown: views on opportunity during the depression, 66
Miller, Dr. John: on drugs and diligence, 156

Moralistic guides to living: attacks on the pleasure and consumption ethic in the 1920s, 58–59; attacks on success in the 1920s, 49, 58, 59; characteristics of, 24–26; definition, 4; emphasis on religion during World War II, 97–98; limitations on care and reform, 26–27, 125–126; from 1947 to 1955, 112, 125–126; and peace, 25; and self-reliance, 24–25; similarities to success ethic in 1950s, 122–124, 126; social function of, 4.
See also Harry Emerson Fosdick; Bill Graham; Peter Marshall; Giovanni Papini; Religion; Fulton Sheen

Morgan, Anne: on success ethic as a religion, 6

Morgan, Henry: on post-World War II confusion, 109

Morgan, J.P.: on New Deal, 80

Murphy, T.E.: on wartime sense of usefulness, 92

Neil, Judge Henry: on success ethic as a religion, 6

New Deal, 75–78; attitudes toward success ethic during, 79–80; conservative reactions to, 78–82; effects upon poverty, 173; Reader's Digest positions on, 78–80

New Thought Alliance: 40–41

Nixon, Richard: on the American as a child, 171–172; compared to Kennedy, 141–142; presidency of, 161–163

Nock, Albert J.: on materialism and idealism, 58

Optimism: characteristics of, 120; Emile Coué on, 44–45; as a defense mechanism, 14–18, 44–45, 120; versus hope, 120; and service clubs, 44; and suffering, 133, 135.
See also Positive thinking

Orwell, George: popularity of Nineteen Eighty-Four, 115

Other-directedness: and Barton, 48; and Brande, 84–85; and Carnegie, 84–85; as a defense mechanism, 44; development during World War I, 39–40; and Fairbanks, 42–44;

relation to corporatism and self-reliance during 1930s, 85, 89.
See also Conformity

Overstreet, H.A.: The Mature Mind, 112

Packard, Vance: on status and success, 139

Palmer, Gretta: on luck in entertainers' success, 94

Papini, Giovanni: The Life of Christ, 49

Paranoia: and anomie, 114; characteristics of, 114; description, 18–19; encouragement of by success writers, 19, 115; and House Committee on Un-American Activities, 87; individualism as a cause of, 167–168; and McCarthyism, 115–118; in post-World War II America, 113–118; and success ethic, 18–19

Passivity: and Alger, 35, 116; and Charlie Brown, 1, 29, 134–135, 167, 170; and Andrew Carnegie, 36–37; and childishness, 169; and Emile Coué, 45, 85; cultural emphasis on, 166–167, 169–172; death, pleasure and, 148–154; Graham, Sheen and, 27, 125, 155–156, 166; humanism, moralism and, 26, 29, 166; and Link, 85, 166; and Peale, 137, 166; and Social Darwinism, 35; urged during depression, 68.
See also Tension

Paxton, Harry: on wartime workers, 91

Peace: of mind, 25; of soul, 25

Peale, Norman Vincent: and abnegation of will power, 129; on anxiety, 109; on anxiety and positive thinking, 16; contradictions and misgivings in statements of, 122; and corporate obedience, 171; corporate subscriptions to works of, 10; and Coué, 123; on individualism, 137; on individual responsibility for success, 121; and passivity, 166; politics of, 121; popularity of, xii, 121; on positive thinking, 121–122; on power, 123; on public exhaustion, 136; and religion, 122–123; on success, happiness and maturity,

137; on youth, sex and self control, 156

"Peanuts": and the changing American Dream, 132–135; humanistic dilemma of, 29; indication of middle class childishness in, 170; and passivity, 166–167; popularity of in 1960s, 147

Phillips, H.I.: on 1950s Congressional investigations, 117

Pitkin, Walter: and boredom of work, 92; on diligence, 72–73, 74; on success, pleasure and friendship, 20, 21, 22

Pleasure and consumption ethic: and alienation from work, 20–21; beginnings of, 56–57; characteristics of, 19–24; as a compulsion, 22–23; corporate use of, 22–23, 138–139; and counterculture, 21–22; as a defense mechanism, 23–24; definition, 3; during the depression, 66, 72–73; differences from success ethic, 19–20; as escapism in 1950s, 126–127; and friendship, 19–20; humanistic and moralistic attacks upon, 58–59; in nervous 1960s, 148–151; and politics, 21; and positive thinking, 127; similarities to success ethic, 22–24; social function of, 3–4; and violence, 23–24, 150–151; and World War II, 92, 106.
See also Consumption

Popular magazines: positions on success ethic, 1897–1917, 39–40.
See also Content analysis

Populism: and success ethic, 38–39

Positive thinking: advocated during—
Progressive era, 40–41
1917–1929 period, 44–45
the depression, 68–69, 82–84
World War II, 104
1947–1959 period, 110–111, 118–123, 127, 133, 135–138
1960–1969, 155
as a corporate device, 16; and Couéism, 44–45; as a defense mechanism, 15–16; and emotional repression, 15–16; Gabriel Heatter on, 118–120; and New Thought, 40–41; Nixon's politics of, 161–163;

and Peale, 20–21, 121–123;

Poverty: extent of—
in 1920s, 55
in 1930s, 63, 70–71
in 1960, 145
middle class attitudes toward, 11, 172–174; Priscilla Penneypacker's views on, 82–83; rate of decline, 173.
See also Welfare programs

Power: American dream of success's emphasis on, 10; American misconceptions of, 177–178; and authoritarian tendencies, 14–15, 18–19, 86–87, 113–114, 118; and Barton, 49–50; Barton's and Peale's different positions on, 123; and care, 177–178; definition, 177; Fosdick on, 98–100; Liebman on, 101–103; and "Little Orphan Annie," 81; loss of in late 1950s and 1960s, 131, 133–135, 136; preoccupation with from 1917–1926, 45; preoccupation with in 1930s success literature, 86; as problem in 1940s, 91, 93, 95–96, 98–103, 107–108; social leaders' rationalizations concerning, 177–178; as theme in 1950s success literature, 121–123.
See also Will power

Presley, Elvis: success and loneliness, 8

Progressivism: 38–39, 170–171

Psychological stress: inability to change beliefs, 14; mental manipulations, 14–17; and self-reliance, 13–14.
See also Anomie; Guilt; Loneliness; Messianic self-descriptions; Paranoia; Shame

Rand, Ayn: on service and materialism, 144

Reader's Digest: methodology used in analyzing, ix, 192; popularity of, x–xi, 193; readership profile of, xi–xii, 194–195.
See also Content analysis

Reagan, Ronald: 9–10

Reich, Charles: on consciousness and action, 167

Religion: growing popularity during World War II, 97–98; 1950s interest in, 124–125; relation to success

ethic in 1950s, 112, 127; Southern churches' view of the depression, 66; support of the success ethic in the 1920s, 51.
See also Bruce Barton; Dale Carnegie; Harry Emerson Fosdick; Billy Graham; Joshua Liebman; Henry Link; Peter Marshall; Moralistic guides to living; Giovanni Papini; Norman Vincent Peale; Fulton Sheen

Richberg, Donald: on New Deal and individualism, 79

Rickover, Vice Admiral H.G.: on individualism and other-directedness, 144

Rockefeller, John D.: on individualism, 36

Rogers, Dale Evans: on spiritual success, 112

Rogers, Will: on Coolidge's attitude toward consumption, 72; on experts' opinions on the depression, 69

Roosevelt, Franklin D.: beliefs and policies of, 75–78; effects of New Deal on poverty, 173

Rose, Marc: on community self help, 106

Roth, Lillian: *I'll Cry Tomorrow*, 112

Salesmanship: as a defense mechanism, 14–15; as moral behavior, 6.
See also American dream of success; Bruce Barton; Dale Carnegie; Henry Link; New Thought

The Saturday Evening Post: illustrations and photographs, 44, 91; methodology used in analyzing, ix, 192; popularity of, x–xi, 193–194; readership profile of, xi, 194–195.
See also Content analysis

Schactel, Ernest: on childhood, 169

Schisgall, Oscar: reassurance of existence of care, 147–148

Schultz, Charles. *See* "Peanuts"

Schwab, Charles: on changing values during the depression, 71; on positive thinking, 69

Self, the: amnesia and the loss of, 178; anxiety, 5; and avoidance of ten-

sion, 165–166; and creative use of ambivalence, 168–169; corporate erosion of, 40, 41; definition, 2–3; dysfunctional effects of cultural developments on, 5, 29–30, 167; ideological influences on, 3–5; 1950s crisis of, 129–130; social and cultural development of, 1–5; World War II changing attitudes toward, 97–98.
See also Autonomy

Self-reliance: Alger on, 34–35; and autonomy, 168; as cause of guilt, 14, 65, 167–168; as cause of psychological stress, 13–14; conflicts with care, 131, 139–141, 154–155; as corporate scapegoating device, 16, 67–69; as device to simplify problems, 167; and economic opportunity, 12–13; effects on guilty feelings during the depression, 66–67; as factor in paranoia, 18–19, 114; Graham on, 24; Hillis on, 67–68; humanistic guides to living and, 24–25; Liebman on, 25, 101–103; "Little Orphan Annie" on, 80; Middletown's faith in, 66; self help writers' insistence on in late 1950s, 135–137; Sheen on, 25; weakened by ambivalent concept of will power in 1930s, 85.
See also Autonomy; Individualism; Luck; Will power

Sensitivity groups: 149

Sentimentalism: compared to sensitivity, 28

Shame: definition, 64–65; guilt and, 64–67; success writers' concern with in 1930s, 82–87

Sheen, Fulton: on Eisenhower, 128; on guilt, 25–27, 126; Liebman contrasted to, 24–27, 125–126; and materialism, 112, 129; and passivity, 166; on peace of soul, 25; politics of, 26–27, 125–126; on repression and obedience, 26–27; on self-reliance, 25

Shriver, Sargent: and care, 144

Shulman, Morton: *Anyone Can Make a Million*, 160

Significance, sense of: attained in World War II, 92–93; desired in early

1950s, 114–115; lost in late 1950s and 1960s, 131–135

Slater, Philip: 11

Smith, Adam: *The Money Game,* 160–161

Social Darwinism: 34; characteristic in "Little Orphan Annie," 80–81; as a corporate ideology, 35–37; and the depression, 73–74; and free will, 35

Social mobility: of black Americans, 12–13; of business elites, 13; business opportunities, 12; differing class opportunities, 13; and the elderly, 12–13; Vance Packard's views on, 139; and rags to riches myth, 13; rise of the middle class, 12. *See also* Poverty

Songs, popular: during—
1930s, 74
1940s, 94
1950s, 125
1960s, 158–159

Status: emphasized in late 1950s, 137–139; loss of during depression, 64–80

Stevenson, Charles: on self-reliance, 144

Stother, Robert: on community self-help, 144

Stowe, Leland: assurance of existence of care, 148

Sumner, William Graham: and opportunity, 35; on Social Darwinism, 34

"Superman": 95–96, 107–108

Taylor, Myron C.: on lessons of the depression, 69

Temple, Shirley: 87

Tension: American avoidance of, 1, 5, 29–30, 165–166, 176–177; avoidance during—
pre-Civil War era, 31–35
post-Civil War era, 38–39
1917–1929, 42–45, 50
the depression, 74–75, 84–86
World War II, 99–100
1947–1955, 109–110, 125–126, 129
1957–1970, 131, 133, 135–137, 142–143, 149–150, 164. *See also* Ambivalance; Passivity

Thrift: conflicts with need for consumption in 1920s, 56–57; Fairbanks on, 43; effects of the depression on, 71–73, 74, 75

Thruelsen, Richard: and factual success stories, 93

Townshend, Robert: *Up the Organization,* 161–162

Toynbee, Arnold: popularity of his *Study of History,* 115–116

Tragedy: and care, 168–169

Upton, Howard: on happiness, success and free will, 136

Van Buren, Abigail: on loneliness, 135

Vanderlip, Frank: described as a positive thinker, 69

Vietnam War: and success ethic, 9, 152–154, 174

Weeks, Sinclair: on "business climate" in politics, 128

Welfare programs: criticisms of, 55, 79, 82–83, 105, 144–145; Barry Goldwater's views on, 151–152; under Herbert Hoover, 70–71; inadequacies of, 172–173; middle class misconceptions of, 11, 173; Richard Nixon's attitudes towards, 141, 161; under Franklin Roosevelt, 76–78, 173; under Harry Truman, 173; War on Poverty, 146

White, Mrs. Thomas J.: on censorship of Robin Hood, 117

Wiggam, Albert: on achievement traits as religious qualities, 6

Willie and Joe: 96–97, 107

Will power: abnegation of, 35, 40–41, 45, 84–85, 99–100, 125–126, 129, 136, 137; and Alger, 35; and allegiance to corporate warfare state, 164; ambivalences regarding, 39, 84–85, 99–100, 135–137; and Brande, 83; and Carnegie, 84–85; and childhood experiences, 169; and Couéism, 45; and defense mechanisms, 14; Emerson on, 33; Fosdick's views on, 99–100; functional and dysfunctional uses of, 174–175; liberation, freedom and, 175–177; Rollo May's attitudes toward, 154–155; and messianic

self-descriptions, 40–41; and New
Thought, 40–41; 1957–1959
ambivalences regarding, 135–137;
Peale on, 137; and Progressivism,
39; and resistance, 175; and
security, 175; and Social Darwinism,
35; Howard Upton's defense of,
136; World War II effects on concept of, 93–94
Wilson, Charles: on General Motors
and government interests, 128
Winsloe, Christa; on achievement
traits as religious values, 6
Woodbury, David: on wartime

workers, 91–92
World War I: development of organization man, 39–40
World War II: effects on success and
the self, 90–98; and wartime
controls, 104–105
Wylie, I.A.R.: on care, 144

Young, Vash, 67 on diligence as
religious virtue, 7

Zinsser, William: on frantic pursuit of
leisure, 149–150; on James Bond,
150–151